The Aesthetic Life of Infrastructure

The Aesthetic Life of Infrastructure

Race, Affect, Environment

✦

Edited by Kelly M. Rich, Nicole M. Rizzuto, and Susan Zieger

NORTHWESTERN UNIVERSITY PRESS
EVANSTON, ILLINOIS

Northwestern University Press
www.nupress.northwestern.edu

Copyright © 2023 by Northwestern University. Published 2023 by Northwestern University Press. All rights reserved.

Printed in the United States of America

10 9 8 7 6 5 4 3 2 1

Library of Congress Cataloging-in-Publication Data

Names: Rich, Kelly Mee, editor. | Rizzuto, Nicole M., editor. | Zieger, Susan Marjorie, editor.
Title: The aesthetic life of infrastructure : race, affect, environment / edited by Kelly M. Rich, Nicole M. Rizzuto, and Susan Zieger.
Description: Evanston, Illinois : Northwestern University Press, 2022.
Identifiers: LCCN 2022036143 | ISBN 9780810145504 (paperback) | ISBN 9780810145511 (cloth) | ISBN 9780810145528 (ebook)
Subjects: LCSH: Comparative literature—Themes, motives. | Infrastructure (Economics) in literature. | Postcolonialism in literature. | Infrastructure (Economics)—Social aspects. | BISAC: LITERARY CRITICISM / Comparative Literature
Classification: LCC PN56.I594 A38 2022 | DDC 809.933553—dc23/eng/20220802
LC record available at https://lccn.loc.gov/2022036143

CONTENTS

ACKNOWLEDGMENTS

The editors would first like to thank all the contributors to this volume, who turned in superlative essays under conditions of shuttered libraries, online teaching, childcare, and other unexpected pandemic-related exigencies. We are grateful for their brilliance, hard work, and professionalism, which helped bring this volume to fruition.

This project began as a session at the Modern Language Association Annual Convention in Seattle in 2020, whose panelists and participants helped us conceptualize the volume's interventions. Its development then benefitted from generative conversations with colleagues, especially those in the University of California Humanities Research Institute's Summer 2020 seminar Reading for Infrastructure, which Susan co-convened with Adriana Johnson. We are particularly grateful for the careful readings of a draft of our introduction by Brian Hochman, Dehn Gilmore, Devin Griffiths, Aaron Matz, Sarah Raff, and Beatrice Sandford Russell, whose comments and expertise helped sharpen the volume's interventions.

Thanks go to the editors at Northwestern University Press, including Trevor Perri for encouraging the project from the beginning, as well as Faith Wilson Stein for guiding it to completion. The reports by anonymous readers provided crucial insights and provocations, which in turn helped strengthen our articulations of the volume's arguments and commitments. Thanks also go to Lauren Hammond at University of California, Riverside, for help with permissions and manuscript preparation.

We would also like to acknowledge each other: steadfast conavigators along the long, bumpy road of editing a collection in the age of pandemic mayhem.

Chapter 1

✦

Reading Infrastructure

Kelly M. Rich, Nicole M. Rizzuto, and Susan Zieger

The word *infrastructure* comes to us from nineteenth-century French railroad engineers, but since the 1950s and '60s, it has meant "the basic equipment and structures (such as roads and bridges) that are needed for a country, region, or organization to function properly": in simple terms, public works.[1] Commensurate with the extraordinary scope of their task, infrastructural projects are enormous. Take the Dubai Creek Tower, soon to be the tallest man-made structure; the Grand Ethiopian Renaissance dam, whose reservoir will take seven years to fill; or the Guangzhou football stadium, which will seat over one hundred thousand spectators. Analysis grounded in the traditional definition would dwell on their technological affordances, scale, and novelty, but a newer definition, drawing on anthropology, critical geography, and political theory, yields timelier and more nuanced interventions. This volume thus updates and redefines infrastructure as the flexible and temporally unstable structures that organize biological and social life: the assemblages that ground the living nexus of modernity as an ongoing project of racialization, affective embodiment, and environmental praxis. Under such a definition, a project like the Guangzhou stadium begins to signify beyond its status as a testament to modern engineering and a source of national pride. Instead, its giant lotus petals recall the project's organic underpinnings, their glitzy ornamental form expressing social functions and environmental relations. The petals also suggest the carbon footprint of the stadium's afterlives and their networks of extraction and waste. And they encourage us to investigate the whole range of sensorial experiences that meet its materialization, including its image's circulation. In turn, these elements direct attention to the people who financed, designed, and are building the stadium, those who will maintain it, and those whom its construction displaces. Such queries must be mindful of the Chinese government's effort to create a culturally Chinese workforce through human rights abuses, amounting to genocide, of Uyghurs and other Turkic Muslims—a dimension that demands renewed scrutiny of the organizational force and biopolitical life of infrastructure.[2]

Such analysis reveals that infrastructure's aesthetic and political life are one and the same and need to be taken as such.

Infrastructure has already come a long way as a category of academic analysis. Twenty years ago, a critic could provoke readers merely by claiming that infrastructure was not boring.[3] Yet in the last decade scholars from numerous disciplines have amply demonstrated infrastructure's versatility. Setting aside the public works definition, they have used it to think through everything from women's gossip in Cairo, to chemical residue in West Virginians' bloodstreams, to oyster reefs in Staten Island.[4] Now infrastructure is emerging as a keyword for literary studies. As the first to closely read the aesthetics and politics of infrastructure together, this volume of essays demonstrates the value of literary and cultural studies approaches to the subject. As Jennifer Wenzel asks, evocatively conjuring the stakes of infrastructural analysis: "Study literature and neglect its myriad imbrications with infrastructure—e.g., its material embeddedness in literary sociology and circulation; its imaginative work in ground-laying processes of 'infrastructuring' or 'infrastructural inversion'; its thematic representation (or elision) in shaping infrastructural imaginaries—and what do you miss?"[5] As it turns out, an entire critical idiom that, like literary and visual culture itself, uses aesthetics to transform relationships between the state, capital, and the commons. Conversely, to study infrastructure without attending to aesthetics is to miss the human experiences that constantly reconsolidate and subvert its interfaces. To account for the multiform manifestations and functioning of infrastructure from the eighteenth century to the twenty-first, from the economies and polities of the colonial state to contemporary globalization, our volume critiques the oppositions that the public works definition assumes: people versus objects, natural versus built environments, the virtual versus the actual.

In infrastructure studies, the strongest formulation of the relationship between infrastructure and aesthetic form can be found in the work of anthropologist Brian Larkin. In a piece often cited by our contributors, Larkin argues that infrastructures need to be studied not only for their technical capacities but also as "concrete semiotic and aesthetic vehicles oriented to addressees."[6] He offers two definitions of the aesthetics of infrastructure. The first, working from Roman Jakobson's analysis of the speech act, posits a "poetics" of infrastructure, a mode in which "form is loosened from technical function."[7] The second, drawing from Aristotle's *aisthesis*, signifies forms of "embodied experience governed by the ways infrastructures produce the ambient conditions of everyday life: our sense of temperature, speed, florescence, and the ideas we have associated with these conditions."[8] These definitions are oppositional: one suggests focusing on form as divorced from its technical or even social and political function, while the other insists on infrastructural aesthetics as having a necessary, profoundly shaping effect on life itself. As an anthropologist, Larkin is not invested in thinking them together, that is, reading the poetics of infrastructure as its mode of address (its promise or social fact, as opposed to material existence) and the aesthesis of infrastructure as the experience of its material qualities (e.g., the dampening effect of asphalt, the hardness of concrete). By contrast, our volume theorizes the relationship between form and function as it manifests in and around the concept of infrastructure. This is what we miss if we neglect literature's imbrications with infrastructure: we miss the ways infrastructure shapes aesthetic experience and the ways it depends upon it. We miss a fuller understanding of how infrastructure works. And most importantly, we miss the ways infrastructure determines what gets counted as "life" at all.

As infrastructure attracts scholarly analysis, its integrality to human life becomes increasingly legible: the ways it engages our bodies, habits, sensoria, aesthetic categories, health, communities, labor, environments, politics, and identities. On this terrain, we find ourselves observing detail, establishing patterns, weighing contexts, and developing interpretation—in a word, we find ourselves reading. "Reading" here simultaneously denotes the technical methods of literary and cultural studies, the more general interpretive approaches practiced across the humanities, and the intuitive practice of nonacademic audiences. To read something—a poem, a building, an expression, the room—is to critically interpret its communicative details. Because this breadth proliferates and defamiliarizes objects of inquiry, it lends itself to reimaginings of infrastructure, a category that can seem everywhere and nowhere, material and abstract, designed for people and yet absent of them. As early modern scholar David Alff conjures this process, "Critics can analyze how words create the emptiness that allows infrastructure to happen and grasp this emptiness as an object of inquiry itself."[9] When reading infrastructure, our desire becomes more nuanced and curious; our attention attunes to varied historical moments; and our politics begin to focus on race, affect, and the environment.

When we do so, we learn that we must also depart from another assumption that has long governed infrastructure studies in the humanities, which we call the "visibility thesis." This phrase summarizes a paradigm articulated by Susan Leigh Star in which infrastructure becomes visible or detectable only or primarily through extraordinary collapse, failure, breakdown, or glitch.[10] This thesis has recently been criticized for its political inattention, as most of the world lives with semifunctional, delayed, and extractive infrastructure that remains highly visible. Of course, it isn't entirely possible, nor desirable, to scour metaphors of visibility from our writing. And visual studies and methods have much to offer critiques of infrastructure, as several of the essays richly demonstrate.[11] Yet we launch our collection from a series of counterpropositions that challenge the assumptions underwriting the visibility thesis. First, we assert that from cores to semiperipheries to peripheries, infrastructural failures, delays, and malfunctions so often form the rule rather than the exception that infrastructure requires no such exposure. Second, we suggest that these infrastructural conditions elicit collaborative acts of repair, renovation, and resistance by groups they would exclude. Infrastructure may activate new collectives who engage in compensation and innovation to cope with them. Finally, while infrastructural dysfunction often elucidates creative agency rather than abject oppression, this fact does not relieve the state's obligation to provide working infrastructure to sustain life. On the contrary, grassroots compensatory strategies remind us of the urgent need for renewed commitments to public services and more equitable distributions of access to them. Taken together, these counterpropositions acknowledge and imagine the diverse forms, times, and politics of infrastructure: critical interventions achieved by attending to infrastructure's aesthetic life.

Because our contributors are committed to reading infrastructure, rather than merely rediscovering it or pointing it out, they do not seek to render the invisible visible. Rather, they aim to make it legible. How does legibility differ from visibility? In answering this question, we articulate the volume's three principal interventions. First, to read is to place an object in context, attuning oneself to its chronology and setting, to test its narrative against itself. Whereas the visibility thesis implies a developmental narrative—that infrastructure is planned, built, operates, and fails before it becomes visible—a "legibility thesis" opens different temporal possibilities. One such powerful iteration is the "promise" of infrastructure, as a recent group of critics termed it.[12] The promise is a proleptic and even utopian gesture of development, efficiency, and modernity. Yet it also discloses ruin, disrepair, disappointment, decay, and deferral, demanding analysis of units and axes of time that depart from linear development. Such disparate temporalities generate a range of legible affects, aesthetics, and politics. Second, reading trains us to assess the social and political production of infrastructural space, a practice that requires imaginative investigation beyond the visible. Infrastructure's geographic scales oblige reconsideration of analysis grounded in conventional locations and identities. They draw our attention to specific, even idiosyncratic forms of sociality and location, from the regional or the microregional to their iterative communities and publics. Such reading practices advance our inquiry well beyond Larkin's important critique of the visibility thesis. When Larkin recommends dwelling in infrastructure's aesthetic details, he means primarily sensual experience. While the human sensorial experiences with infrastructure are central to literary reading, if not made fully legible, their politics never emerge. This adjustment represents our third intervention. Rather than imagine a return to literary formalism or universal phenomenology, the essays in this volume contend that infrastructural aesthetics are inseparable from their political economies. Reading the aesthetic life of infrastructure reflects the wisdom that "life" acquires urgency in political crises that bear on death, whether biological, social, or planetary.

These three interventions, in the temporalities, spatialities, and political aesthetics of infrastructure, emerge in each of the volume's interconnected subparts: part 1's spatial histories of racial capitalism, part 2's engagement with affect and technologies, and part 3's focus on environments and energy. The first part's focus on spatial history follows in the tradition of Henri Lefebvre's *The Production of Space* (1974) and the racial capitalism of Cedric Robinson's *Black Marxism* (1982).[13] If, as Jodi Melamed glosses the latter, "racism enshrines the inequalities that capitalism requires," the first third of the volume makes infrastructure legible as the aesthetic and political spaces of these inequalities.[14] Our continuing focus on the nexus of race and infrastructure begins with a set of inquiries into how the building of empire in the eighteenth- and nineteenth-century Americas reframes the visibility thesis. Spanning the topics of slavery and sexual labor, the plantation system, practices of frontier medicine, and resource extraction, our contributors turn to the visual arts, Black feminist geography, and architectural design to show how infrastructure built and maintained early American capitalist networks and how these oppressive networks in turn spurred unauthorized efforts to manage life differently. Documenting the endurance of forms and ideologies of centuries-old infrastructure, or what Ann Laura Stoler has called the "duress" of imperialism, these essays show how infrastructures from road construction to care work leave both ruination and resilience in their wake.[15]

Affect and embodiment are the focal points of our second part, in which contributors consider the film, ethnographies, clinical writings, art, and fiction of decolonization, postcoloniality, and globalization. Their attention to affect and embodiment forwards our conviction that infrastructure must be approached through a lens other than subject-centered humanism; instead, they address hybrid assemblages and technical networks. These contributors write in tune with Judith Butler's observation that "the body is less an entity than a relation, and it cannot be fully dissociated from the infrastructural and environmental conditions of its living."[16] Affect happens at the intersections between bodies and minds, individuals and collectives, people and environments; it simultaneously opens wide the field of inquiry and focuses precisely on events that otherwise go unnoticed.[17] Infrastructure engages complex interactions and distributions of agency that transcend discrete individual humans, objects, and nature. Such interactions occur under technoscientific regimes of propaganda, surveillance, and entertainment as the nation-state is proleptically called into being, as it is guarded during crises of global migration and asylum seeking, and as it contends with the failures of structural adjustment programs. In our volume, infrastructures throw into a vertiginous abyss the distinction between the visible and the invisible, shifting attention to auditory, tactile, and haptic perceptions and challenging the optical emphasis that has organized infrastructure studies.

Exploring the affective and embodied dimensions of situated infrastructures leads to the last third of *The Aesthetic Life of Infrastructure*, which makes "environment" legible at the intersection of energy, embodiment, and extraction. Taking its cue from recent work that identifies the frontiers of capital in living, laboring human bodies within natural and built environments, this part expands our sense of "extraction" from ordinary referents of logging and fracking as well as our sense of infrastructure, which transforms from static structure to dynamic transfer.[18] Ruth Wilson Gilmore models this creative rethinking of extraction in relation to infrastructures of incarceration: "People extracted from communities, and people returned to communities but not entitled to be of them, enable the extraction of money on rapid cycles. What's extracted from the extracted is *the* resource of life—time."[19] While the first two parts of the book had considered colonial and postcolonial resource and labor extraction in the Caribbean and Africa, and the recontouring of environments throughout the Middle East and Europe, the third part shifts to other regions, providing a multiscalar approach to each. The infrastructures that extract and harness energy from bodies, the earth, and the atmosphere drive both legitimate and shadow economies, elucidating the mutually reinforcing and even co-constitutive relationships between the state and private actors across transnational geographies. Genres ranging from nonfiction novels to documentary and narrative film to art and advertising photography disclose the ironic landscapes and environmental and human precarities induced by infrastructures under neoliberalization, nuclear energy regimes, and efforts to manage climate change in an advanced stage of the Anthropocene.

Our contributors' wide-ranging analyses demonstrate that reading infrastructure helps us imagine possible futures of humanistic inquiry. Infrastructure exerts a varied and near-limitless impress upon cultural production, from design to cinema, fiction to nonfiction, radio technologies to immersive video art installations. Working the seams between aesthetics and infrastructure, the essays generate rigorous humanistic readings. In the next section of this introduction, we offer a critical genealogy of the method.

Infrastructure and the Humanities

Infrastructure might only have recently come to the forefront of literary and cultural studies, garnering increasing attention at conferences, colloquia, and special issues of journals, but it has long been a subject of some of the most important philosophical and theoretical studies to inform these disciplines. Scholarly analysis of infrastructure has traditionally defined it in relation to the modern state, to capital, and to empire. Many begin with Adam Smith's argument in *The Wealth of Nations* (1776) that public works such as highways, bridges, canals, and harbors be made and maintained by tolls on the commercial vehicles that use them.[20] Understood by this canonical model as public works, infrastructure nurtures capital by facilitating its circulation, making possible a tacitly national, now globalized concept of "the economy." In the process, state and capital together settle territory, manage populations, routinize technoscientific practices, and cultivate affective orientations, so that it becomes impossible to imagine the workaday life of the world without infrastructure.[21] In ancient and modern times alike, this world-making power goes by the term *imperialism*. That icon of infrastructure, the road, extended the Roman Empire to Britain; Britain built roads and railways in colonial India; and if completed, the Belt and Road Initiative would open European markets to ever more Chinese goods. The restless expansion of capital means that the naturalized, national concept of public works is inseparable from imperial and neoliberal tendencies to occupy territory, extract resources from the environment, and enact biopolitical programs.

Walter Benjamin's famous idea that "there is no document of civilization which is not at the same time a document of barbarism" demarcates the longue durée of imperial infrastructure.[22] Benjamin was writing about "cultural treasures," but his comments apply equally to the grand nineteenth-century projects and works that were transforming modern European life in the late nineteenth and early twentieth century. Accelerating the circulation of capital and labor, such infrastructure as railway stations and artificial lighting played a crucial role in the critical drama of modernity drawn from Karl Marx. Without ever mentioning the word *infrastructure*, Marshall Berman observes the luminosity of Marx's prose in *The Communist Manifesto* when he describes great bourgeois infrastructural achievements: "steam navigation, railways, electric telegraphs, [the clearance] of whole continents for cultivation, canalization of rivers, whole populations conjured out of the ground." And yet these vast monuments and works, driven by capital and refueling its illusions of commodity fetishism, are destined for obsolescence, as Marx's prose culminates with the famous pronouncement, "All that is solid melts into air."[23] In Marxist critical traditions, infrastructure has quietly facilitated cultural effects: the evanescence of meaning, addictive consumer desire, the erosion of older customs and folkways, the alternating thrills and alienation of mobility. It appears as the technological condition of the cultural experience of modernity. The concept of alternative modernities expanded the field to postcolonial studies and the Global South, without necessarily problematizing or dismantling their technocratic preconditions.[24]

The advent of neoliberalism and the end of the Cold War brought the modern history of infrastructure into the light. Disciplines such as anthropology and media studies, inspired by critiques of neoliberal development and financialization, pivoted to discuss infrastructure as such, interrogating the ways it fulfilled or exceeded its status as technocratic capital expression. Such scholarship has been invested in the study of space, including critical geography, architecture, and design. David Harvey's work, for instance, spans the Haussmannization of Paris in the 1860s and the Chinese turn to massive state-funded projects such as the Three Gorges Dam, opened in 2003.[25] Keller Easterling interprets contemporary infrastructure space as capital's use of the state for its own purposes: in her term, as "extrastatecraft."[26] The anthropology volume *The Promise of Infrastructure* (2018) analyzes infrastructural projects in the Global South and China, contrasting them to the decay of infrastructure under austerity measures in the United States and United Kingdom since the financial crisis of 2008. Such analysis offers a scaffold to a new generation of scholars to analyze infrastructure from the point of view of platform, circular, and postscarcity economies. These scholars will find help from a second recent upsurge of critical interest within media studies. This scholarship, finding its roots in the work of Marshall McLuhan and Harold Innis, has excavated the imperial and Cold War histories of digital infrastructures. Nicole Starosielski's *The Undersea Cable* (2015), Tung-Hu Hui's *A Prehistory of the Cloud* (2015), and Starosielski and Lisa Parks's collection *Signal Traffic: Critical Studies of Media Infrastructure* (2015), among many others, demonstrate how infrastructure can be innovatively approached through attention to its micro- and macroscales, the affects of its users, its materiality, and its relationality—especially with respect to labor and the environment. In this vein, the scholarship most energized by our current crises reads infrastructural contests as the scene of the collapse of both biopolitics and politics, as the United States continues to move "from welfare to warfare" on its Black citizens and the state abandons its people to capital predation.[27]

By making infrastructure central to the history and definition of settler colonialism, critical Indigenous studies scholars offer a valuable perspective on this warfare and abandonment. As Glenn Coulthard writes, "Settler colonialism refers to contexts where the territorial infrastructure of the colonizing society is built on and overwhelms the formerly self-governing but now dispossessed Indigenous nations."[28] In this formulation, infrastructure is the tool of settlement, colonization, and dispossession; as Deborah Cowen and Winona LaDuke put it, "Infrastructure is the how of settler colonialism." Tlingit scholar Anne Spice sharpens such an observation in her analysis of the Canadian and US governments' discourses of "critical infrastructure" that these settler states deploy against terrorism—a term by which they classify Indigenous resistance. Against this violence, Spice demonstrates that Indigenous people "contes[t] the very category of infrastructure itself, asserting alternative ontological and epistemological modes of relating to assemblages that move matter and sustain life"—for example, the ecology of salmon, bears, berries, and Unist'ot'en people.[29] Such reimaginings of infrastructure also reconfigure temporality in response to the ongoing settler violence of modernity. Coulthard proposes "resurgence"; Audra Simpson, "interruption"; Eve Tuck and C. Ree, "haunting"; Max Haiven, "relentless presence."[30] Indigenous theorizations are often joined to those of Black people and people of color, under the sign of haunting that is familiar from critical race studies and post-Marxist studies. These alternative formulations all reject linear time, that technique of the dominating rationality of settler colonialism; accordingly, they rearrange, collapse, or intensify past, present, or future.[31] Indigenous redefinitions of infrastructure have enormous analytic potential to rethink the topic along with critical race studies, the environmental humanities, and post-Marxist thought.[32]

While infrastructure has proved a revitalizing topic with respect to the study of indigeneity, race, sexuality, disability, and postcoloniality, and within the disciplines of the social sciences, science and technology studies, media studies, environmental studies, logistics, and urban planning, literary studies has been slower to take the infrastructural turn. Early work on infrastructure in the subfields of Victorian and modernist studies has examined histories of technology and their relation to empire, focusing largely on the novel: take, for example, Jonathan Grossman's *Charles Dickens's Networks* (2012), Richard Menke's *Telegraphic Realism* (2008), and Michael Rubinstein's *Public Works: Infrastructure, Irish Modernism, and the Postcolonial* (2010). More recently, Jessica Hurley's *Infrastructures of Apocalypse: American Literature and the Nuclear Complex* (2020) assesses the array of literary responses to the invention of the atom bomb and subsequent commitment to nuclear infrastructure, turning this literary analysis toward a theorization of the political possibilities that might unexpectedly emerge from the cultural scene of nuclear apocalypse. Each of these works exhibits a strong historicist tendency, interested more in the influence of institutions on literary periodization than transhistorical patterns.

Other recent scholarship has emphasized the importance of form and genre to literary analyses of infrastructure. Caroline Levine, for instance, proposes "infrastructuralism" as a "post-poststructuralist method" that resembles New Criticism. What she means by infrastructure, however, branches out from the imperial roads and data centers at stake in the Marxist tradition to include cultural and aesthetic forms. For Levine, "infrastructuralism investigates what lies beneath or behind apparently powerful institutions to see what organizes social life. And what it uncovers are . . . an extensive range of incommensurable forms."[33] Jennifer Wenzel rigorously calculates the impact of theories of distributed agency for literary analysis: "What happens to narrative when setting becomes character, plot becomes setting, objects become subjects? When . . . the capacity to be a protagonist . . . is distributed across human and nonhuman entities? When the . . . foundation of plot is dilated across . . . the dimensions of setting?" she asks.[34] Wenzel's afterword to this volume continues to inquire how literary studies can engage infrastructure, emphasizing the importance of doing so without tacitly reinforcing structures of power.

Taking up this question from the perspective of cultural studies, queer theory, and poetry, Lauren Berlant asks the question of how broken social systems can be repaired without reinstantiating unjust social relations. She insists on infrastructure's dynamic and transformative properties; it is "that which binds us to the world in movement and keeps the world practically bound to itself."[35] For Berlant, infrastructure is an assemblage of sociality, collective affect, and poetry, the latter being "a technology in which all objects are granular and moving toward each other to make new forms of approach from difference and distance."[36] In its effort to describe social change in nontraditional terms, Berlant's analysis may verge on vagueness. Yet it also offers another model for thinking of literature and media not as cultural epiphenomena of a technical base but as infrastructure itself—an affective transformation required to sustain self and sociality. At the same time, it remains attuned to Harvey's critique of neoliberalism as it attempts to put into action a reparative critique.

Our volume extends Berlant's call to read infrastructure as the occasion to imagine and instantiate sociality otherwise than in slavery, settler colonialism, postemancipation, and postcoloniality. Our contributors do so by turning away from oppositions of visibility and invisibility, absence and presence, and toward other modes of sensation—for example, hearing. In their essays, we discover that new, anticolonial collectives come into being during the Algerian War through the act of learning to listen for the eruption of radio-mediated noise. And we learn that in contemporary Lagos, sound technologies such as the phonograph offer refuge from the coercive cacophony of repressive socialities, instigating compensatory reparative acts and creating space for nontraditional development. The sense of touch and processes of orienting bodies in space also potentially reestablish relationships between individuals and collectives. The proprioceptive and tactile dimensions introduced by different media, from cinematic representations tracking the effects of nuclear radiation on human bodies and celluloid film, to digital art installations that reveal the indistinction between visible and invisible border infrastructures, foreground the link between form and function in infrastructural aesthetics. These aesthetics transform spectators from passive consumers of information and art to active users pushed to confront their own complicities in maintaining social and energy systems propped on economic, climatological, and corporeal precarities. Inspired by this broadened conceptualization of infrastructure and its rethinking of the transmutations of life, our volume turns to the concept of "life" as a heuristic for infrastructural critique. As we elaborate below, "life" provides a crucial lever for the other keywords in our volume's title—aesthetics and infrastructure—balancing the former's focus on form and the latter's emphasis on institutions.

Infrastructural Life

What are the specific political interventions that are made by imagining the aesthetics of infrastructure through the heuristic of "life"? We use this term to redefine the aesthetics of infrastructure from the perspective of the participating subject rather than the external observer. The work of our contributors attends to the experience of infrastructure, as well as the experience of being infrastructure, drawing attention to individual lives, the lives of communities, and their social, embodied, and sensual dimensions. As discussed earlier, in this way the volume evokes the aesthetic life of infrastructure, building on Larkin's sense of aesthetics as *aisthesis*, or sensory and embodied experience. Theorist Jacques Rancière also employs *aisthesis* to restore the political and revolutionary capacities of art, insofar as it counters the distanced approach that situates the critic as the unveiler of a hidden truth.[37] This characteristic role of the critic also lurks within the visibility thesis: only the master interpreter possesses the insight to see when infrastructure has broken down. By contrast, approaches that foreground ordinary people and everyday life rethink the critic as savior, state and capital as benefactors, and infrastructure as a gift.

The volume moves beyond the visibility thesis partly through the concept of "people-as-infrastructure," an influential formulation proposed by sociologist AbdouMaliq Simone. Focusing on the everyday lives of urban residents in the Global South such as Johannesburg, Jakarta, and Dakar, Simone highlights their infrastructural activity and agency as "a tentative and often precarious process of remaking the inner city now that the policies and economies that once moored it to the surrounding city have mostly worn away."[38] This thesis, as well as its subsequent mobilizations, has shown the concept of "people as infrastructure" to be bottom-up and improvisatory, attuned to feeling and precarity, and alive to the possibilities of social transformation. It is not just a rhetorical move. Instead, to describe people as infrastructure is to show that infrastructures require the interactions and extractions of laboring bodies at all points, from construction to maintenance to cleanup as they decay, explode, or fall apart. Doing so challenges the visibility thesis but also traces state and nonstate actors' actual and figurative deployments of humans as inhuman and partially human. It does so across the disparate eras of the Anthropocene, or what feminist, postcolonial, Indigenous, and Marxist theorists, to accurately reflect the inequality between perpetrators and victims of climate change, term the "Capitalocene." This era extends from the Plantationocene to the nuclear age and beyond.[39] As our contributors limn the nuances that differentiate these epochs, infrastructure comes to name the dynamic transfers that rely upon, propagate, and enforce normative power structures while also permitting negotiation and resistance to reconstellate them.

Here again we witness the gap between consumers of infrastructure and its producers, maintainers, and caretakers, who are often gendered and racialized by this unequal relationship. State and corporate projects require the management of Indigenous, migrant, and enslaved populations to erect the systems that make modern life function, while barring those populations' knowledge formations and ecological practices from entering into the calculus of how and why such infrastructures are made. The earliest British settler colonists in Barbados could not conceive the private transportation systems undergirding their ventures without also physically and emotionally damaging Black and Indigenous subjects to build them by coercing their labor and refusing to fund and maintain hospitals and salubrious dwellings. It has been just as impossible to imagine the smooth functioning of nuclear power plants, from Oklahoma to Chernobyl to France, without subjecting laboring bodies to the insidious "slow violence" of their toxic effects, including the highly gendered humiliation that results from inevitable malfunctions and decontamination procedures—a violent cure to a violent, if all too ordinary, radiation poisoning.[40]

But if infrastructure from the colonial to the postcolonial and neoliberal global age coerces and extracts human energy, generating humiliation, disgust, and all manner of what Sianne Ngai calls "ugly feelings," it also provides raced and gendered subjects with unintended opportunities for social mobility and transformation.[41] Antithetical to its purpose, the building of hard infrastructures such as the Panama Canal spurred Caribbean women of color to develop soft infrastructures of self-fashioning and entrepreneurship in the form of hospitality, care work, and education. When French colonists erected radio infrastructures in Algeria, the colonized responded by creating new infrastructures, reappropriating the airwaves for their own revolutionary purposes. These are two among many of the examples of resilience, improvisation, and enabling sabotage that our contributors describe and analyze.

This reframed idea of infrastructural life resonates with another term used to describe the state's management of the life of its population, including those it has colonized—biopolitics.[42] Because biopolitics intimately relates infrastructure to racial formation and domination, it is not possible to make three centuries of infrastructural development in capitalist modernity newly legible without nuanced attention to its racializing operations. Drawing on a lineage of antiracist theory and criticism, from Black feminisms to anticolonial Marxism, as well as recent scholarship in energy studies, disability studies, sound studies, and the digital humanities, the essays throughout the volume analyze how infrastructures designed to circulate goods and services also enforce biopolitical regimes of uneven racialization. Contributors examine infrastructures as modes of "racializing assemblages," to use the term Alexander Weheliye employed in his provincializing of Giorgio Agamben's universalist model of biopolitics. Racializing assemblages are processes that constitute the differential apportioning of the nonhuman, not quite human, and fully human.[43] The essays demonstrate infrastructure's participation in these processes during slavery and colonialism, and in their aftermaths. This emphasis innovates on Eurocentric approaches in literary studies that dwell in US and Anglo-Irish historical contexts and conventional genres. Most importantly, it highlights the primary role racialization plays in, and as, infrastructure: to extract value. Here we build on Daniel Nemser's view that race operates as infrastructure, "a sociotechnical relation that enables the ongoing functioning of specific machineries of extraction and accumulation."[44]

Race, racialization, and racism are not dematerialized metaphors for social infrastructure. Race is infrastructure because whatever else it may be or do, it has a long and enduring history of mediating relations between states, capital, people, and the spaces, technologies, environments, energies, and affects that both connect and partition them. As states in the Global North and South further consolidate capital and intensify policing to make war on their racialized citizens and inhabitants, this perspective is crucial to a progressive politics of infrastructure, as well as to a study of its aesthetic effects. In visual, sonic, and literary texts, our contributors read racializing assemblages, disclosing the depredations and resistances to race-as-infrastructure.

The asynchronous rhythms of infrastructure that our contributors document bear directly on the management of collective human life, its affective dimensions, and its relation to natural environments. Far from the prevailing attitude that there are two times of infrastructure—when it is functioning for users-as-consumers and when it is not—our volume instead traces the "shadow histories," "present absences," "suspended presents," and "nostalgic futures" by which Ashley Carse and David Kneas have typologized the ubiquitous "unbuilt and unfinished infrastructures," a norm too often treated as anomalous.[45] Nikhil Anand, Akhil Gupta, and Hannah Appel have borrowed the vocabulary of literary theory to describe infrastructure's effects and affects as "chronotopes" extending beyond the boundaries of human lifetimes, iteratively constituting their populations and publics.[46] Across the world, infrastructural projects impose themselves on landscapes, imaginaries, and structures of feeling as torsions of linear and progressive temporalities. They often exist in subjunctive states, as promises unfulfilled, ruins of alternative futures, or relations to ongoingness. Nuancing the temporality of infrastructure reframes conventional narratives of "life," history, and even sequence.

Outline of the Volume

In three parts, the volume's contributors explore infrastructure's role in racial management, its affective dimensions, and its ability to reconfigure ecologies and bodies. Part 1, "Spatial Histories of Racial Capitalism," reframes the visibility thesis by examining instead how infrastructures become legible as biopolitical projects. Focusing on capital and the building of empire in the eighteenth- and nineteenth-century Americas, the essays range from the plantation system to slavery and sexual labor, practices of frontier medicine, and resource extraction. These infrastructures were designed not merely to modernize colonies but to manage unruly populations who would thwart and redirect the aims of capital. Through creatively reassembled archives of visual arts, Black feminist geography, public and private architectural design, and sensory technologies, these essays show how infrastructural labor built and maintained early American capitalist networks—and how these oppressive networks prompted unauthorized efforts to manage life differently. Ramesh Mallipeddi approaches infrastructure as a form of "calculative reason" in an essay examining the role of roads and of the larger built environment—including bridges, ports, and dikes—in resource extraction and colonial governance in eighteenth-century Barbados. Louis Moreno's essay interprets Sally Hemings's private apartments within Monticello's grand Palladian architecture as the racialized space that underwrites and helps perpetuate not only the techniques of financialization required for enclosure but their cultural and aesthetic lineage as well. Samantha Pinto's essay explores the "public speech" of the diasporic writers Mary Seacole and Anne Hart Gilbert, whose entrepreneurial engagements with projects from the Panama Canal, to churches, to the Crimean War demonstrate how Black women deploy infrastructural discourses including publishing and care work as modes of institution and industry building to carve out sites for gendered self-making that extend beyond and complicate the oppositional politics of anticolonial resistance. Taken together, these pieces model the necessity of interdisciplinarity when reading infrastructure, illustrating the stakes and mission of the collection.

Part 2, "Affect and Technologies," pushes the first part's theme of human responses to imperial infrastructures further, developing Simone's idea that people function infrastructurally when they appropriate the biopolitical projects developed around them. Building as well from Larkin's idea that political aesthetics engage unfulfilled promises of infrastructure, these essays read those broken contracts in affective engagements with technology in postwar and contemporary sound, media, and literary aesthetics.[47] From novelistic realism to speculative aesthetics to sonic, visual, and digital technologies, the materials here display infrastructure's necessary fiction making. Building on the first part, they chart the affective relays of racialized infrastructure's uneven imperial temporalities, from their proleptic stagings of modernity to their sheltering of residual pasts, across texts of decolonization and postcoloniality. Yanie Fecu's examination of Frantz Fanon's 1959 essay "This Is the Voice of Algeria" demonstrates how, during the Algerian War of Independence, the French introduction of radios created an unauthorized counterpublic of listeners who used static to assemble a revolutionary community. Janice Ho reads ad hoc and improvisational acts of compensation and repair in Chris Abani's novel *GraceLand* (2004) as coping mechanisms in the face of persistent infrastructural and institutional breakdowns, affective responses that challenge the apocalyptic image of the failed African city and the impoverished and abject African subject. Sangina Patnaik elucidates the racial aspects of immigration infrastructure in Mohsin Hamid's *Exit West* (2017) and Diller Scott + Renfro's immersive art installation *EXIT* (2017), texts that experiment with the difficulties of representing both human movement and the infrastructures that track or thwart it. And Jeannie Im's piece on Namwali Serpell's *The Old Drift* (2019) brings into relief the elaborated narrative of Matha Mwamba, the Zambian astronaut trainee whose pregnancy ends her engagement with the infrastructure of space exploration. In such examples, writers and artists remake infrastructures as alternative technologies of knowing, written in and on bodies and their affects. Their interventions demonstrate that infrastructure, far from being merely oppressive, can be seized and transformed, rewritten and replaced.

Tilting this exploration of infrastructural embodiment toward global and local ecologies and climates, part 3, "Energy, Environment, Extraction," interprets the aesthetic life of infrastructure to retheorize the nexus of living labor, capital, and environment. "Living labor" is the individual worker's energy, which is required to vivify the dead labor of capital but which vibrates with a spontaneity that can also thwart and misdirect productive flows.[48] The temporalities of infrastructures are not only those of promises made, expected, miscarried, and renegotiated, as the volume's earlier parts demonstrate. They are also temporalities of extraction, broadly reconceived beyond the expected examples of mining and fracking. Discussing nuclear, wind, and human energy, the essays in this part read embodiment and environment together to make infrastructure's extractive force within neoliberal regimes fully legible. They demonstrate how both "dirty" and putatively clean energy infrastructures influence modes of embodiment, sparking hybrid genres and experimental forms. Interpreting infrastructure's aesthetic life to foreground uneven experiences of precarity and hazard, our contributors attend self-reflexively to the performance and spectacle of infrastructure, asking how we read, witness, and even inhabit narratives of its power. In so doing, they build on the intervention of *Infrastructure, Environment, and Life in the Anthropocene* (2019), which emphasizes the eroding division between the natural and built environment. Georgiana Banita illuminates how the lifelike forms of wind power infrastructure finesse its infringement on the environment. Her essay shows how the visual logic of wind farms in contemporary photography by such figures as Erwin Olaf, Kim Stringfellow, Mitch Epstein, and Edward Burtynsky makes legible the short life cycle of wind turbines and their potential to create vast amounts of unrecyclable waste. Rahul Mukherjee analyzes the aesthetic address of nuclear reactors in documentaries, TV series, and cinema in an essay that traces radiation's effects in and on the bodies of their workers, questioning the promise of sustainable futures that these monumental, seemingly sublime objects perform. Susan Zieger's reading of cocaine as an extractive "soft" infrastructure in two "nonfiction novels," Luca Rastello's *I Am the Market* (2010) and Roberto Saviano's *ZeroZeroZero* (2013), explores how the work of growing, harvesting, and distributing cocaine, as well as the physiological capacity to sustain cocaine habits, act as a palliative for intensive labor, its informal economy sustaining the formal one of globalized brands. As these essays demonstrate, visual and literary aesthetics render the shadow histories and itineraries encased in infrastructural aesthetics, attenuating the collective futures their forms promise.

Jennifer Wenzel's afterword responds to the interventions and themes that anchor the volume. She approaches the shifting dynamics between the disabling and enabling, the ordinary and spectacular, and the material and metaphorical aspects that shape our contributors' efforts to think of infrastructure in terms of the aesthetic and to imagine aesthetics as contoured by, or even grounded in, infrastructure. Wenzel offers a sober reading of the affordances of infrastructure, asking us to examine the limitations and exclusions built into the networks designed to form connection and society. She recommends attention to the ongoing negotiations and mundane practices of survival and resistance enacted by those disenfranchised by infrastructural projects undertaken in the name of egalitarianism and modernization. In asking how humanists should "attend imaginatively and responsibly to what infrastructure is and does," Wenzel urges us to undertake the interdisciplinary work infrastructural study necessitates. Her answer is to remain attentive to infrastructure's figural dimensions—its capacity to surpass its referential message as concrete fact—while simultaneously remaining attentive to its materiality as historically situated, affectively structured, and conditioned by political, social, and biological life. Under this motto, this volume studies infrastructure to document the intertwined, sustaining power of material ground and figure, aesthetics and life.

Notes

1. On the term's history, see Peter A. Shulman, "What *Infrastructure* Really Means," *Atlantic*, July 13, 2021; the definition is from Merriam-Webster online.

2. Human Rights Watch, "Break Their Lineage, Break Their Roots: China's Crimes against Humanity Targeting Uyghurs and other Turkic Muslims," *Report*, April 19, 2021. See also Jesus Jiménez, "U.S. Holocaust Museum Says China 'May Be Committing Genocide' against Uyghurs," *New York Times*, November 9, 2021.

3. Susan Leigh Star, "The Ethnography of Infrastructure," *American Behavioral Scientist* 43, no. 3 (November–December 1999): 377–91.

4. See Julia Elychar, "Phatic Labor, Infrastructure, and the Empowerment of Women in Cairo," *American Ethnologist* 37, no. 3 (2010): 452–64; Michelle Murphy, "Chemical Infrastructures of the St. Clair River," in *Toxicants, Health, and Regulation since 1945*, ed. Soraya Boudia and Nathalie Jas (London: Pickering and Chatto, 2013), 103–15; and Stephanie Wakefield and Bruce Braun, "Oystertecture: Infrastructure, Profanation, and the Sacred Figure of the Human," in *Infrastructure, Environment, and Life in the Anthropocene*, ed. Kregg Hetherington (Durham, NC: Duke University Press, 2019), 193–215.

5. Jennifer Wenzel, "Forms of Life: Thinking Fossil Infrastructure and Its Narrative Grammar," forthcoming in *Social Text* 40, no. 4 (December 2022).

6. Brian Larkin, "The Politics and Poetics of Infrastructure," *Annual Review of Anthropology* 42 (2013): 329.

7. Larkin, "The Politics and Poetics," 325.

8. Larkin, "The Politics and Poetics," 336–37.

9. David Alff, "Make Way for Infrastructure," *Critical Inquiry* 47 (Summer 2021): 629.

10. See Star, "Ethnography of Infrastructure."

11. See, e.g., Adriana Michele Campos Johnson, "Visuality as Infrastructure," 36, no. 3 (September 2018): 71–91.

12. See Nihkil Anand, Akhil Gupta, and Hannah Appel, eds., *The Promise of Infrastructure* (Durham, NC: Duke University Press, 2018).

13. Henri Lefebvre, *The Production of Space*, trans. Donald Nicholson-Smith (Chichester, England: Wiley-Blackwell, 1992); and Cedric J. Robinson, *Black Marxism: The Making of the Black Radical Tradition* (1983; Chapel Hill: University of North Carolina Press, 2000).

14. Jodi Melamed, "Racial Capitalism," *Critical Ethnic Studies* 1, no. 1 (2015): 76–85.

15. Ann Laura Stoler, *Duress: Imperial Durabilities in Our Times* (Durham, NC: Duke University Press, 2016).

16. Judith Butler, "Rethinking Vulnerability and Resistance," in *Vulnerability in Resistance*, ed. Judith Butler, Zeynep Gambetti, and Leticia Sabsay (Durham, NC: Duke University Press, 2016), 18.

17. For readings of the intersections among aesthetics and affect, see, e.g., Lauren Berlant, *The Female Complaint: The Unfinished Business of Sentimentality in American Culture* (Durham, NC: Duke University Press, 2008); and *Cruel Optimism* (Durham, NC: Duke University Press, 2011); Sianne Ngai, *Ugly Feelings* (Cambridge, MA: Harvard University Press, 2009); and *Theory of the Gimmick: Aesthetic Judgment and Capitalist Form* (Cambridge, MA: Harvard University Press, 2020). For a model of "infrastructure of feeling," see Ruth Wilson Gilmore, "Abolition Geography and the Problem of Innocence," chap 14. in *Futures of Black Radicalism*, ed. Gaye Theresa Johnson and Alex Lubin (London: Verso, 2016).

18. See, e.g., Macarena Gomez-Barris, *The Extractive Zone: Social Ecologies and Decolonial Perspectives* (Durham, NC: Duke University Press, 2017; Anna Lowenhaupt Tsing, *The Mushroom at the End of the World: On the Possibility of Life in Capitalist Ruins* (Princeton, NJ: Princeton University Press, 2015), 270–74; and Sandro Mezzadra and Brett Neilson, *The Politics of Operations: Excavating Contemporary Capitalism* (Durham, NC: Duke University Press, 2019).

19. Gilmore, "Abolition Geography."

20. Adam Smith, *The Wealth of Nations Books 1–3*, ed. Andrew Skinner (London: Penguin, 1982), 251.

21. Michelle Murphy, *The Economization of Life* (Durham, NC: Duke University Press, 2017).

22. Walter Benjamin, *Illuminations*, trans. Hannah Arendt (1968; New York: Mariner, 2019), 200.

23. Quoted in Marshall Berman, *All That Is Solid Melts into Air: The Experience of Modernity* (New York: Penguin, 1988), 93–95.

24. See Dilip Parameshwar Gaonkar, "On Alternative Modernities," in *Alternative Modernities*, ed. Dilip Parameshwar Gaonkar (Durham, NC: Duke University Press, 2001), 1–23.

25. David Harvey, *Paris: Capital of Modernity* (London: Routledge, 2005); *A Brief History of Neoliberalism* (Oxford: Oxford University Press, 2007).

26. Keller Easterling, *Extrastatecraft: The Power of Infrastructure Space* (London: Verso, 2014).

27. On recent moves from "welfare to warfare" against Black citizens, see Brian Whitener, "Detroit's Water Wars: Race, Failing Social Reproduction, and Infrastructure," *Comparative Literature and Culture* 22, no. 2 (2020); on abandonment, see Mark Duffield, "Total War as Environmental Terror: Linking Liberalism, Resilience, and the Bunker," *South Atlantic Quarterly* 110, no. 3 (Summer 2007): 757–69.

28. Glen Sean Coulthard, *Red Skin, White Masks: Rejecting the Colonial Politics of Recognition* (Minneapolis: University of Minnesota Press, 2014).

29. Anne Spice, "Fighting Invasive Infrastructures: Indigenous Relations against Pipelines," *Environment and Society* 9 (2018): 45. See also Cowen and LaDuke's Ojibwe concept of "alimentary infrastructures" and Dana Powell's Diné philosophy and practice of Sa'ah Naagháí Bik'eh Hózhóón. Deborah Cowen and Winona LaDuke, "Wiindigo Infrastructures," *South Atlantic Quarterly* 119, no. 2 (April 2020): 250; Dana Powell, *Landscapes of Power: Politics of Energy in the Navajo Nation* (Durham, NC: Duke University Press, 2018), 11–12.

30. Coulthard, *Red Skin, White Masks*, 216; Audra Simpson, *Mohawk Interruptus: Political Life across the Borders of Settler States* (Durham, NC: Duke University Press, 2014); Eve Tuck and C. Ree, "A Glossary of Haunting," in *Handbook of Autoethnography*, ed. Stacy Holman Jones, Tony E. Adams, and Carolyn Ellis (London: Routledge, 2013), 642–43; and Max Haiven, *Revenge Capitalism: The Ghosts of Empire, the Demons of Capital, and the Settling of Unpayable Debts* (London: Pluto Press, 2020). See also Mark Rifkin, *Beyond Settler Time: Temporal Sovereignty and Indigenous Self-Determination* (Durham, NC: Duke University Press, 2017).

31. See, e.g., Nick Estes, *Our History Is the Future: Standing Rock versus the Dakota Access Pipeline, and the Long Tradition of Indigenous Resistance* (London: Verso, 2019), 14.

32. On the problem of homogenization, see Rifkin, *Beyond Settler Time*, 32.

33. Caroline Levine, "Infrastructuralism, or the Tempo of Institutions," chap. 2 in *On Periodization: Selected Essays from the English Institute*, ed. Virginia Jackson (Cambridge: English Institute, 2010).

34. Jennifer Wenzel, *The Disposition of Nature* (New York: Fordham University Press, 2019), 19.

35. Lauren Berlant, "The Commons: Infrastructures for Troubling Times," *Environment and Planning D: Society and Space* 34, no. 3 (2016): 394.

36. Berlant, "The Commons," 408.

37. See Larkin, "Politics and Poetics," 336; and Jacques Rancière, *Dissensus: On Politics and Aesthetics* (London: Bloomsbury, 2015).

38. AbdouMaliq Simone, "People as Infrastructure: Intersecting Fragments in Johannesburg," *Public Culture* 16, no. 3 (2004): 411.

39. "Capitalocene" is the term Andreas Malm coined to underscore that the Anthropocene's fundamental cause is fossil capital. See Andreas Malm, *Fossil Capital: The Rise of Steam Power and the Roots of Global Warming* (London:

Verso, 2016), 472. For a careful reading of the use of alternatives to the broader term "Anthropocene" that highlight the unevenly distributed effects of capital on climate and environment on Indigenous communities and those of the Global South, see Elizabeth de Loughrey, *Allegories of the Anthropocene* (Durham, NC: Duke University Press, 2019).

40. Rob Nixon, *Slow Violence and the Environmentalism of the Poor* (Cambridge, MA: Harvard University Press), 2011.

41. Sianne Ngai, *Ugly Feelings* (Cambridge, MA: Harvard University Press, 2005).

42. See Michel Foucault, *The History of Sexuality, Volume I* (1976; New York: Viking, 1994), 142–43.

43. Alexander Weheliye, *Habeas Viscus: Racializing Assemblages, Biopolitics, and Black Feminist Theories of the Human* (Durham, NC: Duke University Press, 2014).

44. Daniel Nemser, *Infrastructures of Race: Concentration and Biopolitics in Colonial Mexico* (Austin: University of Texas Press, 2017), 5.

45. Ashley Carse and David Kneas, "Unbuilt and Unfinished: Temporalities of Infrastructure," *Environment and Society: Advances in Research* 10 (2019): 9–28.

46. See Anand, Gupta, and Appel, *Promise of Infrastructure.*

47. Brian Larkin, "Promising Forms: The Political Aesthetics of Infrastructure," in *The Promise of Infrastructure*, ed. Hannah Appel, Nikhil Anand, and Akhil Gupta (Durham, NC: Duke University Press, 2018), 177.

48. For a helpful discussion, see J. Lubin-Levy and A. Shvartz, "Living Labor: Marxism and Performance Studies," *Women and Performance* 26, nos. 2–3 (2016): 115–21.

Part One

✦

Spatial Histories of Racial Capitalism

Chapter 2

✦

Roads, Bridges, and Ports

Infrastructures of Plantation Agriculture in the British Caribbean, 1627–1840

Ramesh Mallipeddi

> The planting interest of these islands may be characterized as one of unqualified selfishness. . . . Theirs was not the broad, grasping selfishness of a powerful oligarchy wise enough to combine their own aggrandizement with that of the nation at large; but it has been from first to last a narrow-minded selfishness that pursued crooked paths to accumulate gain at the expense of the public weal, to the infinite detriment of the colonial credit.
>
> —William G. Sewell, *The Ordeal of Free Labor in the British West Indies*

In 1837, the American antislavery activists James Thome and Horace Kimball traveled to the West Indies to study the condition of apprenticed laborers. Three years earlier, on August 1, 1834, the British parliament had instituted apprenticeship, a transitional period of mixed bound and free labor, to prepare slave societies for full emancipation six years later in 1840. The system was designed, according to the historian William Laurence Burn, "to educate the master or planter beyond the coercive method" and to "train the ex-slaves for the responsibilities of free citizenship, in particular working regularly for wages."[1] Thome, the son of a Kentucky slaveholder, and Kimball, editor of the New England–based *Herald of Freedom*, were sent by New York's Anti-slavery Society to counter the proslavery campaign at home, which suggested that the proposed emancipation in the Caribbean was a failure and that a similar measure in America would be ruinous and destructive. In their interviews with apprentices, managers, and colonial officials, the visitors discovered the willingness of Blacks to work for wages, deemed the transitional period unnecessary, and called for immediate emancipation. But their critique of Caribbean plantation societies ran deeper. During their visit to various public institutions—schools, hospitals, prisons, churches, and workhouses—Thome and Kimball found the colonies' physical structures in a state of disrepair. The correctional facility in Morant Bay, Jamaica, seemed to them "horribly filthy, more like a receptacle for wild beasts than human beings."[2] Likewise, they found the buildings of Codrington College, one of the oldest educational establishments in Barbados, to be "ill constructed" and the grounds, although well laid out, "much neglected," wearing a "rather waste appearance."

> Indolence and inefficiency among the whites, was another prominent feature in slaveholding Barbadoes. Enterprise, public and personal, has long been a stranger to the island. Internal improvements, such as the laying and repairing of roads, the erection of bridges, building wharves, piers, &c., were either wholly neglected, or conducted in such a listless manner as to be a burlesque on the name of business. It was a standing task, requiring the combined energy of the island, to repair the damages of one hurricane before another came. . . . Having no personal cares to harass them, and no political questions to agitate them—having no extended speculations to push, and no *public enterprises* to prosecute, (save occasionally when a wreck on the southern point throws them into a ferment) the lives of the higher classes seem a perfect blank.[3]

The neglect of roads, wharves, and bridges is of a piece with the disregard for other public institutions, such as colleges and hospitals. Visitors to Barbados often noted that the colony was nearly destitute of shared spaces and organizations, including parks, public baths, museums, theaters, and literary or agricultural societies. More generally, the unrepaired public facilities testify to a "political economy of neglect," "a divestment of economic capital, political concern, and personal care."[4] Indeed, the planters' failure to join together and act in concert to build and maintain what Bonnie Honig calls "public things" or a "holding environment" necessary for the maintenance of collective life is symptomatic of a deeper and more pervasive social malaise: the ruling class's indifference to public welfare.[5]

Barbadian planters may have been deficient in "public spirit" but certainly not in private enterprise. The charge of indolence and inefficiency in executing public works is contradicted by their proven entrepreneurial spirit and business acumen. The large, integrated sugar plantation—combining cultivation and manufacture—that became the hallmark of Atlantic colonies was a revolutionary innovation of Barbadians. Between the mid-seventeenth and early eighteenth centuries, Barbados was the most valuable British possession in the Americas. In fact, Thome and Kimball visited the colony because "notwithstanding the insignificance of its size, Barbadoes ranks among the British islands next to Jamaica in value and importance," where "there is scarcely a foot of land that is not brought into requisition."[6] Such intensive exploitation of land was made possible by infrastructure—roads and ports, as well as the windmills and boiling houses that dotted the landscape. Unsurprisingly, one of the first pieces of legislation that the Barbados assembly enacted soon after its founding related to the construction of a bridge and the appointment of commissioners to supervise the laying and mending of highways and causeways. By the early eighteenth century, Barbados had a functioning internal transportation system and Bridgetown emerged as a major port city whose prominence in the transatlantic trading system matched, if not occasionally rivaled, that of Boston, Charleston, and Philadelphia.

Notwithstanding this astounding economic prosperity, the colony's roads and buildings wore, in the estimation of contemporary observers, the look of decay. During a visit in 1807, the surgeon John Waller found Bridgetown "every-where ill-built, with crooked and unpaved streets."[7] Daniel McKinnen, another traveler, found the streets "in a great measure unpaved" and the buildings exhibiting a "crumbling and dilapidated appearance." He attributed their warped exteriors in part to the tropical climate but above all to the planters' transient ethos: "Most of the principal inhabitants of the towns intend their dwellings merely as places of temporary residence, till they have acquired the means of removing to a more temperate climate, and naturally feel less solicitous to dispose of their money in objects of unprofitable and temporary concern."[8] Likewise, to William Sewell, correspondent for the *New York Times*, Bridgetown seemed "an exhausted city" where ostensibly "no attempt had been made to repair [the buildings'] dilapidated condition within half a century."[9] In one of the most thoroughgoing diagnoses of postemancipation societies, reflected in this chapter's epigraph, Sewell ascribed imperial abandonment to the rapaciousness of the white oligarchy. Indeed, the planters' assiduousness in managing plantation affairs is the obverse of their apathetic disregard for public works in Barbados and elsewhere in the British Caribbean.

The antithesis between care and neglect, the owners' responsible stewardship of private properties, and their corresponding indifference to public works is reflected in the visual aesthetic of colonial landscapes, which routinely contrasted urban decay and squalor with the beautiful rural plantation scenery. Thus, upon leaving the "dirty," "disagreeable" environs of Bridgetown, McKinnen was surprised by the "extremely picturesque" countryside, where he beheld "the masters' dwelling-houses with the negro-huts adjoining; and over a rich vale, abounding with cotton shrubs and maize, the hills at a small distance spotted with wind-mills, sugarworks, and a few lofty cabbage-trees, or cocoa-nuts." As he succinctly put it, "Nothing appears more like a garden than the sugar plantation under good cultivation."[10] More generally, using the period's discourse of landscape aesthetics, travelers described the rugged, unsettled mountainous terrain as sublime and terrifying; cultivated areas—neatly planted sugar fields, bordered by fruit orchards and provision grounds—as scenic and beautiful; and urban landscapes as ugly and unpleasant. Contemporary Caribbean authors like Derek Walcott, Michelle Cliff, and Jamaica Kincaid reactivate this discourse of landscape aesthetics to reflect on the ruination that underwrote capitalist agriculture.

This essay considers the role of infrastructure—physical structures designed to enable the movement of things, people, and information—in resource extraction and colonial governance. In Caribbean colonies, the plantation was the basic socioeconomic unit; it was an agrarian enterprise that relied on enslaved African labor to produce export staples for the world market. Founded on principles of racial hierarchy and subordination, plantations were regimented labor systems whose organization mirrored those of the colony. While historians have documented the role of legal codes, racial ideologies, and labor practices in legitimizing racial slavery, attention to infrastructural violence—and to the built environment more generally—illuminates how, as the anthropologists Dennis Rodgers and Bruce O'Neill have put it, "relationships of power and hierarchy translate into palpable forms of physical and emotional harm."[11]

Planters employed Black people in the building and maintenance of roads, bridges, and ports both during slavery and after emancipation, but the planning, construction, and use of these structures also triggered violent confrontation. The armed opposition of Indigenous people—maroons in Jamaica and Black Caribs in St. Vincent—limited or significantly altered the course of colonial expansion in these two colonies. Likewise, the roads and ports built to facilitate the movement of export commodities were also traversed by African Caribbeans to carry foodstuffs and livestock raised in kitchen gardens and provision grounds to Sunday markets, vibrant economic institutions all over the Caribbean. Finally, urban slaves employed in large port cities such as Bridgetown and Kingston had numerous opportunities for mobility and freedom. After emancipation, when planters imposed road and tollgate taxes to limit the mobility of freedmen, they rose up in revolt. Beginning with an overview of the role of roads in resource extraction in Barbados, I then turn to Jamaica to trace how infrastructure was a site of incommensurable desires. In particular, the efforts of the plantocracy to use infrastructure as a form of "calculative reason" and the attempts of their subjugated counterparts at placemaking often collided, as I show below, on the installation and use of transportation networks.

Barbados: Roads to Plantocratic Power

English colonization of the Caribbean commenced in the first quarter of the seventeenth century when Thomas Warner established a settlement on St.

Kitts (or St. Christopher) in 1624 for his sponsor Ralph Morrisford. Three years later, Captain Henry Powell reached Barbados with forty Englishmen and ten African slaves with an injunction from William Courteen, a prominent Anglo-Dutch merchant, to "plant and possess" the island. While the Spanish were drawn by the prospect of silver and gold to the Greater Antilles (Hispaniola, Jamaica, and Trinidad) and to Peru and Mexico on the mainland, English colonists sought to exploit the agricultural resources of the smaller colonies. In seeking to grow tobacco commercially, they hoped to replicate the success of their Virginian counterparts, who exported two hundred thousand pounds of that staple to England in 1624. The formidable presence of Kalinagos, the Native inhabitants of the Lesser Antilles, checked the growth of settlements in St. Kitts. In fact, the English and French partitioned the island in 1626 and entered into a military alliance to defend themselves against their Indigenous rivals. Barbados, however, lacked a native presence when English settlers arrived, and by 1629, the colony's population had risen to nineteen hundred.

The early arrivals in Barbados were the agents of merchants and courtiers whose main aim was to generate wealth out of the colony. The commercial nature of their agrarian undertakings is evident from the location of their houses and farms by the sea because, as the historian Richard Pares observed, "at the first foundation of the colonies all settlers had to enjoy an equal chance of sea transportation for their produce, which was the only kind of transportation then in existence."[12] Likewise, access to shipping seems to have determined the choice of spot for the first town, Bridge (which was later renamed Indian Bridge and then Bridgetown), although it was close to a tidal swamp and hence deemed insalubrious. According to one of the colony's first historians, "The convenience of landing and shipping their goods was doubtless the reason that a healthier situation was not selected by the settlers."[13] Access to coastal transportation appeared to be the overriding imperative in the colonists' desire to fix both their houses and the first town by the seaside.

During the first years, cultivation was undertaken by smallholders who cleared small patches of the land close to the coast and raised, in lots ranging from 1.2 to 2 hectors, tobacco for export and some subsistence crops for self-consumption, primarily with the help of indentured servants and a handful of African slaves and Native Arawaks. Tobacco was a native cultigen; it matured in a year, required only a field laborer or two to cultivate, and could be processed without costly equipment, obviating the need for major capital input. The period between 1627 and 1640 is considered the tobacco age in Barbados, but as Barbadian tobacco was deemed inferior to that produced in Virginia, the settlers switched first to cotton and then to sugar, introduced in the early 1640s from Brazil by the island's powerful and most enterprising planters, including James Drax, William Hilliard, and James Holdip. In the mid-seventeenth century, the Dutch were the principal suppliers of sugar to the European markets from the Portuguese colony Pernambuco in Brazil, but after being expelled by Portuguese planters, they assisted the English by providing credit and physical equipment (three-roller mills and copper furnaces) for processing sugar. By 1650, sugarcane exports were valued at 3 million pounds, an astonishing figure by contemporary standards. More significantly, the English planters who visited Pernambuco to learn about sugar making also witnessed the use of African slaves, a practice they transplanted to Barbados. But whereas in Brazil cultivation and processing were in separate hands, English planters preferred integrated units, which required considerable capital investment. Because a sugar estate needed to be between one hundred and two hundred acres to be financially viable (unlike tobacco farms, which ranged between ten and twenty acres), wealthy owners enlarged their plantations by acquiring adjacent estates. Hence, the number of landowners between the 1640s and 1660s is estimated to have fallen from 11,200 to 745.

Notwithstanding the rise of larger units, most of the plantations continued to be established along the colony's leeward shore. In 1650, roughly 50 percent of the properties (118 out of 259) were coastal because of the lack of adequate transportation in the interior. In fact, much of the island was densely wooded with no paths or mud tracks, and, even if these existed, they were not wide enough to admit horses, let alone carts and wagons. Hence, goods were carried on the heads of slaves. The rudimentary state of inland communication is evident from an anecdote in Richard Ligon's *A True and Exact History of the Island of Barbados* (1657), based on his stay on the island from 1647 to 1650. As he recalls, the dinner table at Colonel Walrond's waterside estate was well supplied with imported wine, olives, and oil because "his Land touching the Sea, his house being not half a quarter of a mile from it, and not interposed by any unlevel ground, all rarities that are brought to the Island, from any part of the world, are taken up, brought to him, and stowed in his Cellars in two hours time, and that in the night."[14] By contrast, these perishable items could not be carried without spoilage even a few miles inland because "the ways are such, as no Carts can pass; and to bring up a Butt of Sack, or a Hogshead of any other Wine, upon *Negroes*' backs, will very hardly be done in a night, so long a time it requires, to hand it up and down the Gullies." In the absence of proper roads and bridges, the deep gullies cut by torrential rains proved hazardous. As one resident recalled in 1651, the rains "beginneth aboute Agust, and lasteth till Christmans, in which time wee have often Land flood, which fall into Severall gullies, that many lose their lives. Not three Weekes since above a dozen were drowned, as alsoe some horses and Asuogos [donkeys] Lauden with Suggar."[15] Given the hazardous nature of inland travel, the asinego became the principal haulage animal, according to Ligon, as they "pick and choose their way, and sometimes choose out little ways in the wood, such as they know are fit for them to pass, which horses cannot do, because the ways are too narrow for them."[16]

It is perhaps in recognition of the wretched condition of internal roads—and hence of the obstacles to resource extraction—that the Barbados assembly enacted a series of laws for the construction and maintenance of roads and bridges, beginning with the 1652 "Act for the mending of the High wayes," which was expanded and reenacted a year later. Although there were earlier attempts at road legislation, the 1652 Act was prompted by the "Complaint that the High-ways of this Island are very bad, to the great hinderance of Trade." These two legal acts required the appointment of commissioners of the highways for each of the eleven parishes in the colony. The importance the assembly attached to roadbuilding and repairs is evident from their selection of some of the most powerful planters on the island as commissioners, including James Drax, Thomas Modyford, James Holdip, and Colonel Codrington, who were given the authority to levy a tax and set the rates of labor contribution from parish residents for the construction of roads that are "firm and good, for the Inhabitants of the Island, to pass too and fro on foot, and on their Cattle, Horse, and other beast about their occasion."[17] Smallholders with fewer than five acres and landless freemen were mandated to work for one day each month, and the rates of contribution by large owners were set according to the size of their holdings. The acts also stipulated the laying of gravel paths to Bridgetown from adjoining estates as well as the construction of a new stone bridge across the estuary.

But the legislative acts of the 1650s were only partially effective in improving transportation because the 1661 "Act for the Better Amending, Repairing, and Keeping Clean, the Common High-ways and Known Broad-paths within This Island" begins by acknowledging that, although "divers good Laws and Statutes have been hithertofore made and enacted in this Island," they have "not wrought the desired effect" because of "remisnes and want of due execution."[18] The 1661 act stipulated that highways should be no less than twenty-four feet wide in open land, forty feet in timber on one side of the road, and sixty feet through "standing wood." Carl and Roberta Bridenbaugh see the opening of the forests and jungle as "a phase of the Great Clearing" inasmuch as roads facilitated the hauling and carrying out of timber and subsequently commodities.[19] By 1700, according to David Watts, "Barbados had the best roads" in the Caribbean that were fit for carriages, carts, and horsemen.[20]

Roads—and the built environment more generally—irrevocably transformed the colony's topography. The rapid transformation of the colony's landscape is evident in Richard Ligon's 1657 map, which can be contrasted against Richard Ford's rendition from 1675. Ligon's map identifies 285 plantations by the names of their owners, the majority situated along the coast. Much of island interior is overgrown by tropical forest and virtually inaccessible, for the roads leading inland from the coast quickly peter out. In the middle of the island are ten thousand acres of land owned by London merchants. Other vignettes depict camels, horses, and donkeys, planters hunting

Fig 2.1. Richard Ligon, *A Topographical Description of Barbados* (1657).

wild hogs, and militia chasing slaves (see fig. 2.1). Richard Ford's map, prepared three decades later, shows the island fully inhabited, with barely an uncultivated patch. Whereas in Ligon's map there is only a single route connecting the northern and southern extremities of the island, in Ford's version, the entire territory is crisscrossed by roads. And the latter map lists 875 plantations by name, with more than 50 percent of the choicest land in the hands of two hundred big planters (see fig. 2.2). The colony's prosperity is evident in Samuel Copen's 1695 painting of Bridgetown, in which various physical structures like domestic buildings, fortifications, a church, and windmills make Bridgetown virtually indistinguishable from any English or Dutch port town (see fig. 2.3). Copen's painting captures the colony's preeminent status as the richest spot in the British Atlantic, whose economic value was "greater than that of all the English colonies put together."[21] Likewise, Bridgetown was the epicenter of transatlantic commerce, accounting for more than 50 percent of exports from the Caribbean to England.[22]

Barbados's emergence as the most important producer of sugar in the Atlantic world was thus enabled by the transformation of the natural environment by the built environment, a transformation guided by the statutes relating to highways enacted by the colonial assembly. Historians of New World slavery from Elsa Goveia to David Barry Gasper have pointed to the significance of the Barbados Slave Act of 1661 (enacted in the same year as

Fig 2.2. Richard Ford, *A New Map of the Island of Barbados* (1675).

the Act for the Better Amending, Repairing, and Keeping Clean, the Common Highways) as the basis for racial slavery in the Atlantic. By giving institutional form to a labor regime founded on the subjugation of enslaved Africans, the law provided a model for the slave codes of plantation societies in Jamaica and South Carolina. While legal violence enacted on raced bodies has garnered considerable scholarly attention, the violence of infrastructure—the suffering and harm entailed by the installation and maintenance of physical structures—is less understood because of challenges involved in archival retrieval. That is, while labor conditions in commodity production on plantations can be reconstructed based on existing sources, the same cannot be said of infrastructural work. As one of the foremost historians of the colony, Richard Pares, admitted, "The making of roads, [like the building and repairing of houses], was a matter of some decades . . . the process of fencing, road-making and building is the hardest of all to trace."[23]

The term "trace" in Pares's statement—which etymologically means a track, road, way, or path on the one hand, or a textual sign or nonmaterial mark denoting the existence of an event or thing on the other—encapsulates

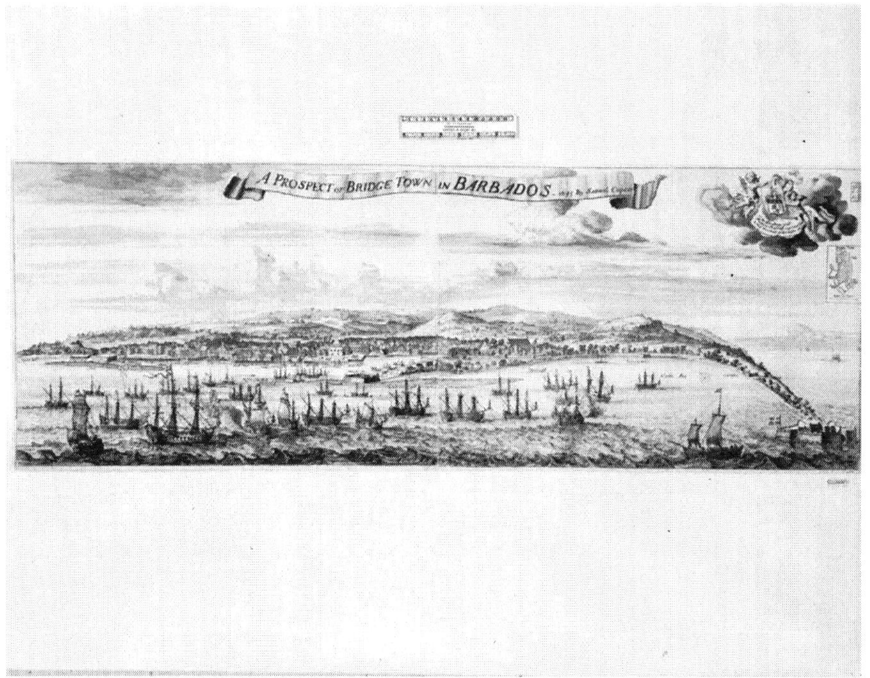

Fig 2.3. Samuel Copen, *A Prospect of Bridge Town in Barbados* (1695).

the obstacles inherent in the archival reconstruction of roads and other physical structures from surviving records. Physical structures are subject to both natural deterioration and modification by humans, thereby complicating scholarly attempts at retrieval. Commenting on the ephemeral evidence of the English medieval road system, Valerie Allen and Ruth Evans have observed how, during that era, "few roads were intentionally planned and built, in contrast to modern civil engineering" and "most have disappeared, having been paved over, or ploughed, or built upon," making it "hard to identify with certainty any field evidence for a medieval road."[24] Recent work on infrastructure has broached the problem of evidentiariness in terms of visibility, emphasizing the Latin prefix "infra" (which means below or under) because, despite constituting the hidden foundation of social life, infrastructure is noticed only during moments of failure or breakdown. Hence scholars have advocated the method of "infrastructural inversion" to bring these recessive, embedded, underground systems into view.[25] But this critical procedure, premised on the logic of concealment and exposure, of depth and surface, is of limited usefulness in tracing the racialized nature of infrastructural work in plantation colonies because of the paucity of archival sources. In a methodological reflection on the archive of slavery, Saidiya Hartman notes that the lives of enslaved people constitute "a history of an unrecoverable past."[26] Indeed, it is only after the abolition of slavery, as the condition of apprentices and free Blacks became a topic of metropolitan concern, that colonial officials began recording infrastructural labor, especially that of penal gangs in the building and upkeep of roads and public works. As J. W. Pringle documented in his landmark *Report on the Prisons of the West Indies* (1838), while women were employed in breaking stones, male prisoners, chained in pairs, worked on highways or were hired out to dig cane holes. The continuity between plantation and prison labor regimes is reflected in the use of the term "driver" to refer to supervisors of penal gangs as well as plantation overseers.[27]

Roadwork and plantation work were inextricably linked, both under slavery and after emancipation. Attention to the history of roadmaking in conjunction with patterns of migration, labor practices, and demographic changes reveals the brutalizing nature of infrastructural labor. Indentured servants constituted the majority of the workforce in the tobacco era (1628–40), and African slaves began to predominate following the introduction of sugar in the 1640s. From a negligible minority in the 1630s, the number of Africans grew to 5,680 in 1645 and to 46,600 in 1684. The number of whites declined from 23,980 to 19,568, of whom 2,381 were servants. By the turn of the century, African slaves accounted for 90 percent of the labor force and Blacks became demographically dominant. The demographic ascendancy of Africans also coincided with the removal of tropical forest in the interior, growth of transportation networks, and the expansion of plantation agriculture, suggesting the primacy of slave labor in all three undertakings. Although estate owners were required to send their slaves to work on roads, they seem to have recruited jobbers—slaves owned by small proprietors who hired them out for specific tasks—especially to dig cane holes on plantations. They worked, like their counterparts in cane fields, under a slave driver wielding a whip. As a contemporary observed, "Digging cane holes, making and repairing roads, and such like employment, commonly falls to their lot. They may be compared to hackhorses, hired by the planter, to perform the most laborious part of the work of the estate;—work which he finds it politic not to extort from his own animals."[28] Orlando Patterson notes that jobbers were also made to clear forests and, given the arduous nature of their labor, "the life expectancy of such a gang was estimated at seven years."[29]

The demands of roadwork were thus equivalent to the most onerous of plantation tasks: digging holes. Rodgers and O'Neill suggest that infrastructure is not "just a material embodiment of violence" but rather, its "instrumental medium, insofar as the material organization and form of a landscape not only reflect but also reinforce social orders, thereby becoming a contributing factor to reoccurring forms of harm."[30] The daily life of plantation slaves in late seventeenth-century Barbados exemplifies the "reoccurring forms of harm" engendered by infrastructure, inasmuch as the ecological devastation caused by the structures they helped build intensified their privations.[31] The network of highways and roads brought virtually every acre of land under cultivation. With woodlots and the tropical forest nearly eliminated, planters began to import timber for construction and fuel. The establishment of monoculture also led to soil erosion, as reports from colonial officials to the Board of Trade and Plantations attest. The colony's ecological degradation entailed difficult work routines because the methods of responsible husbandry that planters adopted to counter the loss of soil fertility—the cane hole technique of planting, the application of manure, the building of walls to arrest soil runoff, and replantation every year instead of ratooning—were all burdensome tasks. Thus, while an acre of sugar typically required one slave, in Barbados, it required two, and Barbados's slave regime was considered the harshest throughout the period. Finally, in the early days of slavery, planters set aside land for provision cultivation, but in the wake of declining profits, they began planting virtually all available land in cane and importing food from North America to feed their workers. The slaves' starch-heavy, protein-deficient diet, combined with overwork, was a source of numerous disorders and a contributor to high mortality rates. In 1689, the sugar planter Edward Littleton complained that "he that hath but a hundred Negroes, should buy eight or ten every year to keep up his stock."[32] The colony as a whole needed four thousand new slaves to maintain existing numbers. The loss of soil fertility, combined with mounting overhead costs of production, made sugar cultivation barely profitable by the first decade of the eighteenth century, prompting Barbados planters to migrate to Jamaica and South Carolina.

Jamaica: Infrastructure as Calculative Reason and Placemaking

Planters succeeded in establishing their authority so fully and decisively in Barbados because of topography. At about twenty miles long by fourteen miles wide, with a total surface area of 166 square miles, the island has 106,000 acres of arable land. It is relatively flat and had no Indigenous presence at the time of settlement. It became one of the most densely populated colonies in the Americas. But the British West Indian colonies were by no means topographically uniform. For instance, St. Christopher, colonized around the same time as Barbados, is highly mountainous, and the island had only one highway connecting the eastern and western extremities. The colony's rugged terrain with its impassable mountains hindered limitless expansion. The unique physical features of each colony thus not only shaped the outcome of projects of spatial integration envisioned by the colonists but also offered opportunities of self-assertion for enslaved people, as evidenced by contests over space in Jamaica, England's largest and most valuable colony in the eighteenth century.

With a surface area of 4,244 square miles, Jamaica is twenty-six times larger than Barbados. The island is long and narrow, traversed by several tall mountain chains rising steeply from the narrow coastal plains. A mere 14.5 percent of the island's total area is flat. The existence of innumerable rivers and creeks, with their rapid currents during the rainy season, made travel hazardous. The existing roads in the eighteenth century were mostly bridle paths and trails. In his 1774 *History of Jamaica*, the planter-historian Edward Long observed: "The settlers in this island have always been forced to contend against this arduous obstacle. They used at first to tread in the old Spanish tracks, which were mule paths, carried without art through thick woods, and over the highest, rudest summits of the mountains in a direct line."[33] Indeed, for nearly two centuries, from the moment of Jamaica's capture from Spain in 1655 until emancipation in 1838, various parishes on the island seem to have existed in relative isolation due to the absence of surface transport. According to a nineteenth-century visitor, lack of communication was the source of insularity: "If the island abounded in facilities for intercommunication, its towns, villages, and countrysides would exert on each other an assimilating efficacy. But the ends of the earth have more intercourse than the extremes of Jamaica." It was considered cheaper to transport produce by boat from one end of the island to another than to move it by road between adjacent parishes. Travelers were surprised, as they passed through the colony, "to find the price of provisions halved or doubled in contiguous parishes."[34]

Given these challenges posed by topography and the near absence of internal transport, the island remained sparsely populated for nearly a century after acquisition. The population of whites rose from 3,000 in 1673 to a modest 7,000 in 1715 and Blacks from 3,500 to 55,000. By contrast, in the latter year, Barbados had a population of nearly 17,000 whites and 50,000 Africans. Landownership was extremely concentrated in Jamaica, where, in 1754, 467 large planters owned on average 1,000 acres each, possessing 77.8 percent of arable land. Still, governor Edward Trelawny reported to the Board of Trade in 1752 that the island had one million acres of uncultivated patented area and 0.6 million acres of unclaimed arable land, citing "the absence of good roads being . . . a drawback to [their] settlement."[35] Edward Long reiterated the governor's view: "Much of the finest land in this island lies waste, for want of good communications leading through it."[36] In the first half of the eighteenth century, the Jamaican assembly and the British government experimented with several land schemes to attract landless whites and small farmers, but not successfully because of the challenge posed by maroons, Africans who, after Cromwell's 1655 conquest, had escaped into the mountainous interior in the northeastern parishes of St. George, St. Elizabeth, and St. James. They held lands in common and raided plantations, using the methods of guerilla warfare. The maroons were openly at war with the plantocracy between 1729 and 1739, when a peace treaty between the native leaders Colonel Cudjoe and Captain Accompong allowed the maroons to trade freely and retain tenure over fifteen hundred acres of land, in return for capturing and handing over runaway slaves. Perhaps most significantly, article 13 of the treaty stipulated that "Captain Cudjoe with his people shall cut, clear, and keep open, large and convenient roads from Trelawney Town to Westmorland and St. James's, and if possible to St. Elizabeth's."[37] This last clause addresses questions of security and colonial governance. Jamaican planters sought to create roads both to enhance economic production and achieve political integration. In his *History*, Long presents a series of recommendations on the construction and maintenance of roads not only with a view to make "untrodden recesses" of the island productive and profitable but also because wide, well-maintained roads facilitate the movement of militia during times of slave unrest—a paramount concern for a colony where Blacks outnumbered whites by ten to one.

It was only in the wake of the 1739 peace treaty that Jamaica emerged as the wealthiest colony in the British Empire. Between 1750 and 1800, the number of slaves grew from 122,000 to 337,000; sugar mills from 525 to 800; sugar output from 20,000 tons to 70,000; and the value of exports from 1.02 million to 3.9 million pounds. The colony's economic supremacy was simply unmatched. While Barbados exported 11,664 tons of sugar to Britain in 1815, Jamaica's stood at 73,849.[38] The colony's economic growth was supported by the growth of Kingston as a major maritime hub, whose population in the 1790s was 26,000, at a time when Boston had 18,000 and New York had 33,000 residents, making it the third largest town in the English-speaking Atlantic. It was also home to 2,690 free coloreds and 570 free Blacks. A notable feature of Jamaica's maritime trade was the growth of smaller port towns along the coast. Although Barbados had another port town, Speightstown, in addition to Bridgetown, it was of negligible importance. By contrast, Jamaica had four ports of entry—Kingston, Savanna-la-Mar, Montego Bay, and Port Antonio—as well as smaller ports. Finally, the cities of Hanover, St. James, Trelawny, St. Mary, and Portland were close to creeks and bays that allowed them to transport produce to the shore on small decked vessels. This system of smaller port cities was especially vital for inter- and intraisland trade in the absence of adequate surface transport.[39]

Ports in these large and small cities offered people of African birth and descent a measure of mobility that was unavailable for plantation laborers. Recent work on urban slavery has emphasized connections between the rural hinterlands and urban borderlands, between the plantation and the port. Blacks were employed in numerous vessel maintenance occupations, such as caulking, sail making, ship carpentry, and block making. Black mariners sailed on large merchant vessels traversing the Atlantic, but also on seagoing carriers of different sizes in a multitude of roles. In Jamaica, slave sailors served as canoe men and pilots, who were needed to guide incoming vessels to safe anchorage. Some small owners also operated wharfs independently of estates to provide coastal access to interior properties, relying on slave labor. Another vital means of coastal transportation was the "drogging" trade, conducted by colonial merchants to carry goods between ports. Olaudah Equiano begins his life as a sailor in Montserrat working on Robert King's droggers: as he recalls, "Mr. King dealt in all manner of merchandize. He had droggers of different sizes, which used to go about the island; and other places to collect rum, sugar, and other goods."[40] Equiano not only masters several skills of the trade such as the pulling, rowing, and piloting of boats, but also accumulates petty cash with which he eventually purchases freedom. Equiano's life, of course, is exemplary, but even common slaves seem to have found work at ports deeply self-affirming, as the following anecdote from an English visitor testifies:

> There being no anchorage for ships at Hope Bay, they usually lie at Annatto Bay, 20 miles to leeward, or at Port Antonio, ten miles to windward; and send their shallops (ten or twelve hogshead boats) for the sugars, & c. Sailors and Negroes are ever on the most amicable terms. This is evidenced in their dealings, and in the mutual confidence and familiarity that never subsist between the slaves and the resident whites. There is a feeling of independence in their intercourse with the sailor, that is otherwise bound up in the consciousness of a bitter restraint, that no kindness can overcome . . . *in the presence of the sailor, the Negro feels as a man;—in that of the man who lives in the continual view of his degradation, he feels as a slave.*[41]

In language analogous to Frederick Douglass's famous chiasmus in his 1845 autobiography— "You have seen how a man was made a slave; you shall see now how a slave was made a man"—Kelly underscores the dignity and independence of Black sailors.[42] But it was not only urban slaves who found means of self-affirmation; their rural counterparts did as well. In Jamaica and other British colonies such as Antigua and Trinidad, slaves cultivated provision crops both for self-consumption and exchange. Working on kitchen gardens near their homes or on grounds located at a distance from plantations, enslaved people raised a range of root crops and vegetables. Orlando Patterson notes that by the 1760s, enslaved people dominated the internal marketing system of Jamaica. About ten thousand Blacks attended the Sunday market at Kingston, traveling at times twenty to twenty-five miles on foot carrying produce on their heads that weighed between thirty and fifty pounds. These markets were not confined to big towns but existed near "ports, villages, cross-roads and the residences of large and wealthy families."[43] James Kelly noted that "it is a remarkable fact, well worth noticing, that a very considerable portion of the ground provisions, fresh pork, eggs, fruits, &c., consumed in the towns, or supplied to the shipping, is the growth and produce of the slaves."[44]

An important feature of the postemancipation era was the rise of a class of Black freeholders. The growth of an independent peasantry in Barbados was hindered by the unavailability of land, where landless freedmen had no other alternative than to perform estate labor. In contrast, Jamaica had vast tracts of "waste land" and unoccupied crown territory. Jamaican ex-slaves quickly acquired small patches of land, ranging from three to five acres, by purchase or simply squatting. A contemporary visitor was not only "surprised to find how general was the desire among the negroes to become possessed of a little land" but was impressed by their economic enterprise:

> Upon their little tracts they raise not only what they require for their own consumption, but a surplus which they take to market, usually in small panniers upon donkies, or upon their heads. Nearly every coloured proprietor has a donkey, which costs from seven to ten pounds, upon which he packs his produce, and under the custody sometimes of a woman, often of a child, he sends it to town, to be converted into money, with which he purchases such articles of necessity or luxury as his land does not produce, and he can afford. One of the most interesting spectacles to be witnessed about Kingston, is presented on the highroad through which the market people, with their donkeys, in the cool of the morning, pour into the city from the back country. They form almost an uninterrupted procession four or five miles in length.[45]

With the assistance of Baptist ministers, ex-slaves also formed numerous free villages throughout the colony, relocating themselves away from the plantations. These practices of placemaking were not only at odds with the ends of commercial agriculture but also threatened to imperil the colony's export-oriented economy. In response, the planter class used taxation to undermine the spirit of economic independence and restrict the physical mobility of freedmen. The Jamaican assembly raised import duties on articles widely used by common people—clothes, salt fish, flour, cornmeal, candles, and salt beef—in an effort to impose economic hardship and reverse Black flight. In addition, duties on haulage and working animals were made exorbitant. Within two decades after emancipation, the tax on "donkeys and horses owned by the people went up 1580 percent and 1220 percent respectively."[46] Perhaps more significantly, the colonial assembly also enacted the Main Road Law, tax proceeds from which were used to maintain roads leading to big estates at the expense of parochial roads that the Black peasantry needed to carry produce. As one of the Baptist missionaries complained: "Vast sums are spent on the main roads, and on those which lead to estates or pens, or to gentlemen's country mansions, whilst those which lead to the villages and freeholds of the people are sadly neglected, and many of them are dangerous to travel over."[47] Unsurprisingly, one of the most significant protests in postemancipation

Jamaica—the 1859 Westmoreland Toll Gate Riots—erupted in opposition to road tolls, when irate Black peasants and itinerant peddlers demolished toll bars and toll keepers' houses.

The white oligarchy thus weaponized infrastructure to thwart the socio-economic initiatives of Black freedmen in the postemancipation era. From the earliest days of settlement, infrastructure facilitated the optimal exploitation of natural resources and raced populations. The planters' single-minded pursuit of profit through monoculture eviscerated the natural environment and the colonies' social fabric. For instance, planters chose to send their children to England to be educated rather than investing in local schools or universities. They worked their laborers to death, rather than making health a priority. By failing to invest in structures and institutions that did not directly contribute to the sugar economy, the ruling class impeded the growth of domestic manufacture and, by extension, a diversified local economy throughout the eighteenth century. After emancipation, the planters used infrastructure to perpetuate existing inequities through their steadfast opposition to the construction of roads and other public amenities.

The plantation complex was thus a social and ecological catastrophe. The disastrous aftermath of export-oriented agriculture is the subject of several influential literary texts, including Sam Selvon's "Cane Is Bitter" (1979), Eric Walrond's "Vampire Bat" (1926), and Jean Rhys's "The Imperial Road." In the Caribbean, colonies became nations, imperial rule gave way to national autonomy, yet the effects of ecological destruction, engendered by capitalist agriculture, persist, both in tangible and subliminal forms. In *Imperial Debris*, Ann Laura Stoler names this ongoing, corrosive process "ruination," in that it "binds human potentials to degraded environments, and degraded personhoods to the material refuse of imperial projects—to the spaces redefined, to the soils turned toxic, to the relations severed between people and people, and between people and things."[48] Few writers have captured the experience of ruination the way Michelle Cliff and Jamaica Kincaid have.[49] In *A Small Place*, her fictionalized memoir about postcolonial Antigua, Kincaid reactivates the language of eighteenth-century landscape aesthetics to insistently characterize the island's natural environment as beautiful, too beautiful in fact to seem real, and the white sojourners—descendants of itinerant planters—and the decaying physical structures they erected as ugly. Kincaid makes the project of national reconstruction equivalent to the building of durable public amenities, such as schools, hospitals, libraries, and roads. Throughout the book, the destructive effects of plantation agriculture and the postcolonial nation-state's efforts at rebuilding are reflected in its faltering infrastructure, prompting one to ask if human flourishing is possible in decimated landscapes. *Imperial Debris* and *A Small Place* also invite us to think about memory, inheritance, and obligation. It is self-evident to many of us that capital accumulates over time, that things and possessions gain value as time progresses. Stoler and Kincaid seem to suggest that debilities and disadvantages too accumulate and accrue over time such that, for some people, dispossession becomes their only inheritance. We need to take an unflinching look at the racialized dimensions of infrastructural harm, enacted through the built environment, to begin a meaningful dialogue about catastrophe and compensation.

Notes

1. William Laurence Burn, *Emancipation and Apprenticeship in the British West Indies* (London: Jonathan Cape, 1937), 366.

2. James Thome and Horace Kimball, *Emancipation in the West Indies: A Six Months' Tour in Antigua, Barbados, and Jamaica in the Year 1937* (New York: American Anti-slavery Society, 1838), 292.

3. Thome and Kimball, *Emancipation*, 189, 249.

4. Christopher Taylor, *Empire of Neglect: The West Indies in the Wake of British Liberalism* (Durham, NC: Duke University Press, 2017), 33.

5. Bonnie Honig, *Public Things: Democracy in Disrepair* (New York: Fordham University Press, 2017).

6. Thome and Kimball, *Emancipation*, 214.

7. John Augustine Waller, *A Voyage in the West Indies* (London: Sir R. Phillips, 1820), 4.

8. Daniel McKinnen, *A Tour through the British West Indies in the Years 1802 and 1803* (London: J. White, 1804), 14, 15.

9. Sewell, *Ordeal*, 18.

10. McKinnen, *Tour*, 18, 57.

11. Dennis Rodgers and Bruce O'Neill, "Introduction to the Special Issue," "Infrastructural Violence," special issue, *Ethnography* 13, no. 4 (2012): 402.

12. Richard Pares, *Merchants and Planters* (Cambridge: Cambridge University Press, 1960), 62.

13. Robert H. Schomburgk, *The History of Barbados* (London: Longman, Brown, Green and Longmans, 1848), 241.

14. Richard Ligon, *A True and Exact History of the Island of Barbados* (London: Humphrey Moseley, 1657), 88.

15. "A Breife Discription of the Ilande of Barbados," in *Colonising Expeditions to the West Indies and Guiana*, ed. V. T. Harlow (ca. 1652; London: Hakluyt Society, 1924), 42–43.

16. Ligon, *True and Exact*, 111.

17. John Jennings, ed., *Acts and Statutes of the Island of Barbados* (London, 1654), 141.

18. Richard Hall, ed., *Acts Passed in the Island of Barbados, from 1643 to 1762* (London, 1764), 45.

19. Carl Bridenbaugh and Roberta Bridenbaugh, *No Peace beyond the Line: The English in the Caribbean, 1624–1690* (New York: Oxford University Press, 1972), 273.

20. David Watts, *The West Indies: Patterns of Development, Culture and Environmental Change since 1492* (Cambridge: Cambridge University Press, 1987), 359.

21. Hilary McD. Beckles, "The 'Hub of Empire': The Caribbean and Britain in the Seventeenth Century," in *The Oxford History of the British Empire*, ed. Nicholas Canny (Oxford: Oxford University Press, 1998), 218–40, 225.

22. Pedro Welch, *Slave Society in the City: Bridgetown, Barbados, 1680–1834* (Kingston: Ian Randle, 2003), 54.

23. Pares, *Merchants and Planters*, 9.

24. Valerie Allen and Ruth Evans, introduction to *Roadworks: Medieval Britain, Medieval Roads*, ed. Valerie Allen and Ruth Evans (Manchester: Manchester University Press, 2016), 14.

25. Ashley Carse, "Keyword: Infrastructure: How a Humble French Engineering Term Shaped the Modern World," in *Infrastructures and Social Complexity: A Companion*, ed. Penny Harvey, Atsuro Morita, and Casper Bruun Jensen (New York: Routledge, 2016), 45–57; Susan Leigh Star, "The Ethnography of Infrastructure," *American Behavioral Scientist* 43, no. 3 (1999): 377–91.

26. Saidiya Hartman, "Venus in Two Acts," *Small Axe* 26 (2008): 12.

27. J. W. Pringle, *Report on the Prisons of the West Indies* (1838).

28. Thomas Cooper, *Facts Illustrative of the Condition of the Negro Slaves in Jamaica* (London: J. Hatchard and Son, 1824), 66.

29. Orlando Patterson, *The Sociology of Slavery: An Analysis of the Origins, Development and Structures of Negro Slave Society in Jamaica* (Rutherford, Vancouver: Fairleigh Dickson University Press, 1969), 66.

30. Rodgers and O'Neill, "Infrastructural Violence," 404.

31. Rodgers and O'Neill, "Infrastructural Violence," 404.

32. Edward Littleton, *The Groans of the Plantations* (London: M. Clark, 1689), 16.

33. Edward Long, *The History of Jamaica* (London: T. Lownudes, 1774), 2:466.

34. David King, *The State and Prospects of Jamaica* (London, 1851), 26.

35. Quoted In Frank Wesley Pitman, *The Development of the British West Indies* (New Haven, CT: Yale University Press, 1917), 125.

36. Long, *History*, 2:466.

37. "Articles of Pacification with the Maroons of Trelawney Town, Concluded March the first, 1738." The full text can be found at https://cyber.harvard.edu/eon/marroon/treaty.html.

38. Robin Blackburn, *The Making of New World Slavery, from the Baroque to the Modern* (London: Verso, 1997), 405.

39. Julius S. Scott, *The Common Wind: Afro-American Currents in the Age of the Haitian Revolution* (London: Verso, 2018), 1–37.

40. Olaudah Equiano, *The Interesting Narrative and Other Writings*, ed. Vincent Carretta (New York: Penguin, 1995), 64.

41. James Kelly, *Voyage to Jamaica, and Seventeen Years' Residence in that Island: Chiefly Written with a View to Exhibit Negro Life and Habits* (Belfast: J. Wilson, 1838), 29–30 (emphasis mine).

42. Frederick Douglass, *Narrative of the Life of Frederick Douglass, an American Slave* (New York: Penguin, 1983), 107.

43. Patterson, *Sociology of Slavery*, 226.

44. Kelly, *Voyage*, 17.

45. John Bigelow, *Jamaica in 1850* (London: G. P. Putnam, 1851), 115, 117.

46. Don Robotham, "The Notorious Riot: The Socio-Economic and Political Bases of Paul Bogel's Revolt," *Anales del Caribe del Centro de estudios del Caribe* (1983): 77.

47. *Accounts and Papers of the House of Commons* (London, 1865), 13:174.

48. Ann Laura Stoler, "'The Rot Remains': From Ruins to Ruination," in *Imperial Debris: On Ruins and Ruination*, ed. Ann Laura Stoler (Durham, NC: Duke University Press, 2013), 7–8.

49. The protracted or enduring effects of environmental devastation in the wake of European imperialism is a recurrent concern of Cliff's novels, including *Abeng* (1984) and *No Telephone to Heaven* (1987). In an extraordinary reflection on ruination, Cliff writes:

> The civilizer works against the constant danger of the forest, of a landscape ruinate, gone to ruination. *Ruinate*, the adjective, and *ruination*, the noun, are inventions. Each word signifies the reclamation of land, of cultivation, civilization, by the uncontrolled, uncontrollable. When a landscape becomes ruinate, carefully designed aisles of cane are envined, strangled, the order of empire is replaced by the chaotic forest. The word *ruination* (especially) signifies this immediately; it contains both the word *ruin*, and *nation*. A landscape in ruination means one in which the imposed nation is overcome by the naturalness of ruin. As individuals in this landscape, we, the colonized, are also subject to ruination, to the self reverting to the wildness of the forest.

Michelle Cliff, "Caliban's Daughter: The Tempest and the Teapot," *Frontiers: A Journal of Women Studies* 12, no. 2 (1991): 40.

Chapter 3

Internal Empire

The Neoclassical Architecture of Racial Capitalism

Louis Moreno

> Racial regimes are unrelentingly hostile to their exhibition.
>
> —Cedric Robinson, *Forgeries of Memory and Meaning*

The Opaque Zone

Of all the competing efforts to define the term "infrastructure," the entry for the eighth edition of *Dictionnaire de l'Académie française* (1932–35) is distinguished by its simplicity. Infrastructure is plainly described as the "lower part of a construction. Also known as Earthworks, the works of art of a railroad."[1] Formulated in a time when infrastructural questions were largely the concern of engineers, if the presence of railroads, bridges, ports, sewers, electrical systems, and so on intruded on the space of everyday life, the role of architecture was to put infrastructure in its place. Infrastructure was something that supported life but was devoid of existence.

Since then, scholars have shown how the significance of infrastructure has expanded, forming a complex presence across every level and dimension of urban space. Keller Easterling argues that with infrastructure's planetarization, urbanism has become overdetermined by its logistical protocols. "Like an operating system," Easterling writes, "the medium of infrastructure space makes certain things possible and other things impossible. It is not the declared content but rather the content manager dictating the rules of the game in the urban milieu."[2] Stefano Harney and Fred Moten similarly describe a transmutation in the infrastructures of power. No longer content with supporting the world, logistical infrastructures want "to live in the concrete itself in space at once, time at once, form at once."[3] On this account, the earthworks of the twenty-first century, whether free ports, smart cities, or golf courses, while no longer described as "works of art," nonetheless represent a powerful kind of landscape aesthetic.

Where did infrastructure learn to act this way? The answer lies in "the zone," Easterling's name for evolving spatial typologies that began with "ancient free ports, pirate enclaves . . . entrepots of maritime trade"[4] but in the twentieth century established a new degree of influence through the spread of logistics and standardization. In the postwar period, nation-states produced deregulated spaces, special economic zones, which blurred public right and commercial interest in a competitive effort to access the global frontier of financial capital. By the early twenty-first century, so successful was the spatialization of free trade, it had become not only the medium of globalization but also its self-replicating form.

Easterling's account is sublime and unnerving, presenting an image of twenty-first-century life wholly dependent on spatial products that elude democratic control. But while the capitalist practices and policies that decide the culture of globalization are rigorously described, the motive forces animating this system are assumed rather than explained. More to the point, what is never clarified is the cultural process that enabled infrastructure to rise from the "urban substructure" to become architecture itself.[5] Therefore, what remains opaque is any sense of the social conditions in which all of the "various and peculiarly shaped feelings, illusions, habits of thought and conceptions of life"[6] become reducible to the logic of property and synthesized into one sprawling "real estate cocktail." Put differently, what the zone avoids is a historical analysis of the class system cultured by the power of infrastructure space.

The eschewal of historical materialism is no accident. According to Easterling the invocation of "Capital" "sends us to the same places to search for dangers while other concentrations of authoritarian power escape scrutiny."[7] For the anthropologist Brian Larkin, the effort to unmask the subjection of social relationships to exchange relations "threatens to" obscure the agency of infrastructure by always "recenter[ing] the human subject as the sole locus of agency."[8] However, both positions indicate a narrow grasp of the struggle, with and within Marxism, to develop a critique of culture that did not subject infrastructure to a reductively economic or humanist interpretation. In the field of cultural studies, Stuart Hall attempted to rethink the question of infrastructure and superstructure to show how in practice "the emergence of new structures of political power"[9] circumvent a political economic analysis. From a different perspective, Fredric Jameson argued that nothing is ever explained when political, social, and cultural phenomena are thought to be determined by capital, but "everything changes"[10] when infrastructure is named as a cultural "problem." Or, as Raymond Williams said, the basis of determination occupies a space of struggle between emergent and residual social forces.[11] More recently, Ruth Wilson Gilmore, drawing on Williams, has described the enduring cultural work of those impoverished, surrounded, and trapped by racist systems of partition and exclusion, as "infrastructures of feeling."[12]

Asking how infrastructure acquired an aesthetic form of life, therefore does not mean abandoning the question of class struggle and spatial production. But the critique of political economy does require geographic reorientation, so we can excavate the "earthworks" that enabled capitalism to become a living system. Thus, far from taking infrastructure to be a fixed system of exploitation, a dialectical approach can draw on radical histories, throwing into relief the colonial designs of infrastructures "founded with the first great movement of commodities, the ones that could speak."[13] The Black radical tradition's interpretations of infrastructure are therefore critical. Take two of the most famous examples; C. L. R. James's *The Black Jacobins* and W. E. B. Du Bois's *Black Reconstruction* both teach us about resistance to sociospatial systems—the plantation systems of the eighteenth and nineteenth centuries—and provide a concrete understanding of how the concept of race and the infrastructure of slavery formed capitalism's conditions of existence. What James and Du Bois introduced, Cedric Robinson explained,[14] was an analysis of the relationship between racism and capitalism that Marx was unable to comprehend. From this perspective, the infrastructures of enslavement that supported the growth of modern capitalism were not only composed of ports, ships, and plantations. Operating this fixed capital required "racial regimes,"[15] Robinson's term for systems of visual and spatial cognition whose perception of individual freedom and human sovereignty was underpinned by the total denial of Black social life, and this underpinning was justified in law by categorizing the enslaved as a peculiar asset class of infrastructure—as real estate.

Prompted by this insight, this essay considers the formative stage of global capitalism to consider why the infrastructure of colonization assumed a particular architectural form. Robinson's fundamental observation is that racial regimes are unstable, always liable to "'collapse' under the weight of their own artifices, practices, and apparatuses."[16] Building on this we shall see how, from the eighteenth century, neoclassical architecture gave colonial infrastructure form and reinforcement, enshrining racial capitalism in a cultural system.

Homes, Gardens, and Plantations

To focus the inquiry, we shall consider one type of architecture—the Italian country villa. This was a design that, while originating in the terra firma of sixteenth-century Italy, moved around the world in a series of arcs: first gentrifying the development of eighteenth-century London and later cultivating the colonial growth of the British Empire with a corporate image.

As Rudolph Wittkower demonstrated in *Architectural Principles in the Age of Humanism*, buildings like Villa Cornaro and Villa La Rotonda represented the culmination of an aesthetic pioneered by Alberti and perfected by Palladio. This project attempted to bring the proportions of the human being into geometric harmony with the building, the city, and the cosmos.[17] More practically, this new architecture provided discrete spaces in which the enjoyment of the countryside could be blended with urbane functions—entertaining and deal making—that were needed by Venice's merchant and political classes. By applying the classical Greek temple front of pediment and portico to the villa's facade, Palladio realized an edifice that made these houses appear the earthly expression of some higher power.

The combination of scale, proportion, and grandeur captured the imagination of the English aristocracy of the eighteenth century. During the Restoration period, the touring classes saw Palladio's architecture as a universal system that could be imported to London. Under the third Earl of Burlington, Palladio's *Four Books of Architecture* provided a means to "fix a standard of architectural taste" for a society in a state of "improvement."[18] What was striking about this transplant was the practical way it ensconced itself in bourgeois and petit bourgeois society. "Palladianism," John Summerson wrote, "conquered not only the high places of architecture—the great patrons, the government offices—but, through the medium of prints and books, most of the vernacular, finding its way ultimately into the workshop of the humble carpenter and bricklayer."[19] So much so that by the mid-eighteenth century, through the proliferation of country houses and urban dwellings, it had established an aesthetic that enabled landowners, merchants, and aristocrats to construct a gentlemanly sense of class interest.

By the time Robert Morris's pattern book *Rural Architecture* was published in 1750, Palladianism had been fully incorporated into the emerging system of "gentlemanly capitalism": fabricating spatial products that could be fashioned and refashioned for town and country. This capacity to give the commercial force of capital a sense of human proportion manifested its growing cultural power. Or, as Raymond Williams put it, the country house refined the violence of dispossession. Although "fashionable to admire these extraordinarily numerous houses," [20] Williams wrote in *The Country and the City*, it was important to inspect the source of their value. When looking at these Italianate structures, with their elegant renewal of classical form and molding of landscape, one needed to ask, By what process was the dictatorship of both land and people *naturalized*? Williams's answer was succinct.

> What these 'great' houses do is to break the scale, by an act of will corresponding to their real and systematic exploitation of others. For look at the sites, the facades, the defining avenues and walls, the great iron gates and the guardian lodges. They were chosen for more than the effect from the inside out; where so many admirers, too many of them writers, they stood and shared the view, finding its prospect delightful. They were chosen, also, you now see, for the other effect,

> from the outside looking in: a visible stamping of power, of displayed wealth and command: a social disproportion which was meant to impress and overawe.[21]

Yet, as Edward Said remarked in *Culture and Imperialism*, Williams was so absorbed in drawing the English architecture of class, the critique fell short in mapping the wider foundations of colonial power. Pushing Williams further, Said demonstrated how a domestic social consciousness was altered by changes in the geographical reach of property. For example, when comparing her expansive Northampton residence to her childhood home in Portsmouth, the heroine of Jane Austen's *Mansfield Park* conveys a sense of disorientation. Fanny is "stunned" by "the smallness of the house" and the "thinness of the walls" in the place where she was raised. Another dimension of compression lies in the way domestic life is ordered at Mansfield Park. While an absent figure, Fanny's benefactor and uncle, Sir Thomas Bertram, maintains a regime of oversight that seems natural in an estate the size of Mansfield Park. In "her uncle's house," Austen writes, there is a peculiarly constant "consideration of times and seasons, a regulation of subject, a propriety, an attention towards every body which there was not here."[22]

This represents a different "stamping of power" to the one Williams had in mind. Bertram's need to personally police the "trouble in Antigua" expresses a fault in the colonial estate felt in the metropolitan interior. Thus, in demonstrating how property forms a complex field of material and cultural forces, Said opened a hidden floor supporting Williams's "structure of feeling." The environment of Mansfield Park is "troubled" by a crisis in the infrastructure connecting colony to metropole, and while Austen never makes the reason explicit, the specter of decline haunts the domestic interior. Belying the balance of neoclassical architecture is a "ghastly . . . infrastructure underlying a chain of people, ideas, places and practices"[23] disclosing the conflict and corruption at the heart of the colonial process.

Even in decline, however, this system has a trick up its sleeve. As Eric Williams wrote in *Capitalism and Slavery*, the ideologies that inhabit the plantation can outlive the immediate form of this system. "An outworn interest, whose bankruptcy smells to heaven in historical perspective, can exercise an obstructionist and disruptive effect which can only be explained by the powerful services it had previously rendered and the entrenchment previously gained."[24] The immediate personifications of capital, such as Bertram's "planter class," may be liquidated, but their ideas survive to "work their old mischief."[25]

To consider how this unfolded, we must shift the critique of property—surveying a venerated monument to landed power *and* a variegated set of infrastructures in perpetual transformation—to launch a thesis, namely, that neoclassical architecture enabled the plantation to exercise an enduring influence over the organization of metropolitan life. To explore this, we must ask how architecture concretized the political authority of the eighteenth-century planter class. Retaining the focus on the country house, we will now pivot from England to eighteenth-century America, to consider the attraction this architecture had for one particular planter, Thomas Jefferson. The third president of the United States is celebrated as a philosopher, politician, and architect. Of interest here, however, is the manner in which this slave-owner used culture to sink the plantation into the foundations of American consciousness.

Expressions of the American Mind

Transplanted to England, the Italian villa indexed a point of translation between the movement of capital and the stasis of land. Which is to say, this aesthetic expressed a general transformation in the structure and culture of the eighteenth century. The colonial "infrastructure of commercial capitalism"[26] expanded the wealth of merchants, bankers, shipowners, insurance agents, and stockbrokers in London, and the stockbrokers in turn provided the gentry and aristocracy with a means for their influence to survive.[27] The import of Palladianism to eighteenth-century England followed, then, a logic: the new architecture sealed an exchange that used commercial capital to restore the financial interests, political influence, and cultural dominance of landed property. But how did this process of translation work in the United States, a republic?

Architectural historians argue that Jefferson's Declaration of Independence identified with the moral as well as mathematical clarity of Palladio's architectural system. According to at least one study, the "relationship established by the Italian architect between architecture and natural law appealed to the American, and the codification of proportion was accepted as most authoritative; and if the first made its appeal to sentiment, the second was based upon intellectual and archaeological grounds."[28] And against the charge that Jefferson was merely a "copyist," it has been claimed that the free use of classical sources manifested a synthesis—of revolution and tradition—similar in manner to the way elements of Aristotle, Cicero, Locke, and Sidney were borrowed in the drafting of the Philadelphia Manifesto.[29]

However, while Jefferson may have seen himself as the spiritual "descendent and willing follower of Palladio,"[30] the designs exhibit deviations. For example, the geometry of Monticello, Jefferson's hilltop villa in Charlottesville, Virginia, betrays the Palladian system with a "preoccupation with polygonal architectural forms." Such idiosyncrasies reflected his desire for the fashionable trappings of the English gentry. This can be seen in the considerable influence Robert Morris's pattern book had on Jefferson. Such was his debt to Morris that the arrangement of his own private utopia was in fact a copy of plate 37 of *Rural Architecture*—"A Little Building intended for

Retirement." Once again, architectural historians are quick to defend Jefferson's reputation as a Renaissance man, presenting the use of templates as merely an *aide memoire*. Even so we might ask, Why was Jefferson devoted to such a peculiarly English "memory model"?[31]

One answer is that, in Jefferson's adaptation of classical form, the architecture was symptomatic of an American "longing for *something other than itself*."[32] In this respect, it conformed to Antonio Gramsci's famous assessment that "Americanism" regenerated rather than broke with European classicism. "What we are dealing with," Gramsci said, "is an organic extension and an intensification of European civilisation, which has simply acquired a new coat in the American climate."[33] The design of the landscape presented an aesthetic means to "understand and absorb" the forces of accumulation. Moreover, and here was the mischievous trick, through the deployment of architecture, these forces could be coded to the grammar of classicism, enabling the founding fathers to obtain an entirely new sense of "natural" history.

Manfredo Tafuri complicated Gramsci's critique by drawing attention to the design of this new coat. Although the stability, clarity, and above all mobility of classical design helped Jefferson conceptualize America as an agrarian utopia, his plans (for universities, observatories, houses, and cities) manifested a feeling of ambivalence about the urbanizing nature of American society. "Agricultural economy, local and regional autonomy as pivots of the democratic system, and the restraining of industrial development . . . were symbols of his fear in face of the processes set in motion by the Revolution. Essentially this was fear of . . . the birth and growth of an urban proletariat."[34]

This fearful ambivalence can be seen in Jefferson's experiments in town planning. As a visiting minister to Paris, Jefferson was impressed by the city's scale, but as a solution to urban form he was convinced more by the American gridiron system than the French capital's baroque convolutions. First deployed in 1638 by English colonists, the nine square plan for the town of New Haven, Connecticut, provided a flexible system that had guided the urban development of America. From what Jefferson saw in Philadelphia, the pattern of radial streets and open squares inhibited the European experience of "density and congestion . . . which he hoped to see avoided in his own country."[35] But the repetitious uniformity of the grid also unsettled Jefferson, recognizing an infrastructure that could generate conditions for disorder and disease. So as with Monticello, which broke with Palladio's geometry through the use of multisided rooms, his design for Jeffersonville attempted to break the grid's monotony. The checkerboard punctuation of buildings with parks was intended to ventilate the streets, prevent epidemics, and evoke a feeling for nature. "The atmosphere of such a town," Jefferson wrote, "would be like that of the country, insusceptible of the miasmata which produce yellow fever."[36]

Jefferson's translation of English neoclassical form was no doubt born of taste, but animating it was the search for what Tafuri called aesthetic "terms of reference for a society continually terrified by the process it has itself set in motion and considered irreversible."[37] Seen in this light, Monticello's architecture manifested an insurance policy disguised as national propaganda. Even if economic and social interests were to be dictated by the urbanization of capital, this American form of power would be cultured by an order "other than itself": namely, the apparent timelessness, effortless superiority, and unquestioned rationality of European humanism. As a theorist whose form was space as well as politics, Jefferson was a policy maker who saw architecture as a medium to regulate the passage of time and motion of society. Faced with the social tumult of urban transformation, the colonial architecture of power—the plantation house—would become the timeless registry preserving the terms of American order.

Real Estate as a Racial Regime

Architecture cracks open a window onto a struggle taking place in the metropolitan and colonial infrastructures of the eighteenth century. Just as the imagined interiors of Mansfield Park are stalked by "trouble in Antigua," Monticello forms the facade to a political unconscious "terrified" by a force that makes freedom uncontrollable. What, though, was the source of this ambivalence and how did it structure the environment? According to Tafuri's spatial dialectic, neoclassical architecture produced a space of inertia, a bulwark protecting the planters from the industrial force of urbanization. However, this analysis observes a clash of forces—plantation slavery of the South versus the industrial complex of the North—without excavating the protocols that preserved, before and after the Civil War, capitalism's racial terms of order. Thus while historical materialism could explain the intersection of infrastructure and culture by making the working class the center of gravity, the emphasis on proletarian urbanization repeated the oversight Du Bois found in Charles and Mary Beard's "Rise of American Civilization":

> Manufacturing and industry develop in the North; agrarian feudalism develops in the South. They clash, as winds and waters strive, and the stronger forces develop the tremendous industrial machines that governs us so magnificently and selfishly today. Yet in this sweeping mechanistic interpretation, there is no room for the real plot of the story, for the clear mistake and guilt of rebuilding a new slavery of the working class in the midst of a fateful experiment in democracy; for the triumph of sheer moral courage and sacrifice in the abolition crusade; and for the hurt and struggle of degraded black millions in their fight for freedom and their attempt to enter democracy.[38]

Following Du Bois, we must dig deeper to investigate the racial regime that underpinned the topography of eighteenth-century capitalism. What underlying instability produced the spatial desire for architectural form? How did the coding of race permeate a neoclassical structure of feeling? Here I want to draw on Hortense Spillers and Nahum Chandler as well as Du Bois to take a second look at Jefferson's architecture. This path clarifies much of what is otherwise cryptic in the spatial dialectic. For example, to grasp the "ambiguous conscience" of neoclassical architecture, the ambiguity does not lie in any notion that the ideology of civil society was troubled by the existence of slavery. It lies rather in the underlying volatility of the category of property that forms liberalism's condition of existence—real estate—a form of value that treated the enslaved not as people but as infrastructure equivalent to a tract of land or a building.

As Spillers explains, the "various civil codes of the slave holding United States" are read in retrospect as if they were "monolithically informed, unified, and executed in their application." But if one reads between the lines, although the slave "is perceived as the essence of stillness (an early version of ethnicity), or of an undynamic human state, fixed in time and space," when one approaches the material facts of slavery we encounter a business "riddled in practice, with contradictions, accidents and surprise." The source of these contradictions comes from the increasing pressure of resistance to the system of plantation slavery. "It is, perhaps, not by chance," Spillers writes, "that the laws regarding slavery appear to crystallize in the precise moment when agitation against the arrangement becomes articulate in certain European and New World communities."[39] How then did this moment agitate the crystalizing form, function, and feeling of the racial regime?

Form

We must first clarify how the practice of slavery grounded the concept of race in the idea of architectural form. Perhaps the best illustration lies in chapter 3 of *Black Reconstruction* where Du Bois indicates a fissure in the master class's racist ideology of freedom. Recounting a speech given at the Southern Congress in February 1861, Du Bois notes that the planters said that the cause of the Civil War was rooted in the American mind's flawed expression. According to Alexander H. Stevens, vice president of the Confederacy, "The assumption of the equality of races" contained in the Declaration of Independence "was an error. It was a sandy foundation, and the idea of a government built upon it; when the 'storm came and the winds blew, it fell.' "[40] Thus according to Du Bois, the Civil War was fought by the planters to eliminate any doubt that the equivalence of African people to real estate was antithetical to American existence, an evil that "somehow or other, in the order of Providence . . . would be evanescent and pass away."[41] Further, such testimony clarified the Confederacy's objective: to geographically extend the right of colonization through a God-granted power to enslave. The racial coding of slavery would form the law that universalized the cosmic "truth" of the Southern empire.

The proof, Du Bois wrote, lay in the slave codes: "Slaves were not considered men. . . . The whole legal status of slavery was enunciated in the extraordinary statement of a chief justice of the United States that Negroes had always been regarded in America 'as having no rights which a white man was bound to respect.'"[42] For the Confederacy, the war was a moment in which this confusion of theory and practice over slavery could be resolved once and for all. Secession would realize a dictatorship of property that no longer had to conceal its base of power, because architecture manifested proof of the sovereign truth of white supremacy. "The architect in the construction of buildings" Stevens said in 1861, "lays the foundations with the proper materials, the granite; then comes the brick or the marble. The substratum of our society is made of the material fitted by nature for it, and by experience we know that it is best, not only for the superior, but for the inferior race that it should be so. It is, indeed in conformity with the ordinance of the Creator."[43] What this indicates is that, beyond the external threat of Northern industrialization, what constituted the American mind was the sense of a threat internal to the design of American democracy. As evidence, Nahum Chandler directs our attention to the *Notes on the State of Virginia*, in which Jefferson records his "trembling" conscience over the "so-called Negro Question."[44] The question at hand, Chandler makes clear, is not any sense of shame over the institution of slavery. Jefferson saw no inconsistency when a slaveholder declared the principle of equality for all self-owning people, precisely because of "his propositional declaration of belief in Negro inferiority in relation to 'Whites' or Europeans."[45] Rather, working in the tracks of Du Bois's method, Chandler argues that Jefferson's trembling turned on the question of possible emancipation.[46] It was caused by the difficulty of establishing, through empirical observation, the grounds for the natural law of racial subordination. Nature did not furnish the white man with the grounds of judgment. "Thus," Chandler writes, "the hesitation and ambivalence recorded" by Jefferson in the following passage:

> To justify a general conclusion requires many observations, even where the subject may be submitted to the Anatomical knife, to Optical glasses, or by solvents. How much more then where it is a faculty, not a substance, we are examining; where it eludes the research of all the senses; where the conditions of its existence are various and variously combined; where the effects of those which are present or absent bid defiance to calculation; let me add too as a circumstance of tenderness, where our conclusion would degrade a whole race of men from the rank in the scale of beings which their Creator may perhaps have given them. . . . I advance it therefore as a suspicion only, that

> the blacks, whether originally a distant race or made distinct by time and circumstances, are inferior to whites in the endowments of both body and mind.[47]

Chandler provides us with a Du Boisian interpretation of the "ambiguous conscience" of architectural naturalism. Jefferson's racism was "organized by the *telos* of preventing, justifying the preclusion of, the mixture and intermixture of any kind among the races." But given that the concept of race awaited some forthcoming proof, the racial segregation of American society was to be constantly enforced and reinforced in view of a threat to the "putative white identity that Jefferson [was] most concerned to affirm,"[48] which meant that, while the slave codes were made, and could only be made, on the basis of pure speculation, the spatial coding of the social environment turned "a suspicion" into a term of order. Thus, just as God revealed himself to Man "only through signs," the founding fathers sought an aesthetic whose symbolic form naturalized the authority of the European order of things. And this belief in architecture would, in naturalizing the racism of the plantation system, constitute the private ground on which civil society would be built.

Function

How did architectural form enshrine the "metaphysical infrastructure"[49] of property? Earlier we acknowledged that the inertia of the eighteenth-century country house was the dialectical expression of the motion of capital. For both Williams and Said, the inert grandeur of such estates articulated a deep sense of trouble permeating the foundations of private property. However, explaining this structure of feeling tests the limits of architectural analysis, as it is extremely difficult to recover the grammar of real estate from the language of form, although another route can be explored by treating the policy regime of real estate as the "generator" of form. On this reading, neoclassical humanism sublimates what Spillers calls the "uneasy oxymoronic character that the 'peculiar institution' attempts to sustain in transforming *personality* into *property.*"[50] The advantage of this move is that it helps us track the correspondence between the division and subdivision of the space of public and private life.

As we have seen, Jefferson's experiments in town planning used geometry to influence the motion of a city, although the most realized experiment in organization is found at Monticello. Here the third president intended his "rich spot of earth" to produce an experience of total space. Unlike the fashion for buildings designed to "communicate the planter's exalted, wealth, status and power,"[51] Monticello was intended to instill a more measured, even cerebral, feeling of control over the environment. Why else "would Jefferson build his house on an isolated hilltop, far from the rivers and roads that linked Virginians to the world? Why would visitors have to struggle over rough terrain, in round-about fashion, in order to see"[52] the so-called Sage of Monticello? The architecture of this particular estate was, scholars conclude, intended to give the plantation a form of self-expression.[53]

However, this leaves us with the "conventional story of the old slave plantation owner and its owner's fine, aristocratic life of cultured leisure."[54] But when the plantation system is looked at not from the perspective of the owner *of* but from the perspective of those owned *as* real estate, then the spatial question is transformed. In a short passage in "The Coming of the Lord" chapter of *Black Reconstruction*, Du Bois proposes that the slave codes formed an environmental policy precipitated by the planters' fear of Black sociality and fugitivity. "Before the war," Du Bois writes, "the slave was curiously isolated; this was the policy, and the effective policy of the slave system," the function of which was a spatial configuration that "made the plantation the center of a black group with a network of white folk around and about, who kept the slaves from contact with each other."[55] Plantation power lay, Du Bois suggested, not only in the direct violence of capitalist extraction but in a *network* preventing social *contact*. If the uncontrolled desire for liberty terrified revolutionary America, then that terror was to be applied to those held captive in a free society. Such terrorism could take diffuse environmental forms, requiring creative modes of sociality to subvert the authority of the slave codes. "Of course, clandestine contact there always was" Du Bois writes, "the passing of Negroes to and fro on errands; particularly the semi-freedom and mingling in cities; and yet, the mass of slaves was curiously provincial and kept out of the currents of information."[56]

Du Bois would later call the urbanization of racial division the construction of a "total environment."[57] Again, Monticello's organization of space prefigured techniques that would become associated with the modern city. For example, Jefferson's tinkering with Palladian templates was not only animated by English fashion but also by a need to accommodate "a whole series of . . . functional inventions." As Tafuri notes, "At Monticello, with its clear distinction of spaces for service and served, Jefferson anticipated something that was to be typical" of the experiments in architecture and urbanism of Frank Lloyd-Wright and Louis Khan.[58] What led Jefferson to anticipate this system of division making? Jefferson scholars inform us that the use of "dumb waiters and revolving service doors" were all intended to ensure the "conspicuous absence of slaves."[59] Thus, the function of served and service space was intended to protect the modesty of guests, providing them the "comfort" of avoiding what Jefferson called in his *Notes* "the whole commerce between master and slave."[60]

Feeling

How do we recover the experience of those trapped inside such a monstrous structure of feeling? Spillers's critique of the bonds of sentiment that underwrite the legal coding of African women and their children as "chattels personal" is fundamental. Addressing a process whose cruelty "manhandled" the body as alienable flesh, Spillers requires us to consider the psychic, social, and sensuous conditions of ownership that made this violence endemic. Specifically, Spillers argues that the vestige of sentiment claimed on behalf of the sexual oppression of captive women indicates the deep level of chaos permeating the infrastructure of civil society—private property.

Faced with Jefferson's concern for concealed space and his desire to protect his precious *sanctum sanctorum*, we need to retrieve the place of Sally Hemings, the enslaved mother of Thomas Jefferson's children. While we know where Jefferson's official family were situated at Monticello, in recent work Spillers has asked about the place of Jefferson's "shadow family."[61] In 2017, archaeologists working on Monticello's restoration uncovered the site. While taking down the fabric of the men's bathroom adjoining Jefferson's bedroom in Monticello's South Wing, Sally Hemings's living quarters were located.[62] The recovery of this living space that measured fourteen feet and eight inches wide by thirteen feet long is said to be architectural evidence of Jefferson's "closeness" to Hemings. Looking at this situation, however, Spillers asks, what does domestic intimacy mean when close proximity and familial ties represent the very opposite of freedom?

Within this thick network of relations, what Spillers throws into relief is another infrastructure subtending the plantation, a system of logistics that polices the expression of intimacy and contact. Spillers's critique is thus indispensable for investigating infrastructure, because when the space of privacy is looked at from the perspective of the owned and not the owner, then the fugitive becomes our guide. For example, based on Valerie Smith's architectonic reading of Linda Brent's (Harriet Jacobs) memoir *Incidents in the Life of a Slave Girl*, Spillers argues that Brent reveals an interstitial space "between the lines and in the not-quite spaces of an American domesticity."[63] Recounting Brent's testimony concerning one Dr. Flint's "sexual designs on the young Linda," Spillers asks, What does the scene of married intimacy look like when property ownership enables a man to instrumentalize his subject position as husband, father, and master in pursuit of self-gratification?

Linda Brent's account presents the chaotic situation. When Dr. Flint's jealous wife visits Brent's garret room, she bends over her, "whispering in my ear, as though it were her husband speaking to me, and listened to hear what I would answer." Here is the horror of possessive individuation, wherein the free woman embodies the abusive power of the self-made man. The uneven distribution of freedom enjoyed by women of the eighteenth century is balanced on the ungendered flesh of the enslaved body. "Since the gendered female *exists* for the male," Spillers writes, "we might say that the ungendered female—in an amazing stroke of pansexual potential—might be invaded/raided by another woman or man."[64] In other words, the system of dispossession Marx called "primitive accumulation"—which removed people from land, processed them as property, and formed the ground of possessive individualism—was, from the very first, ordered by a sensuous mode of exploitation that abstracted flesh from body.[65]

The ramifications of the sexual violence and "founding fatherhood" that nurtured American democracy are critical to measure the depths and dimensions of the infrastructural connection of real estate to architecture. They demonstrate how the unstable coding of another human's *being* as private property produced a "common psychic landscape . . . of dread and humiliation,"[66] one that was rendered in the interior design of the plantation house, an "internal empire"[67] whose service corridors, cramped attics, and crawl spaces subtracted those who were spatialized into service from those who were served by architecture. In the last analysis, what this tells us is that coursing through the architectonics of real estate is an underlying system of degradation, a "pornotropic" mode of exploitation forming the sensuous basis and debased sensuousness of infrastructural power.

Minus

If infrastructure refers, in its most basic sense, to the "lower part of any construction," this essay has argued that to understand its politics, we must understand how the racial terms of social superiority and inferiority have been historically concealed. Over centuries, this art of human appraisal has supported the accumulation process by putting people under and away, out of sight, out of mind. The means of deciding who enjoys a quality of life and who is enjoyed as service has been developed through systems of spatial production forming racial regimes—"constructed social systems in which race is proposed as a justification for the relations of power."[68]

Architecture therefore provides a history of the spatial dialectic whereby real estate—the combination of land, labor, and finance—gave infrastructure the logistical means to possess a life of its own. However, to confront this regime's history, we need to uncover the "makeshift patchwork" of prejudicial conceptions of race, sex, and gender "masquerading as memory and the immutable."[69] All of which gives the architecture of racial capitalism its sense of permanence and purpose. By examining the relationship between the humanism of neoclassical architecture and the categorical volatility of real estate, we can uproot a system of judgment that, when laid into the earth and built into the environment, persists to the present day.

Notes

1. "Partie inférieure d'une construction. Il se dit aussi des Terrassements, des travaux d'art d'une voie ferrée," http://atilf.atilf.fr/academie.htm.

2. Keller Easterling, *Extrastatecraft: The Power of Infrastructure Space* (London: Verso, 2014), 14.

3. Stefano Harney and Fred Moten, *The Undercommons Fugitive Planning and Black Study* (London: Minor Compositions, 2013), 88.

4. Easterling, *Extrastatecraft*, 27.

5. Easterling, *Extrastatecraft*, 12.

6. Raymond Williams, *Marxism and Literature* (Oxford: Oxford University Press, 1977), 76.

7. Easterling, *Extrastatecraft*, 22.

8. Brian Larkin, "Promising Forms: The Political Aesthetics of Infrastructure," in *The Promise of Infrastructure*, ed. Hannah Appel, Nikhil Anand, and Akhil Gupta (Durham, NC: Duke University Press, 2018), 197.

9. Stuart Hall, *Cultural Studies 1983: A Theoretical History* (Durham, NC: Duke University Press, 2016), 96.

10. Fredric Jameson, *Late Marxism: Adorno; or, The Persistence of the Dialectic* (London: Verso, 1996), 46.

11. Williams, *Marxism and Literature*, 121–27.

12. Ruth Wilson Gilmore, "Abolition Geography and the Problem of Innocence," in *Futures of Black Radicalism*, ed. Gaye Theresa Johnson and Alex Lubin (London: Verso, 2017), 237.

13. Harney and Moten, *The Undercommons*, 92.

14. Cedric J. Robinson, *Black Marxism: The Making of the Black Radical Tradition* (Chapel Hill: University of North Carolina Press, 2000).

15. Cedric J. Robinson, *Forgeries of Memory and Meaning: Blacks and the Regimes of Race in American Theater and Film before World War II* (Chapel Hill: University of North Carolina Press, 2009).

16. Robinson, *Forgeries*, xii.

17. Rudolf Wittkower, *Architectural Principles in the Age of Humanism* (Chichester, England: Academy, 1988), 104.

18. John Summerson, *Georgian London* (New Haven, CT: Yale University Press, 2003), 20.

19. Summerson, *Georgian London*, 20.

20. Raymond Williams, *The Country and the City* (Oxford: Oxford University Press, 1973), 105.

21. Williams, *The Country and the City*, 106.

22. Jane Austen, *Mansfield Park* (1816; reprt. Harmondsworth: Penguin 1966), 375-376 Quoted in Edward Said, *Culture and Imperialism* (New York: Vintage Books, 1994), 88.

23. Ruth Wilson Gilmore, preface to *Prison/Culture*, ed. Sharon E. Bliss, Kevin B. Chen, Steve Dickison, Mark Dean Johnson, and Rebeka Rodriguez (San Francisco: City Lights Foundation Books, 2009).

24. Eric Williams, *Capitalism and Slavery* (New York: Russell & Russell, 1961), 211. Quoted in Said, *Culture*, 95.

25. Said, *Culture*, 95.

26. Jairus Banaji, *A Brief History of Commercial Capitalism* (Chicago: Haymarket Books, 2020), 17.

27. Geoffrey Ingham, *Capitalism Divided? The City and Industry* (London: Macmillan, 1984).

28. Clay Lancaster, "Jefferson's Architectural Indebtedness to Robert Morris," *Journal of the Society of Architectural Historians* 10, no. 1 (1951): 3.

29. Buford Pickens, "Mr. Jefferson as Revolutionary Architect," *Journal of the Society of Architectural Historians* 34, no. 4 (1975): 257.
30. Lancaster, "Jefferson's Architectural Indebtedness," 3.
31. Lancaster, "Jefferson's Architectural Indebtedness," 10.
32. Manfredo Tafuri, *Architecture and Utopia: Design and Capitalist Development* (Cambridge, MA: MIT Press, 1979), 36.
33. Antonio Gramsci, *Selections from the Prison Notebooks* (Dagenham, England: Lawrence and Wishart, 1998), 318.
34. Tafuri, *Architecture and Utopia*, 26.
35. John W. Reps, "Thomas Jefferson's Checkerboard Towns," *Journal of the Society of Architectural Historians* 20, no. 3 (1961): 109.
36. Reps, "Checkerboard Towns," 109.
37. Tafuri, *Architecture and Utopia*, 36.
38. W. E. B. Du Bois, *Black Reconstruction in America, 1860–1880* (New York: Simon and Schuster, 1998), 714–15.
39. Hortense J. Spillers, "Mama's Baby, Papa's Maybe: An American Grammar Book," in *Black, White, and in Color: Essays on American Literature and Culture* (Chicago: University of Chicago Press, 2003), 224–25.
40. Du Bois, *Black Reconstruction*, 49–50.
41. Du Bois, *Black Reconstruction*, 50.
42. Du Bois, *Black Reconstruction*, 10.
43. Du Bois, *Black Reconstruction*, 50.
44. Nahum Dimitri Chandler, *X—the Problem of the Negro as a Problem for Thought* (New York: Fordham University Press, 2013), 29.
45. Chandler, *X*, 24.
46. Chandler, *X*, 25.
47. Chandler, *X*, 27.
48. Chandler, *X*, 29.
49. Chandler, *X*, 21.
50. Spillers, "Mama's Baby," 225.
51. P. S. Onuf and A. Gordon-Reed, "Jefferson's Spaces," *Early American Literature* 48, no. 3 (2013): 761.
52. Onuf and Gordon-Reed, "Jefferson's Spaces," 761.
53. Onuf and Gordon-Reed, "Jefferson's Spaces," 757.
54. Du Bois, *Black Reconstruction*, 715.
55. Du Bois, *Black Reconstruction*, 122.
56. Du Bois, *Black Reconstruction*, 122.
57. W. E. B. Du Bois, *Dusk of Dawn: An Essay toward an Autobiography of a Race Concept* (New York: Oxford University Press, 2007), 68.
58. Tafuri, *Architecture and Utopia*, 27.
59. Onuf and Gordon-Reed, "Jefferson's Spaces," 764.
60. Onuf and Gordon-Reed, "Jefferson's Spaces," 763.
61. This essay is indebted to a lecture Spillers gave at Barnard College in 2017, "Shades of Intimacy: Women in the Time of Revolution," February 21, 2017. https://www.youtube.com/watch?v=KPa7KhbuEJo.
62. Michael Cottman, "Historians Uncover Slave Quarters of Sally Hemings at Thomas Jefferson's Monticello," July 3, 2017, https://www.nbcnews.com/news/nbcblk/thomas-jefferson-sally-hemings-living-quarters-found-n771261.

63. Spillers, "Mama's Baby," 223.
64. Spillers, "Mama's Baby," 222.
65. Spillers, "Mama's Baby," 206.
66. Spillers, "Mama's Baby," 223.
67. The essay's title is inspired by Robert Hood's 1994 album *Internal Empire*, whose music underpins Arthur Jafa's 2013 film *APEX*, a cinematic inquiry into the aesthetics of racial regimes.
68. Robinson, *Forgeries*, xii.
69. Robinson, *Forgeries*, xii.

Chapter 4

✦

Infrastructure and Intimacies

Early Black Women's Writing and the Care Work of Colonialism

Samantha Pinto

In 1857, a Jamaican, Creole-identified nurse named Mary Seacole entered into the boom in post–Crimean War narratives with her memoir *The Wonderful Adventures of Mrs. Seacole in Many Lands*. Her work ministering to the tastes and health of laborers building the Panama Canal railway route in the early years of the decade was the precursor to and catalyst for her work as an entrepreneurial nurse on the war front who also ran a general store and "hotel." This service industry enterprise was at once underwriting her ability to serve as a nurse and a cause of skepticism by peers such as Florence Nightingale, who saw Seacole's endeavors as morally questionable. Seacole's memoir and her public reception in the era laid bare the long-standing link between infrastructure and its soft institutional offshoots—including hospitality, health care, and publishing—in defining both the limits and possibilities for women of color under colonialism. Seacole stands at the nexus of frontier infrastructures that defined modernity—the rise of infrastructure capitalism at the building and development of colonial frontiers, the infrastructures of race itself built through chattel slavery, and writing as its own newly accessible infrastructure, one of only a very few ways to mediate support for self-making for Black women in the public sphere.

This essay will explore how Seacole and her precursor Anne Hart Gilbert wrote of and through infrastructure in the eighteenth- and nineteenth-century Caribbean. Their work dovetails with studies of Black women's sexuality in the diaspora, blurring the lines between the intimate affiliations of care work and the public-facing citizenship of institutional belonging in ways that challenge the import and aesthetics of the era of colonial resource extraction. I argue that Black women's writing of the era mobilizes discourses of infrastructure, broadly construed to include built space—transcontinental railways, churches, roads, and so on—and institution and industry building, to locate public speech alongside of and beyond subjection and resistance. While many authors of the era wrote within the frame of Harriet Jacobs's "loophole of retreat"—finding innovative paths to freedom through not just abolitionist politics but also the profession and aesthetics of writing against slavery—this essay focuses on Seacole and Gilbert's deep imbrication with colonial infrastructure and its investments in missionarism, war, exploitative labor, and the unchecked production of global capital.[1] The disciplining and abuse of Black women's sexuality produced models that were characterized by an excess of dissembling[2] for the aesthetic and rhetorical production in Black women's writing and politics in the period; the legacy of Black women's sexual labor exploitation also authorized literal and literary methods of mobility that deeply engaged the speculative economies of settler colonialism, markets that created vacuums and disruptions in conventional white domestic arrangements and demanded the early entanglement of infrastructure and self-articulation in writing. Moving away from a model of reading that values resistance such as the oppositional infrastructure of the metaphor and practice of the Underground Railroad, this essay springs from the material conditions of creating, sustaining, and surveying infrastructures to think about the complicated entrepreneurial aesthetics of Black feminist writing in the New World. Using the work of these two figures who are largely written out of the genealogy of Black women's relationship to frontier infrastructure, I argue for a disruption of development discourse in literary study that takes its cues from critiques of development itself—against progress narratives that define what affiliations and roles Black women's writing should or is allowed to take and what subjectivity they can claim in their life writing as they fashion selves that mirror the excitement and breathlessness of infrastructural expansion with a difference.

This essay then creates the opportunity in the analysis of nineteenth-century writing by Black women "to treat infrastructure not as a foundation, a given, but instead as a tactical medium that opens the possibility of critical infrastructure studies as a mode of cultural studies."[3] The "turn" to critical infrastructure studies in literary and cultural studies—with moves toward the possibilities of affordances, form, and design, as well as their limits—also expands the possibilities of infrastructure.[4] Hart and Seacole represent the exceptional convergence of literary form (epistolary religious history/tract and war memoir/travel narrative) and the height of infrastructural imperialism in the Caribbean, Latin America, and other expanses. *Wonderful Adventures* and Hart's "History of Methodism" in the Caribbean mark a moment where material infrastructure is central and visible—documented breathlessly by the print and later photographic culture of the times. This essay then follows infrastructure to the "frontier" of modernity—colonial "ground" marked for infrastructural expansion through a complex series of what Brett Neilson and Sandro Mezzadra would term "operations of capital" that both make and potentially "remake the world" as we know it.[5] Neilson and Mezzadra's focus on excavating capital as a critical act that cannot be reduced to either "activity nor potentiality"[6] mirrors this essay's turn away from claiming resistance, turning instead to thinking about how participation in infrastructure through life writing allows Black women of the region and period to survey their conflicting, expansive experiences with the infrastructures of race, what Daniel Nemser defines as "the material systems that enable racial categories to be thought, ascribed, and lived, as well as the systems of domination and accumulation these categories make possible as a result."[7] These "more or less durable structures"[8] of built space and community merge with the concept of "people as infrastructure" put forward by AbdouMaliq Simone[9] in Nemser's definition of racial infrastructure and in this essay. I argue that Black women's writing acts as a mediator[10] between these realms as it interfaces with major "hard" forms of infrastructure—transportation systems, war machines—through the "soft" infrastructures that spring up and undergird (authorize, even) Black women's participation in the public sphere. The emergence of Caribbean women's self-writing coincides with the rise of development infrastructure: philanthropy, education, care work, and life writing. How did Black women of the era engage with both the hard and soft infrastructures available to them and those that excluded them, and how did they do so with the materials and systems and forms at hand? Theories of infrastructure that name the exploitation of labor—infrastructure as people—as an undeniable and yet invisibilized racialized formation of the physical objects we usually mark as infrastructure undergird this project, as do concepts of infrastructure that focus not on its role in invention and harm but on how it might mitigate and repair.[11] But I move away from demanding Black women as writing subjects, and my readings of them to perform either subjection or repair in relationship to frontier colonialism; rather I argue that they write in and through complex operations and relations to infrastructure as a form that expands their ability to aesthetically and experientially structure their own lives and representations of self.

Colonial infrastructure included the building of mass agricultural systems, port cities and the industries and literal pathways needed to staff them, and the health, education, feeding, and housing of those building, working, making, and inhabiting the colony, as well as the trade and traffic in the human beings who made up most of this frontier of experiment and innovation in (in)human sociality. For Caribbean authors of the Black Americas, autobiographical writing dovetailed with the economy of colonial infrastructure at their respective times. It aesthetically rendered value to their selves and to their labors. But this writing did so in complicated relationship to the hard and soft frontier infrastructures, offering something other than resistance to the risky and innovative forms of emergent capitalism. Hart and Seacole engage deeply with the possibilities of written forms to enact self-making for Black women in racially, economically, geographically, and sexually diverse diaspora communities. The genres of their writing—travel narrative, autobiographical reflections next to religious treatises, a memoir in a boom of Crimean War media—anticipate and author Black literature's, and Black life writing's, forms and currency as a high-risk/high-reward structure in the postenslavement Americas for those locked out of formal political and economic realms. Infrastructure became the route(s) for their self-making and featured in the thick descriptions of their writings and the very terms and terrain by which they were authorized to come into public view. From the cramped conditions of possibility for resistance to white supremacy in Black women's writing, this essay seeks to consider the architecture and geographies of infrastructure as providing more expansive spaces for institutional engagement. These possibilities marked not retreat from or resistance to colonial structure, but deep investments in building on and from the complex ground where they lived, stood, worked, loved, felt, and wrote.

Faith Infrastructures and Religious Affiliation: Anne Hart Gilbert

In late eighteenth-century Antigua, Anne Hart Gilbert enters this mixed public arena of both willed and forced "development" and self-invention, the daughter of a Black enslaver on an island that was increasingly populated with conflicts between a growing free Black population and a white planter class and the tensions caused by the stirrings of abolitionism. She and her sister, Elizabeth Hart Thwaites, occupy positions as free middle-class Black women that belie the violent intimacies that created the mixed-race identity of their community of fellow free Black Antiguans: the legacy of domestic and sexual arrangements that put some enslaved people in more daily intimate proximity to white enslavers and a system and colonial governance that by custom made room for legal pathways to manumission of slaves even while they remained on the island. As part of a growing free Black population, the family sat in a precarious position as an intermediary of growing networks in abolitionism, Methodism, and colonial-imperial resources in Antigua in the mid to late eighteenth century. Out of this, the Hart sisters emerged through letters in the early part of the nineteenth-century, writing treatises and religious biographies of their kin and inventing themselves as some of the first Black Caribbean women writers through and within the infrastructural and institutional systems that shaped them, including Methodism and abolitionism's emerging structures of thinking and feeling, the emerging markets of philanthropic religious "education" in the colonies, and their own compulsory marriages.

In her 1804 "History of Methodism," written as a letter to a reverend regarding the development of the religion in the West Indies, Anne Hart Gilbert begins by referencing the many histories and missives that have come before her—the vein of writing in which she follows (while also making it clear that she was asked by the recipient and by other parties to contribute): the networks for religious "travel" writing, how colonialism invented both the genre and the infrastructural ability to "arrive" in the Caribbean as a missionary, and how this slim loophole of authorized masculine religious reflection in writing and missionary travel and infrastructural setup (churches, etc.) in Antigua and the surrounding region allowed for the limited participation of a free Black Caribbean woman. Gilbert's "History of Methodism" is an early exercise in Black women's self-invention through the technologies of colonial capitalism—finding a space to write the self through writing about the establishment of religious infrastructure.

Giving a thick (and disparaging) description of Obeah and white pagan practices through the sites of graveyards, she also emphasizes women's and Black Antiguans relationship to the material infrastructure of the church, whereby "our two dear Sisters Mary Alley & Sophia Campbel are mentionable; venture in faith to argue for a spot of land to build a Chapel upon: They were greatly discouraged by all to whom they mentioned it, as an undertaking too great & expensive for so small a Society to engage in; but being embodied by faith tho they knew not the way, they struck for the land & had to pay the cash down."[12] Gilbert's biblical prose stylings emphasize the moral dimensions of literal institution building, appending virtue to labor while highlighting the structural barriers to creating built space for Black communities. Black women's violation of middle-class white womanhood through infrastructural labor is also (and problematically) cast as moral: "The most decent, and creditable of the black women did not think it a labour too servile to carry stones and marl, to help with their own hands to clear the Land of the rubbish that lay about it, and to bring ready-dressed victual for the men that were employed in building the House of God."[13]

The moralistic is paired with the specific for Gilbert, as she uses her epistolary religious history to archive the names and the actions of her community: "Sister S. Campbel went herself with James Watkins (another of our steady old black friends who is now alive & resides in St Christophers) to the Lumber yard & bought materials for building."[14] Mixing the bureaucratic, philanthropic, and sentimental, Hart Gilbert's interface with infrastructure here authorizes the details and occasion for her writing this "History of Methodism" as a history of free Black women's institutional energy—"people as infrastructure," in Simone AbdouMaliq's terms, but in a voluntary capacity. For Gilbert, meaningful and voluntary participation in the making of infrastructure begets both joy and the entrepreneurial spirit of modernity: "They now rejoiced to sell their Ear-rings & bracelets and to buy Lumber & pay Carpenters, to forward this blessed work; and at last they got a comfortable little Chapel, which soon became too small."[15] Expansive and expanding, Gilbert's rhetorical moves from religious humility to archival detail innovate and authorize her as her faith, locale, and community's historian and indeed author. Documenting infrastructure is her way into this public self.

Gilbert also narrates the educational infrastructure set up by a married couple and a separate prayer meeting "for the benefit of young women"[16]—here engaging philanthropy and the burgeoning sphere of education as moral instruction when performed by women and for women and the enslaved. From here, Gilbert's narrative follows the trail of marriage to narrate yet more religious infrastructure, discussing new initiatives that come from moving for her husband's employment opportunities: "To my great but pleasant surprise I found a small society of black and coloured people, consisting of 27 Members & all but a very few in earnest for Salvation. They have never had one half the advantages of the people of St Johns, having no place of worship to go to on Sundays, & very few of them able to read the word of God."[17] Again emphasizing the lack of buildable land or space for Black subjects in Antigua in moral tones, Gilbert narrates her own previous organizing to inspire more pushes for acceptable free Black infrastructure—namely, churches and land to build them on—from the state itself:

> Previous to our coming here they had been in treaty of a house for the purpose of preaching, but the situation is so hot, and so low, that both Preacher, & hearers, run the risk of getting sick as soon as they come into the open air. We have therefore petitioned the Commissioner to give us a Grant of Land to build in a more convenient place & he readily granted the petition. It was written in the name of "the Negroes belonging to His Majesty & others inhabiting English-Harbor." & it was presented by me of the King's negroes.[18]

Narrating inequity through land and built structures, Gilbert engages in the distance of material building and the physical relocation required of marriage and labor to call her writing self into print. Her missionary work and most importantly her circulated writing about her life and work helped to fundraise and establish schools on the island and eventually formed the English support of the Ladies Negro Education Society in response to Gilbert's letters. Always having to ground her rhetoric and her requests in the scale of religious and feminine humility, Gilbert's writing self displaced ambition onto infrastructure and faith even as it made material demands.[19]

Gilbert's writing self emerges, then, through and not against the genres and structures of colonial capital and infrastructures of philanthropy, religion, education, slavery, marriage, and inheritance. Her writings are also cut through with the intimacies and materialities of health—of the constant and lingering presence of disease and death as pathogens and immune systems from different corners of the earth that collide in this ongoing system of brutal invention and contact and hard labor for the free middle classes alongside death-dealing laboring conditions for the enslaved without respite: "From their vicinity to us, and the circumscribed limits of the house they inhabited, several of the children were constant residents at Clarence house, except when, in seasons of ill health, or other peculiarities of circumstance, others by turns took their places. . . . Of this institution It may be truly said, the blessed effects are evident to all who know anything of it."[20] The interruptions of ill health and sudden death, and the need to have built space and resources to cope with both eventualities, pepper Gilbert's missives—and even authorize her completion of her now late husband's autobiography. Speaking of the lack of visiting space for quarantined and ill enslaved workers, Gilbert lays out the built space of the Antiguan plantocracy as she pushes colonial government for better-suited land for church institution building. Managing health sits alongside managing morality as strategies for free Black women's public self-making. Anne Hart Gilbert mines the still-emerging social and material structures of the late eighteenth- and early nineteenth-century Caribbean for ways to author as yet uninvented public selves for Black women—and she does so through an investment in institution building.

Seacole: Infrastructure Capitalism, Medical Intimacy, and Development Discourse

Seacole writes a memoir for several purposes and audiences in the wake of the Crimean War and its technological and media booms. She also engages various genres of the era: the picaresque adventure, the travel narrative to "exotic" colonial climes, the war memoir, the physician memoir, and the celebrity memoir.[21] Of course, these genres exist, in 1857, in the shadow of the enslaved narrative form (Equiano, Sanchez, Prince, Douglass) and the sentimental cross-Atlantic juggernaut of *Uncle Tom's Cabin*. As templates for these Black literary structures are being solidified in an American context,[22] Seacole writes in their wake, addressing race, racism, and ongoing enslavement throughout her memoir through the architecture of the ship and its common spaces (with racist objections by majority-American ships in Central America and Jamaica), urban space (being publicly visible on an early trip to the United Kingdom), the hotel (with its crass American speculators), and then the "frontier" itself—with Indigenous and Black workers who also intriguingly become enforcers and interpreters of the "law" of this contested land of New Granada.

With these complex protocols making demands of readers of her time, as well as expectations of the critical present, Seacole constructs a memoir that stays resolutely on the move—emphasizing the adventures in her title through mobility rather than self-reflection, domesticity, or "staying with the trouble"[23] in any given site or any single life event. So, for instance, the circumstances of her birth, marriage, and widowhood are dispensed with in infamously brief opening paragraphs, sometimes even in one sentence. In this, she is perhaps a difficult paradigm for what Derrick Spires refers to as early African American practices of citizenship—participating in the polis and in community through the practice of writing, the active nature of print culture.[24] Seacole narrates her extraordinary actions with little surface deferral to humility about her professional skills, her observation of others' skills, or her writing prowess. But in the literary infrastructures that haunt her text, the reader catches glimpses of the material infrastructures of both colonial and imperial ventures that have shaped literary form and vice versa—the ways that literary infrastructure can and has shaped structures of feeling around material infrastructures, and particularly around Blackness, race, and difference at and as the site and cost of these infrastructural ventures.

The first half of Seacole's memoir is spent almost entirely amidst the gold rush crowd alongside the continued building of the Panama railroad in the 1840s and 1850s. But even before she sets off, she saves her thickest descriptions of early life in Jamaica not for emotional remembrances of family but for an emphasis on the precarity of property. She speaks of becoming the ideal capitalist subject of empire not through security but through precarity: "I never thought too exclusively of money, believing rather that we were born to be happy, and that the surest way to be wretched was to prize it over much. Had I done so, I should have mourned over many a promising speculation proving a failure, over many a pan of preserves of guava jelly burnt in the making; and perhaps lost my mind when the great fire of 1843, which devastated Kingston, burnt down my poor home."[25] Seacole, however, is not a humble narrator of the self but instead engages in the kind of bildungsroman romanticism of the liberal subject pulling herself up by her bootstraps—save that she attributes this "grit" to her mother's medical knowledge and her connections as a Creole woman running a boardinghouse for white colonial settlers. In other words, it is the history of intimate proximity with white male bodies on which Seacole self-consciously trades—this is her currency of self-invention and reinvention: "But of course, I set to work again in a humbler way, and rebuilt my house by degrees, and restocked it, succeeding better than before; for I had gained a reputation as a skillful nurse and doctress, and my house was always full of invalid officers and their wives from New Castle."[26] Her trade is in the economies of colonial infrastructure, including care, lodging, trade, and war—the infrastructures of speculation.

Here, since Seacole's widowhood is dispatched with in a sentence on the first page of her narrative, widowhood authorizes if not respectability then labor markets for Seacole as a mixed-race woman. Posited as a choice to maintain entrepreneurial property in the self, she declares: "And here I may take the opportunity of explaining that it was from a confidence in my powers, and not at all from necessity, that I remained an unprotected female"[27] and posits further ventures as acts of will and volition, rather than injury: "And it was not long before I grew very tired of life in Cruces, although I made money rapidly, and pressed my brother to return to Kingston."[28] Seacole's positivist assertions of an agentic writing and laboring self fit with her times if not her subject position—a moment when there is an explosion of capital projects seeking to link capital networks and ventures across the globe, alongside an explosion of wars, fronts, and frontiers that introduce an ideal of social and economic mobility for poor white colonial subjects, as well as for nominally free laborers—freed enslaved and indentured or inequitably paid laborers from Indigenous and Asian geographies.[29] In particular, the infrastructural projects of various transcontinental railroads and war efforts mark Seacole's era, and so it is on the thin strip of land in New Grenada where the first half of the narrative largely takes place.

Panama itself stands "as a complex and often vexed conduit of materials and information; as an accessory to modernity as defined by speed and the movement of commodities; and as a vital link of empires contesting control of markets, spaces, and peoples."[30] It was a battleground of foreign interest from the building of the railroad (opened in 1855) to the canal at the turn of the century. But even during railroad construction, it was, as Seacole documents, the locus of speculations—literally, gold speculators traversing the US continent by sea to get to and from California. The laborers were a mix of Indigenous Panamanians, free Black laborers from the Caribbean and the United States, and, in 1854, Chinese laborers. The United States took control of the region starting in 1856 after the "watermelon war"—a specious incident that the United States was waiting for to claim hostility against itself in the region and invoke the Monroe Doctrine to claim ownership of the railroad interests and later the canal. Both became key symbols of US industry–led "ingenuity"[31]—a material Silicon Valley of infrastructural ideals and "innovations" that led to mass worker death.

Seacole makes her own reflections on Panama's (in)famous place in the infrastructural economy of modernity: "All my readers must know," she begins as she describes "a little neck of land, insignificant-looking enough on the map"[32] that signaled the promise of avoiding two other known dangers—a trip by sea around the tip of South America or a trip by land across the United States (which she refers to as "almost impossible" in 1857). Seacole also writes of infrastructure in the aesthetic rhythms of gossip: "I have read and heard many accounts of old endeavors to effect this important and gigantic work, and how miserably they failed."[33] Part of the lure of infrastructure reportage remains the spectacular death count, where "every mile of that fatal railway cost the world thousands of lives,"[34] which was reported on like a war itself. But Seacole is more breathless than reflective—her own memoir, of course, is a product of, and she is an author of, empire—a brand standing for danger, exoticism, newness, violence, and adventure: "It is a gigantic undertaking, and shows what the energy and enterprise of man can accomplish. Everything required for its construction, even the timber, had to be prepared in, and brought from, America."[35] Echoing Gilbert in her emphasis on the materials and energy of infrastructure, Seacole's description nonetheless pivots in scale and sentiment. Where Gilbert emphasizes the moral virtue and fortitude of the volunteer labor of poor Black Methodist converts in biblical prose, Seacole has the confident distance of empire in her style, even as she is describing an infrastructure and event she experienced directly. While she doesn't deploy humor here, her tone is echoed in an 1868 letter that Mark Twain wrote on the railroad: "It is a popular saying, that every railroad tie from Panama to Aspinwall rests upon a corpse. It ought to be a substantial road, being so well provided with sleepers—eternal ones and otherwise."[36] His written account, and the ways that it contains both the same data and the same characterization of the railroad's human costs as Seacole's description a decade earlier, emphasizes the central role that infrastructure had in the global public imagination of the time, constituting "gossip" on the movement of global capital.

Seacole's narrative shows us the contours of infrastructure aesthetics, where her press-like accounts paint the railroad as bloody, costly, and a failure and then also breathlessly larger than life—or the lives it cost, literally—in its material capacity to showcase the "gigantic" scale of imperial modernity, as the "the envy and enterprise of man" removed from the intimacy and sentimentality of death with the language of adventure and venture. Seacole's investments in actual roads seem to narratively harbor this flaneur-ian distance, teeming with description of roads as a means to an end in her entrepreneurial pursuits, where "the road sometimes being made of logs of wood laid transversely"[37] on an excursion to the town of Panama marked it as an "old-fashioned, irregular town, with queer stone houses, almost all of which had been turned by the traders into stores."[38] Taking such note of the repurposing of built structures fits with Seacole's earlier proclaimed detachment from property: the colonial cities themselves become like roads, passed through, easily decimated, "cheaply" rebuilt on the backs of inequitable, racialized labor.

Rendering infrastructure as political, personal, and cultural "gossip," Seacole aesthetically encapsulates the lore of the "road" for public consumption—a tale of death, tragedy, money, depravity, greed, and, of course, business. Julie Livingston, in the context of contemporary Botswana, writes about the key links between roads—built, infrastructural, state-sponsored routes—and all aspects of "modernity"—development, medicine, trade—that promise "freedoms": "Roads are part of the public health vision enabling the ambulance, the medications, and the patients to travel,"[39] even as "the road commands a certain amount of death and damage as a necessary price for its freedoms and opportunities."[40] The railroad, as road, stands as this nineteenth-century promise in Seacole's global world, where "as the road goes, it invents new places."[41] Seacole occupies and defines tense "new places," the interim places built for some subjects to pass through and others to sacrifice their labor and bodies toward. What Livingston marks when she argues that "road making became part of the developmental impetus, an infrastructural expectations of the modern nation-state"[42] is true for nineteenth-century global private capital and the cost of laboring lives for the spread of "modernity." The appetite for stories of and from the "frontier" of the imperially expanding world through what we might call public-private partnerships undergirds

Seacole's moment—a moment when technology makes capturing war or infrastructural chaos in near real time through photography and quick print journalism possible. These twinned appetites—for epic infrastructural entanglements promising future public good and for sordid first-person news of these exotic ventures in far-flung places from the colonial metropole—are the nineteenth-century roots of starstruck development and aid discourse today.

Infrastructure both is and is not a commodity—it is an object, a promise of relation, a vision into a future self and future relations between places, between people. A road, a railroad; these are promises[43] as surely as the other more ephemeral intimacies that Seacole's legacy as a "hostess" to white men in the Caribbean charts.[44] The infrastructure of colonialism begat intimacies—official and unofficial, public and private—that invented new terms, new places, new relations between and among and even within bodies. Seacole lives and writes at the juncture of the legacy of concubinage, of the small-scale yet systemically crucial public-private partnerships that produce other social reproductions—for her, Caribbean health practices, just as nursing itself is becoming "professionalized" by Florence Nightingale. Seacole writes as the hostess of many of the "new places" infrastructure building creates (the hospitality industry) and through her role as a nurse or doctress—an expert on colonial-era disease who even performs an excited narrated autopsy on a baby in Panama in the midst of a cholera epidemic—on the front lines of the climate, race, and epidemiological theories of the time. Her work and her unsentimental narration of her work (even as she is dubbed "Mother Seacole" by the press) sits at the vanguard of infrastructural booms in travel, hospitality, health care, and philanthropy and in the life writing adapted to surround and represent these ventures as adventures, or active practices of assembling the self through trial and error, and through encounters with difference.

Seacole recognizes and distances herself from other known modes of feminine writing by asserting a different relationship to "the streets" and roads of the colonial frontier. Of the women in the borderlands she writes: "I think, on the whole, that those French lady writers who desire to enjoy the privileges of man, with the irresponsibility of the other sex, would have been delighted with the disciples who were carrying their principles into practice in the streets of Cruces."[45] That she provides and builds the services and edifices surrounding more literal infrastructure is a key distinction in her writing of a public self—someone who observes and constructs but does not participate in the economy as a customer. This distancing of her writing self from "the streets of Cruces" is also a counter to the perceptions laid out by Florence Nightingale of Seacole running a "bad house" and the constant association of Creole women who ran hostels for soldiers with sexual intimacy, of course. Her merging of the masculinist language of adventure and ambition with the new narratives for women in care work like nursing (made respectable by Nightingale) and philanthropy[46] results in confessional gendered boasts such as "I am not ashamed to confess—for the gratification is, after all, a selfish one—that I love to be of service to those who need a woman's help."[47] For a woman who eschews all but the most cursory descriptions of familial, marital, or maternal attachments, Seacole's self-invention is "entirely public,"[48] even as she denies the embodied pleasures of "the streets" she has helped to build and sustain.

New Grenada is a place of construction, speculation, and hospitality—hailing us contemporary critics to the work of anthropologist James Clifford, critic Sean Goudie, and theories of hospitability by Derrida on the promise of cosmopolitanism.[49] Seacole's is a wild cosmopolitanism, one being built as it is written about, an interim space where social roles and structures are tested and suspended but where she identifies as "post" what Ann Stoler calls "the education of desire."[50] Even as she name-checks the passing through of entertainment infrastructure icons such as Lola Montez (misspelled as "Montes") "in the full zenith of her evil fame" and wearing "perfect male attire"[51] and details others drinking and gambling to excess, most of her narrative focuses instead on the institutional setups of her locales, rather than the licentious pull of debauchery. She spends long paragraphs walking us through the run-down space of her first hotel-to-be ("Picture to yourself, sympathizing reader, a long, low hut,"[52] she begins) and tells us how much she paid the workers who fixed up another "miserable little hut for sale" that she transformed in another gold rush city. Seacole also characteristically spends long passages describing natural disasters like flooding and fire and the property damage that ensues.[53]

The built space of these hotels puts Seacole in intimate proximity with difference (of gender, race, and nationality)—and here, also, is where her confrontation with openly racist Americans is narrated in brief vignettes that nonetheless mark her authorial subjectivity—such as when her presence on a steamship is protested and she must leave it—as one in tension with the perceived lawlessness of the colonial frontier, where, she says, "I generally avoided claiming the protection of the law whilst on the Isthmus, for I found it was—as is the case in civilized England from other causes—rather an expensive luxury."[54] If the hospitality industry was emerging in the shadow of infrastructure, expanding the reach and means of capital, Seacole also writes of other institutional subjects when she vamps: "There are two species of individual whom I have found alike—wherever my travels have carried me—the reader can guess their professions—porters and lawyers."[55] Aligning law and infrastructure with the "service" industry, Seacole spends a long vignette, for instance, telling us the story of American comeuppance through the tale of a free Black alcalde, or judge,[56] but also making clear the alcalde's corrupt fee system even as she praises the freedmen in the background of her own racism against the Spanish Indians on the isthmus and the government: "Whatever was of any worth in their institutions, such as their comparative freedom, religious toleration, etc., was owing mainly to the negroes who had sought the protection of the republic. . . . Like most fallen nations, they are very conservative in their habits and principles, while the blacks are enterprising, and in their opinions incline not unnaturally to democracy."[57] Seacole's protoethnographic aesthetics are shown here, rendering all of her work in the mode of the authoritative travel narrative.

Seacole's adventures in self-fashioning are also stitched together with her necessary calling card, her skill in delivering health care in these settings where the infrastructure and its multiple operations leave locales "unhealthy," in Seacole's stark terms. Women who would like to earn the public pleasures of men may be pilloried in Seacole's offhanded descriptions, but she unsentimentally narrates performing an autopsy on an infant who died of cholera, a disease that she at one point designates as her "fellow-traveler."[58] Throughout the text, Seacole acts as early epidemiologist in Jamaica: "Our idea—perhaps an unfounded one—was, that a steamer from New Orleans was the means of introducing it to the island,"[59] and then again in the long passage on the death and autopsy of the infant—part of a long chapter on Seacole's skills in treating cholera.[60] Here Seacole does not attempt to hide what Andrea Stone refers to as "the ruled and regulated self"[61] of medical and health authorship: "I was not afraid to use my baby patient thus," she narrates before she bribes someone for the body, arguing that the "daily, almost hourly, scenes of death had made me somewhat callous"[62] before refusing to give her findings. This lurid and yet unsentimental aesthetics of frontier death is meant to shock and to authorize Seacole as an integral part of infrastructure's cold, hard hand—the impartial and yet dishy scientist, once again breathless in her description of infrastructure's costs and possibilities.

"Use" is what propels Seacole's representation of her self, as well as her formal innovation of her genres. It is the lack of actual firm rules and regulations at the frontier of infrastructural expansion—the absence of bureaucracy—that drives Seacole to push to the edges of infrastructural boundaries, as her blistering account of the uselessness and racism of the application procedure to join Nightingale's pool of nurses in the Crimea attests.[63] Here, Seacole, though a nurse, eschews the "repair, care, and maintenance" strand of infrastructure studies engaged in lightly (as moral care) by the institution-building Anne Hart Gilbert. Reading Seacole's narrative through the lens of race and gender offers an interesting wrinkle to the risk-taking nature of colonial capital ventures in that Seacole articulates a particular endurance through loss—the loss of property and hence a lack of attachment to money or stability that is particular to being a Caribbean Black woman subject. She is not afraid to be of use to and through infrastructure—in the wake of the legacy of intimate promises that can never be banked on that undergird Seacole's heritage and colonial chattel slavery. Being of innovative, disruptive service marks Seacole's public campaign—including this memoir and a publicized four-night fundraiser—to recoup her losses from the sudden end of the Crimean War. Seacole is enterprising in her inhabitation of infrastructure's operations, its gray areas and borderlands, and in her inhabitation of literary form.

Conclusion: Black Women's Life Writing in the Age of Infrastructure

Seacole and Gilbert evince critical stances toward built structures not in the sense of critique as resistance but as they survey the uneven, incommensurable ways that a given subject—particularly a given free Black woman subject in the late eighteenth century or first half of the nineteenth century—can engage with infrastructure in relationship to structures and technologies of self-making. Rather than being autonomous and working with or against institutions, their writing selves recognized both the self and institutions as infrastructural formations that were constantly being made and remade—structures and objects that came at great cost, at great failure, and with the promise of heretofore unknown opportunity and possibility (intended and unintended). They stand then as central rather than peripheral critical subjects of understanding infrastructural economies through rather than against their racial and sexual genealogies and identifications.

Contemporary infrastructure policy in the Caribbean emphasizes the region as attached to development discourse, with official documents titled with phrases like "Meeting the Infrastructure Challenge." In literature, too, we talk about development—the emergence and progression of new forms and genres in response to or in the merging of old forms. Anne Hart Gilbert cobbled together material structures by aesthetically rendering demands through available forms of philanthropy, religion, education, and domesticity, as well as emergent abolitionism. Mary Seacole dipped her narrative toe in the thriving market for abolitionism in her narrative's time period but did so while embracing markets themselves and refusing sentimental aesthetics. Critical infrastructure studies, critical race studies, and critical literary studies sit in precarious relation to one another—one emerging, one dominant, one resonant, in Raymond Williams's terms—on the contemporary scene of academic and political urgency. Two of them take systems—the structure of the world as it is, built and social—as their main point of analysis. One seems wed to form if not systemic structure as the humanities "wane" in an era of preprofessional skills-training models of education and a race for STEM. All must respond to the markets for them in institutional infrastructure—and the market for Black women to narrate themselves through resistant life writing while at the same time doing institution building as care and repair work. Tracing different genealogies and forms for self-making for Black women through the act of early life writing can bring infrastructure studies and literary studies together in extraordinary ways—surveying the forms being made and forged alongside infrastructural invention then and now not as opposed but as genres through which to view literary, historical, political, and aesthetic relations anew.

Notes

1. See Katherine McKittrick, *Demonic Grounds: Black Women and the Cartographies of Struggle* (Minneapolis: University of Minnesota Press, 2006).

2. See Darlene Clark Hine, "Rape and the Inner lives of Black Women in the Middle West: Preliminary Thoughts on the Culture of Dissemblance," *Signs: Journal of Women in Culture and Society* 14, no. 4 (1989): 912–20.

3. Alan Liu, "Toward Critical Infrastructure Studies," *Critical Infrastructure Studies* (2018): 5, https://cistudies.org/wp-content/uploads/Toward-Critical-Infrastructure-Studies.pdf.

4. See Caroline Levine, *Forms: Whole, Rhythm, Hierarchy, Network* (Princeton, NJ: Princeton University Press, 2017); Martha Rosler, "In the Place of the Public: Observations of a Frequent Flyer," *Assemblage* 25 (1994): 61–79.

5. Sandro Mezzadra and Brett Neilson, *The Politics of Operations: Excavating Contemporary Capitalism* (Durham, NC: Duke University Press, 2019), 2.

6. Mezzarda and Neilson, *Politics of Operations*, 4.

7. Daniel Nemser, *Infrastructures of Race: Concentration and Biopolitics in Colonial Mexico* (Austin: University of Texas Press, 2017), 4.

8. Nemser, *Infrastructures of Race*, 4.

9. AbdouMaliq Simone, "People as Infrastructure: Intersecting Fragments in Johannesburg," *Public Culture* 16, no. 3 (2004): 407–29.

10. Keller Easterling, *Extrastatecraft: The Power of Infrastructure Space* (London: Verso, 2014).

11. See Lauren Berlant, "The Commons: Infrastructures for Troubling Times," *Environment and Planning D: Society and Space* 34, no. 3 (2016): 393–419; Ara Wilson, "The Infrastructure of Intimacy," *Signs: Journal of Women in Culture and Society* 41, no. 2 (2016): 247–80.

12. Moira Ferguson, ed., *The Hart Sisters: Early African Caribbean Writers, Evangelicals, and Radicals* (Lincoln: University of Nebraska Press, 1993), 64.

13. Ferguson, *Hart Sisters*, 64.

14. Ferguson, *Hart Sisters*, 64.

15. Ferguson, *Hart Sisters*, 65.

16. Ferguson, *Hart Sisters*, 84.

17. Ferguson, *Hart Sisters*, 73.

18. Ferguson, *Hart Sisters*, 73.

19. This prefigures the faith-based political work of Edward Blyden in St. Thomas and then Liberia.

20. Ferguson, *Hart Sisters*, 84.

21. See Stefanie Markovits, *The Crimean War in the British Imagination* (Cambridge: Cambridge University Press, 2009).

22. Markovits, *Crimean War*; Karen Sánchez-Eppler, *Touching Liberty: Abolition, Feminism, and the Politics of the Body* (Berkeley: University of California Press, 1993); Julia A. Stern, *The Plight of Feeling: Sympathy and Dissent in the Early American novel* (Chicago: University of Chicago Press, 1997); Jennifer DeVere Brody, *Impossible Purities: Blackness, Femininity, and Victorian Culture* (Durham, NC: Duke University Press, 1998).

23. Donna J. Haraway, *Staying with the Trouble: Making Kin in the Chthulucene* (Durham, NC: Duke University Press, 2016).

24. Derrick R. Spires, *The Practice of Citizenship: Black Politics and Print Culture in the Early United States* (Philadelphia: University of Pennsylvania Press, 2019).

25. Mary Seacole, *Wonderful Adventures of Mrs. Seacole in Many Lands* (London: Penguin, 2005), 15–16.

26. Seacole, *Wonderful Adventures*, 16.

27. Seacole, *Wonderful Adventures*, 16.

28. Seacole, *Wonderful Adventures*, 40.

29. Lisa Lowe, *The Intimacies of Four Continents* (Durham, NC: Duke University Press, 2015).

30. Joseph W. Childers, review of *Mobility and Modernity: Panama in the Nineteenth-Century Anglo-American Imagination*, by Robert D. Aguirre, *Victorian Studies* 61, no. 2 (2019): 356.

31. See popular titles such as Kevin Baker, *America the Ingenious: How a Nation of Dreamers, Immigrants, and Tinkerers Changed the World* (New York: Artisan Books, 2016).

32. Seacole, *Wonderful Adventures*, 17.

33. Seacole, *Wonderful Adventures*, 18.

34. Seacole, *Wonderful Adventures*, 19.

35. Seacole, *Wonderful Adventures*, 19.

36. Mark Twain, "Letter from Mark Twain," *Chicago Republican*, August 23, 1868, https://www.panamarailroad.org/marktwain.html.

37. Seacole, *Wonderful Adventures*, 62.

38. Seacole, *Wonderful Adventures*, 62.

39. Julie Livingston, *Self-Devouring Growth: A Planetary Parable as Told from Southern Africa* (Durham, NC: Duke University Press, 2019), 94.

40. Livingston, *Self-Devouring Growth*, 96.

41. Livingston, *Self-Devouring Growth*, 94.

42. Livingston, *Self-Devouring Growth*, 98.

43. See Emily Owens, "Promises: Sexual Labor in the Space between Slavery and Freedom," *Louisiana History* 58, no. 2 (2017): 179–216.

44. See Jenny Sharpe, *Ghosts of Slavery: A Literary Archaeology of Black Women's Lives* (Minneapolis: University of Minnesota Press, 2003); and Lisa Ze Winters, *The Mulatta Concubine: Terror, Intimacy, Freedom, and Desire in the Black Transatlantic* (Athens: University of Georgia Press, 2016).

45. Seacole, *Wonderful Adventures*, 26.

46. See Philippa Levine, *Feminist Lives in Victorian England Private Roles and Public Commitment* (Los Angeles: Figueroa Press, 1990).

47. Seacole, *Wonderful Adventures*, 31.

48. Lizabeth Paravisini-Gebert, "Mrs. Seacole's Wonderful Adventures in Many Lands and the Consciousness of Transit," in *Black Victorians/Black Victoriana*, ed. Gretchen Holbrook Gerzina (New Brunswick, NJ: Rutgers University Press, 2003), 77.

49. See James Clifford, *Routes: Travel and Translation in the Late Twentieth Century* (Cambridge, MA: Harvard University Press, 1997); Sean X. Goudie, "Toward a Definition of Caribbean American Regionalism: Contesting Anglo-America's Caribbean Designs in Mary Seacole and Sui Sin Far," *American*

Literature 80, no. 2 (2008): 293–322; Jacques Derrida and Anne Dufourmantelle, *Of Hospitality* (Stanford, CA: Stanford University Press, 2000).

50. See Ann Laura Stoler, *Race and the Education of Desire: Foucault's History of Sexuality and the Colonial Order of Things* (Durham, NC: Duke University Press, 1995).

51. Seacole, *Wonderful Adventures*, 42.

52. Seacole, *Wonderful Adventures*, 25.

53. Seacole, *Wonderful Adventures*, 54–55.

54. Seacole, *Wonderful Adventures*, 47.

55. Seacole, *Wonderful Adventures*, 19.

56. Seacole, *Wonderful Adventures*, 45–46.

57. Seacole, *Wonderful Adventures*, 68.

58. Seacole, *Wonderful Adventures*, 29.

59. Seacole, *Wonderful Adventures*, 17.

60. Seacole, *Wonderful Adventures*, 54.

61. Andrea Stone, *Black Well-Being: Health and Selfhood in Antebellum Black Literature* (Gainesville: University Press of Florida, 2016).

62. Seacole, *Wonderful Adventures* 34.

63. Seacole, *Wonderful Adventures*, 72–74.

Part Two

✦

Affect and Technologies

Chapter 5

Fine-Tuning Frantz Fanon's Infrastructural Affects

Yanie Fecu

The Martinican psychiatrist and political theorist Frantz Fanon was extraordinarily prescient about the significance of infrastructure's material and immaterial dimensions. His 1959 essay "This Is the Voice of Algeria" from *A Dying Colonialism*[1] chronicles radio's dual assimilationist and revolutionary roles in French-occupied Algeria to demonstrate how political struggles transformed this new technology, and telecommunications infrastructure more broadly, into a public utility as valued as roads or water. In her studies of audiovisual media sites, objects, and processes, Lisa Parks identifies a need for scholarship situated at the intersection of infrastructure and affect. She asserts that we need to understand infrastructure's technical operations as well as its capacity for creating "different dispositions, rhythms, structures of feeling, moods, and sensations" through people's material encounters.[2] I posit that Fanon's work anticipates this intellectual gap and provides a model for examining infrastructural developments in relation to affect, or precisely that which resists structure.[3] Scholars such as Susan Leigh Star and Bruce Robbins emphasize that reliable infrastructure does not draw attention to itself or incite questions about its operations. Rather, these organizational systems routinize behavior in ways that ultimately render them invisible. Only during instances of malfunction does infrastructure gain notice. In this essay I ask, What insights might we gain from studying a phenomenon that both begins and ends from the place of breakdown? How can listening to breakdown—in the form of noise—generate new affective relations? And how does affect, embodied but not coterminous with the body, challenge visibility as the primary framework for understanding infrastructural awareness?

In 1953 Fanon traveled to Algeria to work as *chef de service* at the Blida-Joinville Psychiatric Hospital. Just three years later, the *Front de Libération Nationale* (FLN) would launch the clandestine program *The Voice of Fighting Algeria* in order to spread news of a growing resistance. Even as infrastructures facilitate the movement of goods, people, and information on large scales with increasing speed, they also "generate possibilities for their own corruption and parasitism."[4] Throughout the twentieth century, the rise of commercial radio industries necessitated the construction of new sites and systems to oversee licensing policies, frequency allocations, and technical standards. While many recent studies of infrastructure are concerned with moments of equipment failure and government ineptitude, Fanon's essay points to a kind of corruption that instead stems from deliberate state sabotage. When, after a period of wary disinterest, Algerians incorporated the radio into their daily lives, they encountered rebel broadcasts at once interruptive and interrupted. French efforts to jam their transmissions engendered new affects among an unintended audience because the sonic distortion demanded a distinct level of interactivity from listeners. Fanon's essay provides an important case study of infrastructure and embodiment. By mining Fanon's writing for the development and circulation of feeling, I reveal the operations of what I call the "modulating ear." I argue the modulating ear emerges when what one hears not only transmits the producer's intended or overt message but also brings infrastructural instability to the fore.

Colonialism required the construction of large-scale networks of communication and transportation as part of the management of overseas territories where natural resources, labor, and goods were extracted. Nevertheless, we should be careful of thinking about infrastructure solely as the materialization of a domineering and "discrete logic of colonial governance."[5] What interests Fanon is how Algerians negotiated their desire to communicate through systems subtended by imperial power relations. These infrastructures are composed of interconnected relay stations, communications networks, transmission systems, and data terminal equipment that operate in unison. Fanon concentrates on the object of the radio itself and not, for instance, the cables or transmission stations that often remain out of sight. However, he does so using the "soft" infrastructures of market kiosks, hospitals, and changing regulations about access, content, and circulation. By focusing on distribution networks and listeners, he tackles the role of the human element, so often figured as "human capital," in infrastructural planning and development. His decision to highlight distribution is particularly significant in light of the fact that, as Parks notes, production and consumption have tended to overshadow distribution.

These soft infrastructures open toward AbdouMaliq Simone's theory of "people as infrastructure," which reveals how a community's adaptive practices can establish new channels through which goods, services, and knowledge may travel. Drawing on Simone, I uncover the inextricable link between material distribution networks and cultural listening networks to argue that quotidian acts of listening generated not only a counterpublic but also a counterinfrastructure that disrupted the cultural, political, and economic circuits of empire. I offer an analysis of "listeners-as-infrastructure" in light of Brian Larkin's observation that "the sheer diversity of ways to conceive of and analyze infrastructures . . . cumulatively point[s] to the productive instability of the basic unit of research."[6] Although there were no explicit rules for radio listening, audience members used their modulating ears to improvise roles and behaviors around hearing, interpreting, and disseminating news of the revolution. Much like the interlocking grids of pipes and roads that order a city's residents and products, these listeners and their specialized form of audition imposed order on noise and facilitated the flow of information and affect.

Despite Fanon's looming presence in Anglophone scholarship, most studies focus on two major threads in his corpus: the psychological impact of colonialism and the emancipatory possibilities of anticolonial violence. Few critics have made attempts to analyze his interest in media and technology.[7] In the sections that follow, I contextualize radio's complex reception in French Algeria and do a close read of Fanon's ethnographic essay to unveil the human infrastructure at work. In my view, the modulating ear names the extraordinary phenomenon he witnessed in homes, hospitals, and the streets as the Algerian resistance gained momentum. This ear transforms listeners into infrastructure by allowing them to hear unintelligibility as a condition of possibility for, rather than as a foreclosure of, sensorial and political organization. This social infrastructure provides an alternative to sight as the entry point into infrastructural awareness not only because of its provisional, fluid nature and its reliance on aurality but also because it presents deroutinization as the norm rather than the deviation. Although interdisciplinary scholars of auditory culture have productively reframed listeners as agents rather than receptacles, I suggest we examine listeners and listening as an organizing force, one based not on governmental regulations but on social necessity. That affect is so often theorized as "resonance" invites us to recalibrate our own ears and to examine the sounds we dislike, the sounds we dismiss, and the sounds we fail to notice even as they move us.

Broadcasting Empire, Broadcasting Revolution

In thinking through the infrastructural affects of everyday life under colonial rule, Fanon elucidates racialized systems of governance. Throughout the early and mid-twentieth century, communications technologies offered French officials new ways to disseminate and reinforce imperial values. France tackled the administrative challenge of maintaining and monitoring links between the distant corners of its territories through several means, including censuses, surveys, and statistics. Jacques Attali characterizes the state as "a gigantic, monopolizing noise emitter, and at the same time, a generalized eavesdropping device."[8] His description draws attention both to the recapitulation of dominant narratives and the centrality of surveillance. By establishing sound as essential to the ordering of difference and knowledge production, Attali reveals how noise becomes a measure of political power. In the aftermath of

World War II, the French could no longer ignore their waning political power. They began deploying radio sets, relay stations, and shortwave receivers as defenses against the threat of dissolution in a period of increasing uncertainty. In Algeria, subject to French rule for over a century, the radio was but one aspect of a larger sensory regime. But as the global fight for independence began to gain traction, that same technology simultaneously facilitated projects of radical self-determination. Telecommunications systems made France vulnerable to attacks launched on entirely new terrain.

By the time Fanon arrived in Algeria in 1953, Radio-Alger had become critical to the French settlers' continuation of civilized life in an "uncivilized" society. The sentiment "without wine and the radio, we should already have become Arabized" makes plain how daily broadcasts assuaged their fears of cultural contamination.[9] As an echo of transmissions from Paris, these shows offered occasional acknowledgments of Algerian culture in the form of humiliating reminders of France's conquest and references to the failed revolt of 1830. Algerian social life was thus relegated to the margins, and broadcasts consisted of "Frenchmen speaking to Frenchmen."[10] Following Hannah Knox's formulation, politics is "neither prior to nor determined by material structures, but emerges and is reworked through affective engagements with the material arrangements of the worlds in which people live."[11] The material resources that link people to amenities are inseparable from imperial relations of power. Fanon perceives the radio as a concrete manifestation of bourgeois values; it operates in conjunction with their consumption of objects such as cars and refrigerators.[12] But most importantly, it is a metaphorical tether to the metropolis, one offering a powerful version of reality that restored occupiers to their rightful place within the social hierarchy. These class aspirations have particular affective contours intended to shield colonizers from the threat of infrastructural instability. World War I had temporarily curtailed European citizens' constitutional freedoms, while the interwar period further destabilized the French empire. Germany's invasion in 1940 established Vichy rule, and in 1942, British and US forces invaded Algeria, although they did not contest French rule. It is no wonder then that in the aftermath of such upheaval, Fanon explained the French settler's relationship to the radio as being strongly characterized by the feeling of "serenity" it evoked.[13] The desire for tranquility surfaces as a counterbalance less to the chaos of conquest than to the mundane tensions that arise for French citizens who wish to live *in* the colony without being *of* the colony. The more metropolitan France sought to incorporate its overseas citizens, the more stringent their measures for excluding the colonial subject became.

Despite radio's wide distribution among the French, Algerians displayed a "dull absence of interest."[14] I want to emphasize that this apathy, while not an organized form of opposition, is not simply an affective absence or void. Like Raymond Williams's structures of feeling, affects "do not have to await definition, classification, or rationalization before they exert palpable pressures."[15] In Fanon's essay we see an example of how a group may cultivate an affective relationship with a technology prior to any interaction with said technology. Fanon posits two causes for this initial disinterest. The first addresses the significant economic divide within the colonial state: only members of the elite could afford these new commodities. The second is that French cultural norms meant that broadcasts were too vulgar for family consumption. Once he outlines these reasons, however, Fanon dismisses this "sociological approach" as too limited. A few paragraphs later, he weighs in with two alternative explanations, both larger in scope and more nuanced. Because the radio originates with the colonizers, the colonized can see no immediate use for it. And because it extends the colonizers' cultural and sensorial influence, the colonized cannot objectively evaluate any potential merits. Whatever benefits this new technology might offer, its primary function is to create an exclusive system of language and transmissions. Fanon reminds us that an oppressed population "never participates in this world of signs."[16] At the same time, his observations push us to consider the overlooked affective flows spreading through and outside of this codified semiotic realm.

Fanon explicitly links these two ideas when he returns to the occupier's feeling of serenity. The European is enmeshed in this world of signs—it is created by and for him. "Through the triple network of the press, the radio and his travels, [the European has] a fairly clear idea of the dangers threatening colonial society," but this awareness triggers emotional dysregulation.[17] Thus, it is the "visible crumbling away of the settler's serenity," interspersed with episodes of "sudden affability" and "unmotivated bursts of temper," that first reveals France's weakening hold to the colonized subject.[18] Once the FLN tapped into French infrastructure and co-opted radio technology, the colonizers found themselves waging battle on land and on air. The broadcasters who sought to detail the progress of rebel forces at home and throughout the Arab world had no interest in producing a sense of serenity among their listeners. Rather than placate fears, they had to draw civilians into the fight. A "fierce and sudden assurance"[19] would come to replace initial feelings of apathy and disdain. The cultivation of new bodily sensations, postures, and activations were integral to radio's ability to bring Algerian families into intimate contact with the resistance. In his exceptional media history of colonial Algeria, Arthur Asseraf explains, "On the one hand . . . the impact of the radio was not that dramatic. Algerians had long heard news rather than read it in various forms by public readings in cafés and song, so the role of aural culture was not new."[20] However, he goes on to argue that "a specific connection between the development of the radio in 1930s Algeria and new forms of political participation" arose as listeners became aware of and invested in larger international conflicts between communist and fascist nation-states.[21] To this observation, I would add that radio caused an important shift in aural culture because it created new sonic effects—principally static—that in turn created new perceptual modes.

In his writing, Fanon represents not only recognizable emotions but what Brian Massumi describes as an "intensity corresponding to the passage from one experiential state of the body to another and implying an augmentation or diminution in that body's capacity to act."[22] Fanon seeks to capture Algerian listeners on the cusp of world-changing action. Knowing that infrastructures "emerge out of and store within them forms of desire and fantasy and can take on fetish-like aspects that sometimes can be wholly autonomous from their technical function"[23] helps us understand how infrastructural growth in Algeria became ideologically tied to the narrative of colonial progress and the civilizing mission. More importantly, it helps us understand how Algerians could form a psychological and visceral attachment to a radio program that, by conventional standards, never successfully transmitted its message. When Algerian investment in radio technology grew, the French had to develop tactics for maintaining their exclusion from this infrastructural dream. Once it became clear the FLN had co-opted this technology, Algerians were subjected to new laws that prohibited them from purchasing radios. Fantasies, however, are not only invisible and uncontainable but mutable. Fanon's descriptions of affective pulses and flows coalesce around such infrastructural dreaming.

Bad Reception and the Nation's Consciousness

As these collective freedom dreams escaped Algeria's geopolitical borders to circulate throughout North Africa and beyond, so too did stories of France's brutal response. For Fanon, the year 1945, which brought the end of World War II and the massacres in Setif and Guelma, is a line of demarcation. Following these bloody repressions, which resulted in roughly forty-five thousand victims, Algeria was catapulted onto the international stage. The native population became cognizant of global anticolonial movements, and the first widespread distribution of radio sets in Algeria occurred just as broadcasting stations appeared in Egypt, Syria, and Lebanon. Algerian listeners were drawn to programs from the Arab world and beyond. They saw their own anxieties and aspirations reflected in the suffering and resistance of others. By 1951 news of civil unrest came from Tunisia, and in 1952 Morocco waged war for independence. When Algeria aligned itself with the Maghreb Front's anticolonial mission, radio sets finally had something valuable to offer. Fanon describes how the colonized had to counter the enemy's alternative facts with events, figures, and language gleaned from this newly accessible "world of truth."[24]

At the start of the Algerian War the free press was the Algerians' primary news source. Within months, however, local journals offering objective reports or anticolonial sentiments were censored. The distribution networks that brought radio technology into Algerian households and the attendant listening networks that arose in response attest to the fact that infrastructure exists beyond the boundaries of public works. In the context of the settler-colonial state, however, the term "public" is especially fraught. The word may signal the government's operational and regulatory role, but there is little expectation that it would also connote universal access at a time when the conferral citizenship and attendant rights were bifurcated and unequal. Radio sets enabled not only the dissemination of news but access to "a world in which things happened, in which events existed, in which forces were active."[25] Moreover, broadcasts were accessible to the illiterate masses in a way the local presses were not.[26] The lack of consistent news incited rumors both substantiated and otherwise. The Algerian, Fanon writes, "gave the isolated European the impression of being in permanent contact with the revolutionary high command."[27] Given their absolute commitment to the cause, all news had to be good news. What some sociologists described as inexplicable fanaticism Fanon describes as a "collective conviction" that allowed individuals to forge the closest possible bond to the revolution.[28]

Despite growing social unrest, Algerians were still slow to adopt the radio in the early 1950s. At the end of 1956, however, the launch of *The Voice of Fighting Algeria* incited a rapid change. Fanon writes that all the radio stocks were bought in fewer than twenty days. Battery-operated receivers were necessary due to the lack of electrical grids in vast swathes of the country, so access was unevenly distributed. Possession of a radio offered "the sole means of entering into communication with the Revolution, of living with it."[29] The technology lost its negative valence as the enemy's apparatus, not only because the program spoke directly to its listeners but because it spoke to them in Arabic, French, and Kabyle. These three languages were placed at distinct levels of the sociolinguistic hierarchy, with French inhabiting the uppermost rung, Arabic the middle, and Kabyle, one of seven major indigenous Berber languages, languishing at the bottom. *The Voice of Fighting Algeria* strove to be the great equalizer; moreover, it made the subversive move of reclaiming an imposed colonial language and using it to advance an anticolonial vision.

I am less interested in the content of *The Voice of Fighting Algeria* than I am in the modulating ear—that is, the interpretive strategies and affective experiences it provoked in its audience. The proof of radio's power was evident in France's efforts to prohibit sales: an Algerian could not make a purchase unless given a military or police voucher. This prohibition only accelerated the development of an alternative infrastructure by which sets and batteries from Tunisia and Morocco could be smuggled in via underground channels. These objects became as valuable to the political cause as weapons. Attali observes that "it is possible to judge the strength of political power by its legislation on noise and the effectiveness of its control over it."[30] In Algeria, state-supported programming created a transnational community of listeners among French citizens and, in doing so, remade the contours of political and intellectual life. However, the unanticipated capacities of wireless communication subverted France's imperial mission; radio's far reach influenced unintended audiences. If broadcast communication is always "a social process or practice rather than a finished product,"[31] then all transmissions remain subject to interpretation, even within the framework of colonial domination. While the producers and broadcasters whose voices emanated from the speakers were undoubtedly significant social actors, I want to suggest that listeners and their media practices incited the most profound shifts in the increasingly tenuous relationship between empire and colony.

Having gained expertise in previous wars, the French were well versed in "sound wave warfare."[32] They were able to discern the precise wavelengths of broadcasting stations and systematically jam the signals. Algerians were informed via printed tracts to stay tuned for periods of up to two or three hours as the censored speakers migrated from wavelength to wavelength and relayed scrambled messages. Fanon describes the listeners who imagined themselves as combatants fighting to outsmart and outmaneuver the enemy on a different battlefield. The primary operator of the radio set stood or sat with an ear pressed against the receiver, straining to hear. Described as a "privileged interpreter," this listener delivered the results to audience members and attempted to answer the litany of questions that would inevitably erupt.[33] In many cases the group would reach a consensus about what had and had not been covered by the broadcast, since the interpreter could not be expected to parse everything. The "real task of reconstruction" inspired all to recall previous broadcasts, and with them, previous battles won.[34] As David Marriott puts it, this audience demanded "a new kind of listening in relation to which the clarity of transmission is only of a kind of secondary importance, almost without consequence." This broadcast's chronic state of technical malfunction paradoxically fostered a reawakened sense of collective life among the oppressed. At the same time, the FLN's ability to routinely overtake these frequencies revealed new vulnerabilities in France's armor.

Fanon describes a willingness to incorporate what can never truly be heard—another's hearing—into one's affective relations. The Algerians cultivated a practice that enabled one individual to hear another's description of distorted sound and to not only agree that they heard the same sentences and sentiment but to build creatively upon this shared fiction. The modulating ear, then, is a collaborative ear, no longer sequestered in the individual's sensorium but expanded and dispersed. Just as this particular perceptual mode dissolves the presumed edges of the individual, so, too, does affect. I take heed of Teresa Brennan's claim that "the transmission of affect means, that we are not self-contained in terms of our energies. There is no secure distinction between the 'individual' and the 'environment.'"[35] A number of genealogies inform affect theory, including psychoanalytic theory, posthumanism, poststructuralism, and trauma studies. This essay is most informed by an approach Gregory J. Seigworth and Melissa Gregg describe as "hidden-in-plain-sight"; it looks to the quotidian to reveal "where persistent, repetitious practices of power can simultaneously provide a body (or, better, collectivized bodies) with predicaments and potentials for realizing a world that subsists within and exceeds the horizons and boundaries of the norm."[36] An independent Algeria is one such world, and what we witness through Fanon is how a mundane activity such as listening can propel the exchange of potential and kinetic energy between bodies as listeners become narrators who become structuring forces for a future being called into existence.

The visual indeterminacy of the term "shimmer," which Seigworth and Gregg borrow from Roland Barthes, proves useful when exploring a concept that resists definition and description. "Static" is perhaps an effective aural analogy to "shimmer." Both words gesture towards sensations located on the edge of our sensibilities. Static, like shimmer, skirts precision and legibility to instead offer gradients, mergings, and suturings of difference. When people intentionally listen to static, they encounter nonrepresentational stimuli; while static here is not itself affect, it elicits affectivity or "the capacity for the body to be radically creative." Although affects may evade conscious awareness or rationalization, the behaviors they prompt provide an entry point for analyzing political change. Like Fanon, I recognize that Algerians crafted unsubstantiated accounts, statistics, and claims as they integrated the FLN's broadcast into their lived experience. I distinguish this crowdsourced knowledge from the French colonizers' misinformation, because it was never directed at the French as a form of propaganda. This tactic brings to mind Michel Serres's suggestion that noise has both "a value of destruction and a value of construction."[37] These narrative collages circulated among the oppressed in a manner closer to the oral preservation of myth or religious ritual. We must understand this activity in relation to Asseraf's study of what he calls the "full news ecosystem" of French-ruled Algeria, wherein "'modern' news coexisted and interacted with 'traditional' networks of rumour and song."[38] Old and new forms of media did not replace each other but jostled against one another, forming a kind of palimpsest that grew more intense and "electric."[39] If the Algerians' reassembled broadcasts grew in monumentality, it is only because the lengths to which the French settlers went to suppress the truth warranted it. The Algerians' accounts of the war are only outrageous if excised from the framework of colonial domination in which they arose. Whereas the occupiers manufactured propaganda, Algerians used their modulating ears to engage in an act of radical translation. This act involved not only the transformation of static to speech but of their own roles, shifting from listener and newscaster to freedom fighter and citizen of a sovereign nation.

Algerians' acceptance of the radio meant the introduction of multiple voices—"les amis; les complices des ennemis; les neutres"—into the home.[40] The occupier's once domineering speech was no longer amplified above all others. I wish to emphasize that the effect of the fragmentated broadcasts that arose was unlike the "impression of incompleteness, of sketchiness, even of betrayal in the realm of news."[41] The suppression of print journalism cut off knowledge of the colonizer's disintegrating power and thus paralyzed Algerians who wished to act. The crackling and hissing of an interrupted broadcast, however, actually encouraged a form of collusion. But why would the censorship of an audio format lead to such a different outcome? The answer, I believe, is threefold. The first reason has to do with the fact that radios reached a much broader swath of people. While many family members and neighbors would gather indoors to listen to the secret transmissions, in the mountainous Kabylia region, dozens of peasants would congregate around a single radio set. The second element concerns the nature of hearing. Fanon's writing makes clear it is not simply "the simultaneity of listening—not just of hearing the same things at the same time, but of doing the same cognitive work at the same time" that brings an audience together.[42] Lastly, in his study of Fanon's essay, Marriott points out how "the denotative or referential functions of the linguistic sign here coexist with that which is absent, inaudible."[43] This joining of speech, static, and silence was possible on air, whereas censored publications were stripped of any unacceptable material *before* printing. In other words, there was no possibility of reading between the lines. This impossibility highlights the centrality of sound's ephemeral nature in the emergence of listeners as infrastructure and the challenge they pose to the state's scopic regime.

As the French blocked their pirated airwaves, the disembodied voice of the revolution persisted. This resulted in a complex interplay of continuity and interruption. The polysemic nature of static made it particularly well suited for an environment structured by government surveillance and censorship. As John Mowitt puts it, "The more distorted, that is, less expressive the voice of the nation is rendered, the more clearly the nation's existence is, as it were, signaled."[44] That the official word of the revolution was often rendered unintelligible or inaudible was not a hindrance but an advantage. Fanon observes situations wherein, having failed to make contact with the voice, listeners would intentionally tune in to a jammed frequency and search for truth in the static instead. Reassured by their own triumphs in the soundwave war, listeners believed France's collapse to be imminent. If Algerian listeners, wholly unremarkable but committed to the cause, could win their own battles, what force could stop their valiant comrades? This belief heightened the fervor needed to sustain the fight for independence. Fanon's essay demonstrates how listeners engaged with scrambled messages that, even when half heard and half imagined, threatened colonial power. In a time of resistance, the failure itself *is* the message. But what I want to reiterate here is the related observation that in a time of resistance, the listeners themselves are the infrastructure.

When the modulating ear encounters jammed radio frequencies, it simultaneously exposes the underlying infrastructure the French implement to maintain administrative control and the precarity of that infrastructure.

These intercorporeal listenings and the narrative impulse that develops around them transform the audience members themselves into an emergent, living infrastructure. Invisible yet audible, "every Algerian felt himself to be called upon and wanted to become a reverberating element of the vast network of meanings born of the liberating combat."[45] The interdependence at the core of this auditory phenomenon echoes the interdependence integral to the function of conventional infrastructures. These narratives depend upon and cohere around an awareness of infrastructural disruption. The listener-narrators replace the occupier's fallible equipment with their self-assured receiving and transmitting bodies. As Fanon makes clear: "On request, information as to its striking power and plan of operations can be obtained. No one, of course, can give the source of such information, but the reliability is unchallengeable."[46] The modulating ear names both the listener's relation to and response to infrastructure under threat. However, it is crucial to note the listeners' transformation into infrastructure does not reproduce the colonial matrix of global capitalism that seeks to surveil, regulate, and extract labor from them. Instead, Algerian listeners offer a decentralized version of infrastructure, a communal soundscape that functions in sharp contradistinction to Robbins's description of infrastructure as "the object of no one's desire. . . . It is neglected because it belongs to the public domain, all other tokens of belonging effaced, owned in effect by no one"[47] and thus taken for granted by those who most benefit. What we hear in Fanon's own listening is the possibility of an infrastructure stripped of power asymmetries, tended to by those it serves, and linked to an irrepressible will to nationhood.

Resonant Collectives

Fanon emerges as a thinker who constructs an alternative conceptualization of listeners as engaged social actors rather than as the passive, even regressive consumers envisioned by Theodor Adorno and Jean-Paul Sartre. As a trained psychiatrist and Martinican native, Fanon aimed to be both an expert listener and decoder. If one holds this view of his clinical duties, his interest in another colonized culture's improvised strategies for listening and decoding becomes less surprising. He often elides medicine and technology; as Roxanna Nydia Curto notes, he routinely "refer[s] to medical practices as 'the new technique/technology' (*la nouvelle technique*) and doctors as 'technicians' (*techniciens*)."[48] For Fanon, modern medicine, like technology, is tainted by its colonial associations. The negative valence they carry affects their reception among marginalized populations. Nevertheless, in this essay and elsewhere, he insists the oppressed are capable of transforming these instruments and forms of knowledge to support their own needs. Fanon's sustained engagement with media and medical practices provides overlapping entry points into the study of global anticolonial movements. He situates his analysis of communications infrastructure, radio technology, and cultures of listening within a specific material environment: newspaper kiosks, living rooms, and hospitals. I believe Fanon recognized a staging of colonial conflict within these intimate, domestic scenes of radio listening that reiterated what he also witnessed at his clinic. Indeed, he makes no effort to separate these two spheres of observation: his essay includes accounts of radio's changing status in relation to the psychopathological experiences of his Algerian patients. He describes how voices on the radio initially manifested as a threat in their hallucinations and delusions. After radio's incorporation into Algerian society as a positive link to the revolution, those formerly hostile voices were imbued with friendly and even protective tones.[49] Much in the same way listeners sought to fill in the gaps of their static-riddled broadcasts, so, too, did Fanon seek to address the aporias of colonial medicine through theory and praxis.

Richard C. Keller reminds readers that colonial health workers were cognizant of their political function. The French army's Sections Administratives Spécialisées had orders to persuade Algerian patients of the benefits of colonial rule while also providing medical care. Patrick Ehlen details the changes Fanon instituted during his time at Blida: he offered patients regular consultations, integrated separate wards, encouraged relationships between patients and the nursing staff, and ended the use of straitjackets. The 2002 film *Frantz Fanon: Mémoires d'asile* brings to light additional reforms; in interviews, nurses and patients discuss the introduction of a soccer field and concerts by Algerian musicians as well as the reconstruction of the hospital mosque. Most crucially, Fanon took responsibility for failed treatments and responded by reevaluating his French-based therapeutic methods rather than blaming patients. David Macey, however, takes care to remind us of his adherence to other accepted protocols, which included electroconvulsive therapy. Fanon did not reject Western medicine wholesale; instead, he attempted to build "a therapeutic 'neo-society' in which patients could establish a multiplicity of social bonds, fulfill a variety of functions and act out a variety of roles."[50] What may go unnoticed is that so many of these reforms created more opportunities for close listening, not just between doctors and patients but among the patients themselves, whether in newly desegregrated wards or a site of worship. Building on Macey's observation, I want to insist that Fanon's modifications should be read as an attempt to reproduce what he heard unfolding in Algerian homes: another permutation of listeners as infrastructure.

Listening, both in and out of clinical contexts, is vital to what become co-constitutive tasks for Fanon—that is, the reformation of Western colonial psychiatry and universal emancipation. Fanon was a Black man raised in the Caribbean, educated in France, with little knowledge of Arabic; his writing about static is itself marked by a form of cultural static. Nevertheless, these disturbances do not negate the value of his claims. Even as he urges readers to listen to Algerian voices and through Algerian ears, he does not present himself as their spokesperson. Instead, he positions himself as a comrade in the global struggle for liberation. In his essays on Algeria and decolonization more broadly, readers can see how Fanon remained painfully aware of his native country's neocolonial status. Nick Nesbitt, writing on the Haitian Revolution of 1804, explains how the concept of an unqualified freedom that included peoples of African descent exceeded the limits of enlightenment thought.[51] Following in the footsteps of Haiti's revolutionary leaders and first constitution, the FLN made the radical proposition that all people living in Algeria, regardless of race or ethnicity, would be considered citizens of the new nation. This declaration challenged the foundational hierarchies and taxonomies at the heart of colonial logic. The world's first and only successful slave revolt took place on an island that shares the same French colonial history as Martinique, but the latter never achieved independence. It remains an overseas department today. The end of slavery in Martinique did eventually grant legal citizenship to its inhabitants. However, Fanon was sensitive to the partial and limited nature of this change in status. Political autonomy eluded Martinique, but Fanon discovered in Algeria a nascent resistance that might overcome the gaps and failures of a decolonization enacted in name only.

Unlike French broadcasts, Algerian broadcasts were always already a source of deroutinization, one that countered the normalization of colonial occupation. The modulating ear allowed listeners to incorporate embodied and disembodied sounds as they registered the felt reality of a new technology and became the new infrastructures for circulating that technology. Affect, as unstructured potential, moves through and gathers itself in many bodies: in the oft-invisible networks that send and receive electromagnetic waves, in the mechanical wiring of radio sets, in the folds of a listener's bony labyrinth, and in the ephemeral transmissions that spread across a nation. The modulating ear is a particular way of organizing one's attention. It brings infrastructural affect to the fore, juxtaposing our dependence on vulnerable physical hardware with our dependence on vulnerable bodies. In other words, the modulating ear draws us to the sites, objects, and feelings that we most struggle to perceive and incorporate into our understanding of world-making. The French were unable to enforce rigid boundaries and procedures for transmitting and listening because "media are not fixed natural objects; they have no natural edges."[52] Their failure resulted in unforeseen uses of radio technology in the colonial context. France established Radio-Alger to reinforce an unblemished sense of national identity among its own citizens. In doing so, colonizers unwittingly enabled Algerian broadcasts and listener networks that supported the fight for political independence. In studying the conceptual terrain of sensory experience and social belonging, I am reminded of Jennifer E. Telesca's claim that "what we see and hear, how we see and hear, according to whom and where condition the possibilities for the way people in crisis debate meaningfully about how they are governed."[53] Infrastructural affect is an animated and animating circuit that emerges from contact between bodies, systems, and technologies. The modulating ear linked Algerians to a new technical grid imposed by occupiers as much as it linked them to a growing political resistance. Although censorship would force them to create alternative templates for listening, their becoming infrastructure ultimately allowed them to build and sustain a form of belonging not dispensed by the colonial state but forged against it.

Notes

1. All English quotations are taken from the translation of Frantz Fanon's *A Dying Colonialism*, trans. Haakon Chevalier (New York: Grove Press, 1965).

2. Lisa Parks and Nicole Starosielski, *Signal Traffic: Critical Studies of Media Infrastructures* (Champaign: University of Illinois Press, 2015), 15.

3. While Brian Massumi argues that feelings are personal and affects are prepersonal, I follow Sianne Ngai's distinction made in terms of degree rather than kind. I do not see affect as entirely formless but as less organized than nameable emotions attributed to specific individuals.

4. Brian Larkin, *Signal and Noise: Media, Infrastructure, and Urban Culture in Nigeria* (Durham, NC: Duke University Press, 2008), 217.

5. Sunila S. Kale, "Structures of Power: Electrification in Colonial India," *Comparative Studies of South Asia, Africa and the Middle East* 34, no. 3 (December 2014): 455.

6. Brian Larkin, "The Politics and Poetics of Infrastructure," *Annual Review of Anthropology* 42 (October 2013): 339.

7. The work of Rebecca Scales, Roxanna Nydia Curto, and John Mowitt are important exceptions.

8. Jacques Attali, *Noise: The Political Economy of Music*, trans. Brian Massumi (Minneapolis: University of Minnesota Press, 1985), 7.

9. Fanon, *A Dying Colonialism*, 72.

10. Fanon, *A Dying Colonialism*, 74.

11. Hannah Knox, "Affective Infrastructure and the Experience of the State," *Public Culture* 29, no. 2 (May 2017): 375.

12. Fanon, *A Dying Colonialism*, 53.

13. Fanon, *A Dying Colonialism*, 71.

14. Fanon, *A Dying Colonialism*, 72.

15. Raymond Williams, *Marxism and Literature* (Oxford: Oxford University Press, 1977), 132.

16. Fanon, *A Dying Colonialism*, 73.

17. Fanon, *A Dying Colonialism*, 75.

18. Fanon, *A Dying Colonialism*, 75.

19. Fanon, *A Dying Colonialism*, 78.

20. Arthur Asseraf, *Electric News in Colonial Algeria* (Oxford: Oxford University Press, 2019), 131.

21. Asseraf, *Electric News in Colonial Algeria*, 131.

22. Gilles Deleuze and Félix Guattari, *A Thousand Plateaus: Capitalism and Schizophrenia*, trans. Brian Massumi (Minneapolis: University of Minnesota Press, 1987), xvi.

23. Larkin, "The Politics and Poetics of Infrastructure," 329.

24. Fanon, *A Dying Colonialism*, 76.
25. Fanon, *A Dying Colonialism*, 76.
26. It is important to note, however, the classical Arabic employed in these broadcasts was not understood by Algerians of all classes.
27. Fanon, *A Dying Colonialism*, 78.
28. Fanon, *A Dying Colonialism*, 63.
29. Fanon, *A Dying Colonialism*, 83.
30. Attali, *Noise*, 122.
31. Joy Elizabeth Hayes, *Radio Nation: Communication, Popular Culture, and Nationalism in Mexico, 1920–1950* (Tucson: University of Arizona Press, 2020), 7.
32. Fanon, *A Dying Colonialism*, 85.
33. Fanon, *A Dying Colonialism*, 69.
34. Fanon, *A Dying Colonialism*, 86.
35. Teresa Brennan, *The Transmission of Affect* (Ithaca, NY: Cornell University Press, 2004), 6.
36. Gregory J. Seigworth and Melissa Gregg, *The Affect Theory Reader* (Durham, NC: Duke University Press, 2010), 7.
37. Michel Serres, *The Parasite* (Minneapolis: University of Minnesota Press, 2007), 67.
38. Asseraf, *Electric News in Colonial Algeria*, 5.
39. Asseraf, *Electric News in Colonial Algeria*, 9.
40. Fanon, *A Dying Colonialism*, 80.
41. Fanon, *A Dying Colonialism*, 77.
42. Susan J. Douglas, "Some Thoughts on the Question 'How Do New Things Happen?,'" *Technology and Culture* 51, no. 2 (April 2010): 298.
43. David Marriott, *Whither Fanon? Studies in the Blackness of Being* (Palo Alto, CA: Stanford University Press, 2018), 99.
44. John Mowitt, "Breaking up Fanon's Voice," in *Frantz Fanon: Critical Perspectives*, ed. Anthony C. Allesandrini (London: Routledge, 1999), 95.
45. Fanon, *A Dying Colonialism*, 94.
46. Fanon, *A Dying Colonialism*, 79.
47. Bruce Robbins, "The Smell of Infrastructure: Notes toward an Archive," *boundary 2* 34, no. 1 (March 2007): 26.
48. Roxanna Nydia Curto, *Inter-tech(s): Colonialism and the Question of Technology in Francophone Literature* (Charlottesville: University of Virginia Press, 2016), 106.
49. Fanon, *A Dying Colonialism*, 89.
50. David Macey, *Frantz Fanon: A Biography* (New York: Verso, 2012), 320.
51. Nick Nesbitt, *Universal Emancipation: The Haitian Revolution and the Radical Enlightenment* (Charlottesville: University of Virginia Press, 2008).
52. Carolyn Marvyn, *When Old Technologies Were New* (Oxford: Oxford University Press, 1988), 8.
53. Jennifer E. Telesca, "Preface: What Is Visual Citizenship?," *Humanity: An International Journal of Human Rights, Humanitarianism, and Development* 4, no. 3 (Winter 2013): 339–40.

Chapter 6

Embodied Subjects and Infrastructural Failure in Chris Abani's *GraceLand*

Janice Ho

Chris Abani's *GraceLand* is a bildungsroman structured around the trials and tribulations of Elvis Oke—the young Nigerian protagonist who is an aspiring dancer and Elvis Presley impersonator—as he navigates his way through the urban slums of Lagos. The novel begins thus:

> Elvis stood by the open window. Outside: heavy rain. He jammed the wooden shutter open with an old radio battery, against the wind. The storm drowned the tinny sound of the portable radio on the table. He felt claustrophobic, fingers gripping the iron of the rusty metal protector. It was cool on his lips, chin and forehead as he pressed his face against it.
>
> Across the street stood the foundations of a building; the floor and pillars wore green mold from repeated rains. Between the pillars, a woman had erected a buka [food shack], no more than a rickety lean-to made of sheets of corrugated iron roofing and plastic held together by hope.[1]

This opening scene confronts us with a portrait of failing infrastructure: a broken window shutter, rusty and corrugated iron, an unfinished building, a makeshift shop. The materiality of the grating, its metallic rust, generates a physical response, cool against Elvis's skin, a reminder of the corporeal interactions between human bodies and infrastructure. The emphasis on materiality is also visible in Elvis's use of a battery as an impromptu window lever, with it functioning not as a subcomponent of a radio facilitating the transmission of music but rather as an infrastructural tool qua object. Put differently, we are reminded that cultural transmission depends in the first place on the physical infrastructure of media. By the fourth sentence, the scene turns from the infrastructures of sound to the sound of music "drowned" out by the storm, an indication of the difficulties of media transmission in informal settlements where infrastructure is continuously undermined by its state of disrepair and where boundaries between inside and outside, home and the world, private and public spaces, are porous, since Elvis's slum housing affords only frail protection against the elements of nature. This environment produces affective despair in Elvis's sense of "claustrophobic" entrapment; yet the passage also depicts the improvisational and compensatory repairs deployed in the face of this infrastructural decay, in the way Elvis props up the broken window with the battery and the way the buka is "held together" by mere scrap material. There is claustrophobia, the feeling of being hemmed in, but the optimism of "hope" persists in the struggle to live, to listen to music, to earn a living, to erect shelters under impoverished conditions. The opening passage thus stages a nexus of motifs that encapsulates this essay's central concern: *GraceLand*, I suggest, is a novel preoccupied with how infrastructural failure is experienced and how people cope with, compensate for, or repair such failures.

In suggesting that infrastructural failure is *experienced*, this essay parses the interrelations between the materiality of infrastructures, on the one hand, and bodies and subjectivities, on the other—that is, the ways infrastructure shapes both physical responses and psychic life. In a seminal essay, Brian Larkin argues that infrastructure is constituted by a poetics exceeding its technical function. For him, a poetics of infrastructure takes two forms: first, drawing on Roman Jakobson's definition of the poetic as a speech act "organized to the material qualities of the signifier itself rather than to its referential meaning," he reflects on how infrastructures take on symbolic meanings of technological modernity, acting as signifiers that showcase the spectacularity of state power and interpellate citizens in a teleological narrative of national progress, regardless of the uses to which such infrastructures may be put.[2] Infrastructures are embedded in discursive logics of governmentality that, in turn, produce various structures of feeling among those who encounter them in daily life—hope and promise, anger and disappointment, loss and exclusion.[3] The second dimension of infrastructural aesthetics is not semiotic but is instead located in "an embodied experience governed by the ways infrastructures produce the ambient conditions of everyday life: our sense of temperature, speed, florescence, and the ideas we have associated with these conditions."[4] Larkin returns to the etymological origins of the term "aesthetics"—*aisthesis*, or "sense perception"[5]—which, Terry Eagleton reminds us, is "born as a discourse of the body," belonging to the realm of "somatic, sensational life."[6] The materiality of infrastructure provokes sensory responses that are aesthetic experiences in the original sense of the term. The brightness of electric light, the smoothness of tarmac roads, the noise of generators, the warmth of heaters—all these point to encounters with infrastructures that go beyond their utility since our environments are mediated and shaped by them. These structures of feeling and sensory apprehensions underpin *GraceLand*'s depiction of infrastructure when it breaks down; Abani explores what the aesthetic experiences of infrastructural failure feel like.

GraceLand's concern with the failures of infrastructure and the interrelations between embodiment and infrastructure helps reframe infrastructure studies in two ways: first, ever since Susan Leigh Star's ethnography of infrastructure, it has been a truism that infrastructure is always "ready-to-hand" in the background of our existence and therefore, "by definition, invisible" until it breaks down.[7] Yet *GraceLand*'s setting in a postcolonial state under the rule of dictatorship means that infrastructural breakdown is invariably not the exception but the rule, all its faulty operations part and parcel of the fabric of ordinary life. Rather than assuming the invisible smooth workings of infrastructure as the norm, Abani redirects our focus to take infrastructural failures as our starting point and to consider how individuals and communities live with and adapt to these daily. Although these failures index the political shortcomings of the nation-state, functioning as sites of disgust and disappointment, they also generate unexpected and ad hoc strategies of survival such that they are simultaneously sites of repair, repurposing, and resilience that open up improvisational possibilities of self-fashioning and constitute tentative, albeit fragile, affective and social communities. Second, Abani's portrayal of the embodied, ambient, and aesthetic experiences of infrastructure asks us to consider people and human bodies as central constituents of infrastructural systems, not simply as extrinsic end users, thus expanding our definition of what counts as infrastructure. If infrastructures "are matter that enable the movement of other matter,"[8] *GraceLand* suggests that bodies are matter that matter too: the text not only foregrounds the phenomenological interactions between the infrastructural and the corporeal, undermining clear distinctions between material objects and human subjects; it also attends to how human bodies function as infrastructure, especially in places where the failures of infrastructure are ubiquitous and people take their place.

The Aesthetics of Infrastructural Failure

GraceLand is a novel filled with infrastructural absence, decay, and breakdown: in the tenements, the "iron staircase . . . looked rickety and unsafe and was covered in a rash of rust" (*GL*, 79). Lagos is full of "alley[s] with . . . crumbling walls, wrought-iron gates, puddles of putrefying water and piss and garlands of dead rats" (*GL*, 121). In Afikpo, forest fires rage uncontrollably while the fire brigade "lounged around watching the fire" because "it was common knowledge that their water supply had been cut off for days—something to do with a broken generator at the pumping station" (*GL*, 179). The pervasiveness of infrastructural decay acts as material evidence of the political travails of postcolonial Nigeria, rendering *GraceLand* a quintessential example of "failed-state fiction," a genre that, John Marx argues, turns to the "administration of populations" and "pragmatic questions of governmentality" in its depiction of the nation-state.[9] Of course, the trope of political failure has frequently been attached to images of Africa, borne out of decades of Afro-pessimism casting Africa as a "hopeless" continent.[10] *GraceLand* evokes this motif to some extent: the dereliction of state governance is thematized after Elvis observes the large number of pedestrians killed while crossing highways whose corpses are carelessly discarded. When Elvis inquires why the State Sanitation Department does not remove the bodies from the roadside, a stranger replies, "Is dis your first day in Lagos? Dey are on strike or using de government ambulances as hearses in deir private business. Dis is de only country I know dat has plenty ambulances, but none in de hospitals." Elvis disgustedly indicts the state and its citizens with a litany of infrastructural failures: "That is the trouble with this country. Everything is accepted. No dial tones or telephones. No stamps in post offices. No electricity. No water. We just accept" (*GL*, 57–58).

GraceLand is preoccupied with the inadequacies of urban infrastructure given its setting in the historically real Maroko, an informal settlement in Lagos demolished by the state in 1990 whose residents were forcibly evicted, with many killed in the process. Abani returns not to this historical moment but to an earlier demolition occurring in 1983, establishing a longer prehistory to the violent and ongoing processes of slum clearance and gentrification taking place in urban centers. Indeed, the novel furnishes Mike Davis's *Planet of Slums* with an epigraph— "He [Elvis] let his mind drift as he stared at the city, half slum, half paradise. How could a place be so ugly and violent, yet beautiful at the same time?"[11]—and may be read, in many ways, as a fictional counterpart to Davis's account. Davis charts the explosion of informal settlements in the Global South as a consequence of structural adjustment programs imposed by the International Monetary Fund and the World Bank from the 1970s, which opened up national economies to global markets and mandated rollbacks in national state programs and subsidies, causing the decimation of agrarian livelihoods and mass migration into cities, even as states withdrew funding for urban infrastructures. The end of the twentieth century sees the global spread of slums "surrounded by pollution, excrement, and decay," characterized by "overcrowding, poor or informal housing, inadequate access to safe water or sanitation, and insecurity of tenure."[12] This is the socioeconomic backdrop of *GraceLand*—briefly alluded to when the King of Beggars lectures Elvis about the "tiefs in the IMF, de World Bank and the de U.S." (*GL*, 280)—and the novel presents a relentless catalogue of the conditions of slum life without infrastructure.

Elvis experiences this infrastructural absence viscerally as a state of abjection. Early in the novel, "the smell of garbage from refuse dumps, unflushed toilets and stale bodies was still overwhelming [to him]" (*GL*, 4). Returning to his tenement:

> Elvis realized that nothing prepared you for Maroko. Half of the town was built of a confused mix of clapboard, wood, cement and zinc sheets, raised above a swamp by means of stilts and wooden walkways. The other half, built on solid ground reclaimed from the sea, seemed to be clawing its way out of the primordial swamp, attempting to be something else.
>
> As he looked, a child, a little boy, sank into the black filth under one [of] the houses, rooting like a pig. Elvis guessed it was some form of play. To his left, a man squatted on a plank walkway outside his house, defecating into the swamp below, where a dog lapped up the feces before they hit the ground. Elvis looked away in disgust and saw another young boy sitting on an outcrop of planking, dangling a rod in the water. (*GL*, 48)

In descriptions of the "primordial swamp" and "black filth," Abani mobilizes a vocabulary of regression to characterize Maroko, the settlement caught in a liminal, metamorphic space between evolutionary stages, half on "solid ground" and "attempting to be something else," while the other half sinks into a primitive slough of mud. The passage deploys the ubiquitous trope of what Jed Esty has called "excremental postcolonialism": the pervasive use of scatological images in literature from the Global South that symbolize the broken promises of modernity heralded by both colonial regimes and postindependence nation-states.[13] The lack of sanitation makes the body and its waste visible and odorous, present in public spaces rather than hidden in the privacy of the home. When Bruce Robbins describes "the smell of infrastructure" as the "public smell of corrosion, rust, and rottenness," he highlights that infrastructural breakdown is often apprehended only because it is experienced corporeally—through the sight of open defecation, through the smell of shit—and that the self-containment of the body and its subjective autonomy depends in the first place on modern technologies of hygiene: flush toilets and sewer pipes, running water, garbage removal trucks.[14]

Elvis responds to his slum environment with "disgust." David Trotter understands disgust as an embodied reaction belonging to the gut: it is a "dis-taste" caused by the "the ingestion of something which tastes bad" and which "provokes expulsion: vomiting, spitting. A bad smell can have the same effect." Drawing on Mary Douglas's anthropological distinction between purity and danger, he suggests that the affective and visceral experience of disgust occurs when boundaries are crossed, leading to a sense of threat and a physical response that attempts to regulate and reaffirm these boundaries.[15] Disgust is instinctively provoked by a collapse between inside and outside, self and other, body and environment: taste and smell are the sensory experiences that come closest to the disintegration of these ontological differences, since both involve the incorporation of external matter, as staged in the passage above when feces turns into food the dog consumes. Bodily boundaries are porous and permeable in *GraceLand*, eliciting an ambivalence from Elvis, who identifies with his excremental environment while establishing his distance from it: "Shit, he thought, I look like shit. . . . What do I have to do with all this?" (*GL*, 6). Even the spatial experience of life in Lagos is one where bodies and flesh are forcibly pushed up against each other. When Elvis boards an overcrowded bus, he "hated the way he was being pressed against the metal side by the heavyset woman sitting next to him, one ample buttock on the seat, the other hanging in the aisle, supported against a standing stranger's leg" (*GL*, 7).

Disgust, however, is typically experienced along class lines. Much of the scatological apprehension of Lagos is mediated through Elvis, that is, from the perspective of a recent transplant who previously grew up in a middle-class family in the rural township of Afikpo. Elvis employs only "big words" (*GL*, 96), and his speech is written in standard English, distinguishing him from other characters through his linguistically marked class position. This class division is reinforced by the juxtaposition of the scene of public defecation with a "white bungalow" Elvis sees in the distance: "Its walls were pristine, as though a supernatural power kept the mud off it. . . . That sight cheered him greatly" (*GL*, 48). Wealth against poverty, the white bungalow against the primordial swamp, privacy against publicness, cleanliness against filth—these are the key oppositions underpinning Elvis's disgust at their collapse. The distinction between Elvis's focalization and the novel's wider perspective is important because *GraceLand* presents us with a broader range of reactions to infrastructural failure beyond disgust, disappointment, and degradation. To assume that existence in informal settlements is defined solely by wretchedness and abjection is to reproduce the logic of the slum clearance programs that *GraceLand* depicts in the Nigerian state's attempt to raze Maroko in an "Operation Clean de Nation" because these settlements are regarded as a "pus-ridden eyesore on de face of de nation's capital" (*GL*, 247).[16] What the novel also explores is how these "slums" and "ghettoes" can be sites of communal existence and how individuals and communities can transform infrastructural failures through creative moments of repair and resilience. This is visible in *GraceLand*'s treatment of the materialities of media technologies saturating everyday life in Nigeria.

Media, Noise, and Repair

Criticism of *GraceLand* is largely divided into two strands: the first picks up on the sociopolitical forces of the novel's world, the precarities of life in slum settlements, and the economic world systems responsible for such conditions;[17] the second picks up on the novel's expansive and dynamic cultural world, consisting of an eclectic range of literary, musical, filmic, and television references.[18] The texture of urban life that Elvis inhabits comprises a rich mediascape, filled with sound and music from street performers and buskers; loudspeakers installed in marketplaces, shops, and restaurants; and radios blaring across public spaces. Lagos exemplifies what Alexander Weheliye describes as "the greater sonic intensity of urban space" in which various sounds compete, complement, and jostle up against each other, producing a porous auditory boundary between music and noise.[19] As he goes about his day, Elvis encounters multiple genres of music—by his namesake Elvis Presley, as well as Gloria Gaynor and Miles Davis; popular hits from Bollywood films; West African high-life music—and watches movies ranging from spaghetti Westerns to European arthouse films. Many critics have remarked on the novel's myriad allusions, a cornucopia testifying to Lagos's cosmopolitan insertion into a global circuit of cultural production. I am less interested, however, in the symbolic content of the cultural texts referenced and more in how these are transmitted through frequently unreliable media infrastructure. Elvis notes that "next door someone was playing highlife music on a radio that was not tuned properly" (*GL*, 4). In a bar, "Gloria Gaynor screamed 'I Will Survive' from crackly loudspeakers" (*GL*, 26). In a street restaurant, "the buka's radio sounded like someone had drowned its speaker in muddy water" (*GL*, 75). Elvis watches *Dirty Harry* on a television whose "color needed adjusting" and which "had a garish red tint to it that made him nauseous after a while" (*GL*, 190). There is a clear continuum between the infrastructural failures of the nation-state and the degraded media technologies filtering the soundscapes of the city.

But how is media failure registered in these instances? In his analysis of the material conditions of cultural transmission in Nigeria, Brian Larkin has usefully distinguished between "signal" and "noise": whereas signal refers to "the capacity of media technologies to carry messages," noise marks "the technical interference and breakdown that clouds and even prevents that signal's transmission." Noise, then, describes the distortions in all these examples where cultural forms are mediated through malfunctioning infrastructure. Yet noise, for Larkin, is not reducible to or synonymous with failure insofar as it engenders unstable effects in the social practices of everyday life. As an example, Larkin reads video piracy not as the inferior reproduction of an auratic original, but rather as "an aesthetic, a set of formal qualities that generate a particular sensorial experience of media marked by poor transmission" and that have been integral to the flourishing of the Nigerian video film industry.[20] Noise can produce a work of art in the age of failed mechanical reproduction. Noise also evokes embodied reactions, a "sensorial experience" instantiated in Elvis's nausea at the "garish red tint" of the television (*GL*, 190) that resonates with his disgust at slum life. The pervasiveness of media breakdown in the Global South further leads to "repair as a cultural mode of existence for technologies [as] a consequence of both poverty and innovation."[21] Larkin's theorization of noise anticipates recent work in infrastructure studies that takes failure as an object of inquiry, recasts it as normal and quotidian, not as exceptional or pathological, and sees failure and repair as intertwined phenomena. Steven Jackson has proposed an "exercise in broken world thinking" by adopting "erosion, breakdown, and decay, rather than novelty, growth, and progress as our starting points," since this is an increasingly accurate account of our world today, given the myriad cracks in our material and social infrastructures, from potholed roads to collapsing bridges to understaffed hospitals to inadequate welfare services.[22] Instead of the invisible flow of working infrastructures, more and more we are confronted with visible evidence of infrastructural glitches and disrepairs. In this respect, the rethinking of infrastructural failure reimagines "failed-state fiction" not as texts about legal states of exception or political emergency but as fiction that recognizes, as John Marx insists, that "failure is normal" in different degrees in governance.[23] An epistemology of failure further acknowledges those responsible for repair and keeping breakdowns in abeyance—"the subtle acts of care [that maintain] the infrastructures within and against which our lives unfold."[24] Jackson's association of repair with an ethics of care—a key term in feminism for the revaluation of domestic labor—connects the daily, unglamorous work of maintenance to the realm of social reproduction and to the necessary but unrecognized labor that enables systems to keep going. And eschewing the etymological meaning of repair as a return to the original, Stephen Graham and Nigel Thrift suggest that repair is fundamentally a creative act, a "vital source of variation, improvisation and innovation" in the world.[25]

GraceLand rethinks the meanings of failure through its treatment of noise. The conceptual nexus between failure, care, and improvisational repair is apparent in Elvis's interactions with his surrounding mediascape. Consider Elvis's visits as a boy to the theater at the local motor park where "silent westerns and Indian films with badly translated English subtitles were shown after dark"; these films are sponsored by an American tobacco company that distributes cigarettes, and the free entertainment and merchandise signify to locals that "America must be the land of the great" (*GL*, 146). The motor park cinema is, at one level, emblematic of an American cultural hegemony intended to bolster cigarette sales, and the novel obliquely underlines its success insofar as Elvis is repeatedly admonished to stop smoking by his elders, although these paternal figures prove no challenge to the masculine models of cinematic cowboys. Yet the signal of American cultural imperialism, to employ Larkin's terms, is interrupted by the local conditions of noise in a number of ways. Because the audience is mostly illiterate, the subtitled movie is accompanied by the projectionist's oral narration: "Actor is shooting John Wayne Wayne has dodged Oh No! Actor is down actor is down actor's horse is down Oh No! John Wayne is in action John Wayne is a powerful medicine man" (*GL*, 149). This exposition is inflected by the projectionist's habitual drunkenness that produces unintentional generic cross-pollinations between cowboy Westerns and Bollywood films, as "Ganesh sported six-shooters and the name John Wayne, while the Duke morphed into Krishna." But this narrative confusion does not impair the audience's enjoyment, since they "simply invented their own stories, resulting in as many versions as there were people" (*GL*, 148–49). The singular exported signal of American cultural values splinters into a plurality of local noise, fragmented by failures in the soft infrastructure of linguistic translation; but this failure is simultaneously the enabling occasion for improvisational, creative, and diverse modes of storytelling in the audience's reception.

The scene further foregrounds the materiality of the infrastructure of film projectors:

> Still, for him it was magical.
>
> The screens were dirty, hole-ridden, once-white bedsheets stretched between two wooden poles. The projectors, archaic and as old as many of the silent stars, sounded like small tanks. Moody, they tended to burn films at the slightest provocation, melting the plastic into cream-and-brown cappuccino froth. They vibrated so badly, the picture often blurred and danced insanely from side to side, sometimes spilling out onto a nearby wall.
>
> At first, Elvis found it was dizzy work just trying to keep focused, until he learned that the popular trick was to sway from side to side while squinting off to the left. Barring the occasional bout of motion sickness, this worked quite well, and Elvis often wondered what it would be like to stand above and look down. He was sure the crowd made quite a sight: hundreds of people swaying from side to side, chattering away like insane birds, worshipping their new gods. They drowned out the commentary provided by the projectionist, who, undeterred, continued his litany on a battered megaphone. (*GL*, 148)

Although the projectors and screens are dilapidated, the passage imbues this technology with the sensuous and tactile qualities of glamor, much like the "silent stars" appearing on the screen: the infrastructure burns, melts, vibrates, calls forth cappuccino froth. The distorted picture dances, and Elvis finds the process "magical"—a word calling back to an earlier act of infrastructural repair. "Molues were buses unique to Lagos, and only that place could have devised such a hybrid vehicle, its 'magic' the only thing keeping it from falling apart." Made of secondhand components imported from Britain and Japan, as well as "scraps of broken cars and discarded roofing sheets" (*GL*, 8), the molue is the product of a magical act of repair that allows trash and detritus to be reassembled into a mode of transport.[26] Magic, too, describes the phenomenology of this cinematic experience where technological obsolescence remakes an embodied community when the medium produces parallel and rippling corporeal effects: the picture "danced insanely from side to side," so Elvis has to "sway from side to side" to watch the film, along with "hundreds of people [also] swaying from side to side." Although the "worshipping" of "new gods" might gesture at the neoimperial triumphalism of American cultural exports, the literally slanted reception of these filmic texts suggests otherwise, since the audience accommodates its collective body to decaying infrastructure in a way that creates an ad hoc and novel form of sociality and religiosity. This collective here is temporary, the crowd of strangers drawn together by the momentary aesthetic experience of media; but *GraceLand* repeatedly celebrates ephemeral moments like these when the shared phenomena of music, film, or texts coalesce into brief moments of aesthetic communities from the familial to the social-sexual to the political, even if these communities may unravel the very next instant: we see this in the "impromptu little music-and-dance sessions" Elvis shares with his ailing mother (*GL*, 43); in how he crosses the gender divide by dancing with women and winding them and "the records into a frenzy of released pressure," while "the men sniffed, silently disapproving" (*GL*, 80); in the protests of the denizens of Maroko, marching to "the Bob Marley song coming out of the sound system with the large speakers that they had borrowed from the record store down the road" (*GL*, 266).

In the motor park, Elvis is both part of and apart from this collective body as he imagines himself "stand[ing] above and look[ing] down" on the crowd. He prefers the paid-for seats of the new Indian cinema in the next town as "the cheap, jerky silent movies [of the motor park] had lost their appeal" next to the undistorted transmission of the theater (*GL*, 99); Elvis, in other words, prefers signal to noise. Much in the way he distances himself from the perceived abjection of Maroko, Elvis is at odds with his environmental soundscape. In the above scene, the projectionist's commentary from a "battered megaphone . . . was so loud, he annoyed him" (*GL*, 148–49). While trying to rest on a bus, Elvis is interrupted by the advertising spiel of a hustler selling "Pracetmol" and a preacher exhorting passengers to "Repent"—public auditory disturbances that cause Elvis to disembark (*GL*, 9–10). The complaints about malfunctioning media are mostly focalized through Elvis as he traverses the city. Toward the novel's end, after he has been tortured by the state and released, only to find that Maroko has been razed, Elvis is displaced to a poorer and more dangerous settlement, Bridge City. Reflecting on all he has lost, he thinks: "The two things [he] missed most were books and music—not the public embrace of record-store-mounted-speakers, but self-chosen music, the sound of an old record scratching the melody from its hard vinyl, or the crackle of a radio fighting static to manifest a song of the mystery of the ether" (*GL*, 309). He distinguishes between public music in urban life—music relegated as so much sonic noise, part of the cacophony of the city—and music deserving of that designation by virtue of being freely "self-chosen"; music is the signal—"melody" and "song"—fighting to clarify itself out of the noise of "scratch[es]" and "static."

Elvis's remarks offer a way of reading the record player, one of his most prized possessions alongside his books and his mother's leather journal. Like the journal, the phonograph connects Elvis to his dead mother, the maternal absence haunting him in the narrative present, since she purchases the player and holds dance sessions for him as a young boy, offering a developmental space outside the pressures of Igbo masculinity. But the record player is also a media infrastructure: Weheliye reminds us that "the phonograph lends itself well to eschewing the social by allowing the listener to consume music in private, without the presence of a human source responsible for (re)producing these sounds. Historically the phonograph was the first technology to authorize this form of listening."[27] Sounding technologies are constitutive of subjectivity, deployed by modern subjects to "distinguish their own space from others" by demarcating between personal music ("sounds of their own choosing") and impersonal noise in the environment ("sounds imposed upon them by others"). This attempt to draw sonic borders may seem an "individuating gesture, an aggressive retreat from the communal," yet "it only appears as such in relation to some form of sociality."[28] Weheliye's analysis of sounding technologies offers a way to understand Elvis's investment in the record player beyond its literal and symbolic connections to his mother: in a dense settlement where boundaries between the public and private are porous, in a world where agency is restricted by economic and political pressures and gender expression by policed norms of masculinity, Elvis's attachment to the phonograph and its facilitation of "self-chosen music" is a compensatory strategy, an act of self-repair enabling him to construct a measure of autonomy in a world where he has none, an assertion of an individuated self against the forms of repressive socialities imposed on him, constellated as so much urban noise.

The self-fashioning of Elvis's subjectivity through the phonograph is especially visible after he has just been sacked from his construction job. This scene stages a correspondence between the physical repair of the phonograph and the embodied repair of Elvis's affective life. In misery, Elvis begins to apply makeup "with the air of ritual," transforming himself into the image of his musical namesake, Elvis Presley (*GL*, 77):

> The old battery-powered record player scratched through "Heartbreak Hotel," a stack of coins keeping the stylus from jumping through the worn grooves. Elvis nodded along, singing under his breath as he mixed the pressed powder with the talc. The lumpy powder crumbled in cakes of beige, reminding him of the henna cakes Oye [his grandmother] ground to make the dye she used to paint designs all over her body. Satisfied with the mix, he began to apply it

> to his face with soft, almost sensual strokes of the sponge. As he concentrated on getting an even tone, his earlier worries slipped away. Finishing, he ran his fingertips along his cheek. Smooth, like the silk of Aunt Felicia's stockings.
>
> With the tip of his index finger, he applied a hint of blue to his eyes, barely noticeable, but enough to lift them off the white of his face. . . . Drawing quickly and expertly with the black eye pencil, he outlined his eyes, the tip of the pencil dancing dangerously close to his cornea. (*GL*, 77)

The passage accentuates the tactility and sensuousness of Elvis's self-transformation and the phenomenological constitution of his identity: modern makeup calls back to traditional modes of self-decoration by his grandmother, and Elvis's ability to reconstitute himself is achieved through an act of embodied repair that facilitates an escape into a world of song and dance, freeing him from the constraints of masculinity and poverty, if only momentarily. This self-repair occurs in tandem with the phonograph playing in the background: if the phonograph is a sounding technology that carves out an auditory space of private individuation, this space is infrastructurally augmented by the record player being "battery-powered." Writing about the rise of radio as a media technology in Nigeria, Larkin reflects that batteries were central to the developing world, making possible the "mobility of radio" because "electricity supply, in those areas lucky enough to have it, was patchy, and radio sets that relied on mains supply were decorative objects unable to transmit sound."[29] Batteries freed sounding technologies from an unreliable state electricity grid. Elvis's autonomy is thus reinforced not just by a record player that facilitates "self-chosen music" against public noise but by a mobile energy infrastructure. Furthermore, like Elvis, who sees himself as a failed subject, the phonograph too is malfunctioning, requiring improvisational repair—"a stack of coins" to keep "the stylus from jumping through the worn grooves," to keep it from producing noise instead of music. After he finishes making himself up, Elvis "got up to change the record, which was dragging its stylus reluctantly and noisily across the label. He put it into its sleeve carefully and checked the sharpness of the needle by running a fingertip across it. This also cleaned the dust on the needle's point" (*GL*, 78). The imagistic parallels between Elvis's sensuous maintenance of his self and his tactile maintenance of the record player are striking: the "stylus" and the "needle" of the phonograph echo the "black eye pencil" or "the tip of the pencil" that Elvis uses as eyeliner, and he runs a "fingertip" across the record player's needle to clean it, in the same way that "with the tip of his index finger, he applied a hint of blue to his eyes." In the face of affective despair and infrastructural disrepair, Elvis marshals embodied strategies of repair to construct a fragile and temporary respite in his broken world.

Bodies as Infrastructure

The experience of infrastructural failure in *GraceLand* thus generates unexpected and contingent responses, especially in the creative mechanisms devised to cope with these failures, which generate opportunities, however fragile, for the coalescence of aesthetic communities or for moments of individual self-making. The novel attends to failure and repair as sensory phenomena, operations where material infrastructures and human bodies interface with each other. But it is worth concluding this essay by briefly reflecting on another dimension of how Abani explores the interrelation between bodies and infrastructure—to wit, the physical costs incurred when infrastructures are absent and when bodies have to take their place. Using Johannesburg as a case study, the urban theorist AbdouMaliq Simone has suggested that we need to think about "people as infrastructure": when the state fails, social networks and economic collaborations between people emerge as support systems to facilitate "the intersection of socialities so that the expanded spaces of economic and cultural operation become available to residents of limited means." Rather than seeing infrastructure merely as material objects, patterns, systems, and habits of interactions between people can function as infrastructure insofar as they are a "platform providing for and reproducing life in the city," especially among "residents seemingly marginalized and immiserated by urban life."[30] Simone's suggestion that we apprehend people as infrastructure is provocative, but his argument can also be extended, as the geographer Yaffa Truelove has done, to read people not merely in terms of the infrastructural social networks they constitute but as embodied infrastructural subjects in and of themselves. In her analysis of the water supply in Delhi, Truelove argues for the importance of thinking at the scale of the body, a scale often ignored in favor of analyzing infrastructure at the "global, national, regional and community" scales; as she points out, in many informal settlements in India, women are responsible for waiting for state tankers to bring water, filling these containers, and transporting them back to their domiciles; the labor and bodies of these women therefore form a crucial node in the logistics of water provision from state to household.[31] Women's bodies act as a "prosthetic" to the water grid, part of an infrastructural system that enables "water [to] flow across the city."[32]

The human body thus becomes a supplement when infrastructure is absent or when it fails: when taps don't turn on, bodies labor as replacements. Even as *GraceLand* presents infrastructural failures, especially media distortions, as potentially generative of creative acts of repair, it refuses to romanticize such failures by foregrounding their bodily costs. Violence in the novel frequently renders bodies as infrastructure. In Bridge City, Elvis sees a young boy "standing around at a public tap waiting for his bucket to fill up," one of the myriad beggar children "making a fortune by fetching buckets of water to housebound people." Situated directly under a high-voltage line, the boy picks up "a thin piece of metal" and beats a tune, "dancing" to it. A bolt of lightning kills him, leaving "only the smell of burning flesh." "Elvis watched the boy's body float away in the deluge, while another took his place and took the full bucket of water to whatever destination would pay for it" (*GL*, 313–14). Like the women whom Truelove studies in India's informal settlements, children are the substitutes for the infrastructure of piped water. The ad hoc use of detritus—the metal—as a vehicle of aesthetic expression and musical instrument may signal improvisational repair elsewhere, but it is here the cause of the boy's demise, with another boy fatalistically taking his place in a chain of infrastructural bodies. And in *GraceLand*, it is in particular children's bodies that are subjected to such material uses. In the resistance of the denizens of Maroko against the bulldozing of their settlement, "it was decided that the children would join their parents on the picket line as a guarantee that the police wouldn't stampede them" (*GL*, 258). Children are employed in the logistics of war as child soldiers, as seen in Innocence's experience during the Biafran war. And the novel's organ-trafficking plotline—in which Elvis and Redemption unwittingly participate in the transportation of children kidnapped for their organs—literalizes the way bodies in the Global South function as infrastructural life support for those in the Global North.[33] If *GraceLand* is interested in depicting how bodies experience infrastructure when it fails, it is no less interested in how bodies become infrastructure when it fails. And it is at this conjuncture between embodied subjects and infrastructural failures that the novel richly charts a range of affective responses—the recoil of disgust, the improvisation of repair, the care of maintenance—to such failures while also testifying to their bodily costs.

Notes

1. Chris Abani, *GraceLand* (New York: Picador, 2004), 3. Hereafter cited parenthetically in text and abbreviated *GL*.

2. Brian Larkin, "The Politics and Poetics of Infrastructure," *Annual Review of Anthropology* 42 (2013): 334.

3. For an account of urban infrastructure's production of "structures of feeling," see Stephen Graham and Simon Marvin, *Splintering Urbanism: Networked Infrastructures, Technological Mobilities, and the Urban Condition* (London: Routledge, 2001), 123–34.

4. Larkin, "The Politics and Poetics of Infrastructure," 336.

5. *Oxford English Dictionary*, 3rd ed. (2011), s.v. "aesthesis," https://www.oed.com/view/Entry/3234?redirectedFrom=aisthesis#eid.

6. Terry Eagleton, "The Ideology of the Aesthetic," *Poetics Today* 9, no. 2 (1988): 327–28.

7. Susan Leigh Star, "The Ethnography of Infrastructure," *American Behavioral Scientist* 43, no. 3 (1999): 380.

8. Larkin, "The Poetics and Politics of Infrastructure," 329.

9. John Marx, "Failed-State Fiction," *Contemporary Literature* 49, no. 4 (Winter 2008): 598.

10. See, for instance, the front cover of the *Economist* that declared Africa "The Hopeless Continent," May 13, 2000, with an accompanying leader.

11. Quoted in Mike Davis, *Planet of Slums* (London: Verso, 2007), 20.

12. Davis, *Planet of Slums*, 19, 21.

13. Jed Esty, "Excremental Postcolonialism," *Contemporary Literature* 40, no. 1 (1999): 32.

14. Bruce Robbins, "The Smell of Infrastructure: Notes towards an Archive," *Boundary 2* 34, no. 1 (2007): 26.

15. David Trotter, "Disgust," in *The English Novel in History, 1895–1920* (London: Routledge, 1993), 215. Trotter has also written on disgust elsewhere. See, for instance, "The New Historicism and the Psychopathology of Everyday Life," in *Filth: Dirt, Disgust, and Modern Life*, ed. William A. Cohen and Ryan Johnson (Minnesota: University of Minnesota Press, 2015), 30–48; and "British Novel and the War," in *The Cambridge Companion to the Literature of the First World War*, ed. Vincent Sherry (Cambridge: Cambridge University Press, 2005), 34–56.

16. Indeed, Tom Angotti has offered a trenchant critique of Mike Davis's *Planet of Slums* precisely because it understands life in such settlements only in pathological terms. As Angotti writes, *Planet of Slums* employs "apocalyptic rhetoric [that] feeds into longstanding anti-urban fears. [It] is a windshield survey of cities in the South by a stranger from the North. It is an expression of moralistic outrage that one would expect from a Westerner who discovered for the first time that the conditions of most people living in cities around the world are much worse than in Los Angeles and Amsterdam." See Angotti, "Apocalyptic Anti-Urbanism: Mike Davis and His Planet of Slums," *International Journal of Urban and Regional Research* 30, no. 4 (December 2006): 961.

17. See, for instance, Ashley Dawson, "Surplus City: Structural Adjustment, Self-Fashioning, and Urban Insurrection in Chris Abani's *GraceLand*," *Interventions: International Journal of Postcolonial Studies* 11, no. 1 (2009): 16–34; Sarah K. Harrison, "'Suspended City': Personal, Urban, and National Development in Chris Abani's *GraceLand*," *Research in African Literatures* 43, no. 2 (2012): 95–114; Stacey Balkan, "Rogues in the Postcolony: Chris Abani's *GraceLand* and the Petro-Picaresque," *Global South* 9, no. 2 (2015): 18–37.

18. See, for instance, Lauren Mason, "Leaving Lagos: Intertextuality and Images in Chris Abani's *GraceLand*," *Research in African Literatures* 45, no. 3 (2004): 206–26; and Stefan Sereda, "Riffing on Resistance: Music in Chris Abani's *GraceLand*," *ARIEL: A Review of International English Literature*, 39, no. 4 (2008): 31–47.

19. Alexander Weheliye, *Phonographies: Grooves in Sonic Afro-Modernity* (Durham, NC: Duke University Press, 2005), 106.

20. Brian Larkin, *Signal and Noise: Media, Infrastructure, and Urban Culture in Nigeria* (Durham, NC: Duke University Press, 2008), 10, 218.

21. Larkin, *Signal and Noise*, 235.

22. Steven Jackson, "Rethinking Repair," in *Media Technologies: Essays on Communication, Materiality, and Society*, ed. Tarleton Gillespie, Pablo J. Boczkowski, and Kirsten A. Foot (Cambridge, MA: MIT Press, 2014), 221. See also Shannon Mattern, "Maintenance and Care," *Places Journal* (November 2018), https://placesjournal.org/article/maintenance-and-care/.

23. Marx, "Failed-State Fiction," 599.

24. Jackson, "Rethinking Repair," 222–23.

25. Stephen Graham and Nigel Thrift, "Out of Order: Understanding Repair and Maintenance," *Theory, Culture, and Society* 24, no. 3 (May 2007): 6.

26. From one perspective, this renders the molue a perfect example of what Ann Laura Stoler has described as "imperial debris," a material remnant of colonialism and its succeeding regime of economic globalization that disproportionately transforms many parts of the Global South into the ecological dumping grounds of the Global North; the molue encapsulates the "social afterlife of degraded infrastructures," the detritus of what people are "left *with*" as a consequence of the slow violence of ruination. Yet *GraceLand*, I am suggesting, is also invested in depicting the repairs that emerge from infrastructural ruins and ruination as acts of coping and survival. Ann Laura Stoler, *Duress: Imperial Durabilities in Our Time* (Durham, NC: Duke University Press, 2016), 348.

27. Weheliye, *Phonographies*, 62.

28. Weheliye, *Phonographies*, 106–7.

29. Larkin, *Signal and Noise*, 70.

30. AbdouMaliq Simone, "People as Infrastructure: Intersecting Fragments in Johannesburg," *Public Culture* 16, no. 3 (2004): 407–8.

31. Yaffa Truelove, "Rethinking Water Insecurity, Inequality, and Infrastructure through an Embodied Urban Political Ecology," *WIREs Water* 6, no. 3 (2019): 1–2.

32. Yaffa Truelove, "The Body as Infrastructure: Gender and the Everyday Practices and Labour of Water's Urban Circulation," in *Labouring Urban Infrastructures: A Digital Magazine*, ed. A De Coss-Corzo, H. A. Ruszczyk, and K. Stokes, 27, https://hummedia.manchester.ac.uk/institutes/mui/InfrastructuresZine191007.pdf.

33. Here I echo Kelly Rich's astute point, which she makes in relation to Kazuo Ishiguro's organ-trafficking novel in "'Look into the Gutter': Infrastructural Interiority in *Never Let Me Go*," *Modern Fiction Studies* 61, no. 4 (2015): 631–51.

Chapter 7

✦

Border Zones

Infrastructure and Human Migration in *Exit West* and *EXIT*

Sangina Patnaik

As early as 1951, Hannah Arendt warned that rights hinged on citizenship, a precondition she described in *The Origins of Totalitarianism* as "the right to have rights."[1] In recent years, the consequences of this loophole have become all too clear. Climate crises, warfare, and political and economic upheaval result in drastically increased numbers of persons displaced from unstable regions—some eighty-two million in 2020 alone.[2] Meanwhile, developed nations are redoubling efforts to contain migrant bodies. The United Nations announced Global Compacts on Safe, Orderly, and Regular Migration and on Refugees in 2018, but such agreements have been overshadowed by instances of nation-states contravening their terms: the expulsion of the Rohingya people from Myanmar, the rejection of Syrian refugees seeking asylum, the cages holding migrant children in the United States. As Seyla Benhabib contends, "The asylum seeker, the stateless, and the refugee have become *metaphors* as well as *symptoms* of a much-deeper malaise in the politics of late modernity."[3] Border zones play out this failure, indexing the schism between a midcentury investment in rights without borders and the failures of the twenty-first-century order of nation-states to secure widespread protections for a humanity in flux.

This essay takes up two texts that experiment with the difficulties of representing both human movement and the infrastructures that track or thwart it. Mohsin Hamid's *Exit West* (2017) weaves a fable of migration that softens border infrastructure, transforming migration into a journey through "in" and "out" doors in private residences around the world. *EXIT* (2015), a collaboration between French philosopher Paul Virilio and the architecture firm Diller Scofidio + Renfro, sidesteps human characters entirely, combining maps, emojis, statistics, and sound into an immersive art installation that its creators describe as a "narrative about migration." The creative refashionings of border crossing in these works invert the consequences of an otherwise disconcerting conclusion: contemporary border infrastructure and human life seem difficult, if not impossible, to adequately represent together. Elucidating the stakes of *EXIT* and *Exit West*'s aesthetic refiguring of migration requires us to supplement visions of the border as a concrete wall with newer, quieter forms of border maintenance including drones, satellites, and digital surveillance. I direct attention to these emergent infrastructures of the border in order to articulate the predicament of navigating an increasingly mobile, increasingly securitized world, one where digital technology proffers the promise of something like global citizenship for the price of globalized surveillance.

My sense is that there is a missing critical category in discussions of forced migration, something between the geographical boundaries of the nation-state and the universal, that is perhaps best indexed by discussions of infrastructure. Border zones are not just interstitial space between nation-states: their infrastructures form a capillary system of global capitalism. As complex systems of geopolitical boundaries, national and international laws, physical barriers, digital surveillance, and human labor, borders mark the space where the ideological leanings of the nation-state manifest as geopolitical sites of inclusion or exclusion. The titles of *EXIT* and *Exit West* gesture to the enmeshment of humans in motion and the border infrastructures they traverse. Slipping between object and action, noun and verb, "exit" announces the act of leaving and designates the architectural space crossed during departure. *EXIT* alternately blares an injunction and conjures up the emergency exit signs affixed to doorways in public facilities; *Exit West* reads as stage direction and notation on maps of migration patterns. In both cases, departure looms as an imperative while the promise of arrival fades from view. I read this silent rejoinder as a warning: narrative conventions for representing migration as a drama of social incorporation—a variant of the realist novel's investment in producing individuals within their historical contexts—find few moorings in the diminished public and political spaces of the contemporary border zone.

Border Zones as Infrastructure

Border infrastructure today is at once hypervisible and invisible, the dull assault of thirty-foot concrete walls but also the opaque bureaucracy of Immigration and Customs Enforcement detention centers and National Security Agency data storage centers in Utah. In Wendy Brown's influential account, proliferating walls signal the last gasp of the waning nation-state.[4] Today, however, new technologies exist in asymptotic relation to the wall's concrete infrastructure: electronic surveillance, biometric data, artificial intelligence, drones equipped with infrared cameras. Analyzing how states separate "outside" from national "inside," as Brown herself observes, involves recognizing that "the wall and the border have an untethered relationship."[5] As border management dilates and contracts, from the supranational to the corporeal, from drones reading bodies' movement to private security companies reading activists' emails, our notions of what it means to be "inside" or "outside" infrastructural support must modulate as well.

Much infrastructural thinking emphasizes how infrastructures delineate community. They are hailed as "public works," to borrow Mike Rubenstein's evocative phrase, but they are also works that produce a public: as Rubenstein, Bruce Robbins, and Sophia Beal detail in the introduction to an issue of *MFS Modern Fiction Studies* dedicated to infrastructure, infrastructures generate and support the "commons," "civilization," "society," the "public," or the "modern state."[6] Even when such systems accord with a central tenet of infrastructural studies—namely, that infrastructure is the boring stuff in the background that only becomes visible when it breaks down—to account for infrastructure in the novel is to identify a community configured by (or deserving of, although perhaps lacking) its works.[7]

Border infrastructures confound these premises. This is a counterintuitive claim, perhaps, since borders seem ontologically invested in creating an "inside" and "outside." But digital surveillance allows borders to metastasize in unpredictable directions, simultaneously amplifying and confounding the boundaries of the nation-states they are designed to secure. Brian Larkin's reminder that infrastructures reflect collective intentions insofar as they "emerge out of and store within them forms of desire and fantasy" helps explicate the cognitive dissonance produced when one begins to chart the globalized systems required to produce securitized national borders.[8] Nativist fantasies, it turns out, actually require the production of overlapping networks of international data. These networks produce their own material infrastructures, often far removed from the physical site of the border, that themselves elude figuration: personal cell phones are so ubiquitous as to seem innocuous, despite generating data essential to geotracking movement across borders. Conversely, locating the infrastructure of the Internet requires access to vast resources and singularly skilled labor. In order to document the "choke points" where the NSA taps undersea cables supporting the Internet, for example, photographer Trevor Paglen combed through Edward Snowden's NSA archives and trained with deep sea divers.[9] The resultant images—murky, chiaroscuro renderings of cables snaking along the ocean floor—point up the Internet's fragile materiality.

Digital surveillance solicits participation of the very bodies borders are designed to shut out. Debarati Sanyal dwells on a moment when residents of a Calais refugee camp shave off their fingertips to avoid being "read" by border patrol: in an age of biometric surveillance, borders start at the fingertips.[10]

AbdouMaliq Simone reads "people as infrastructure," arguing that human movement generates "conjunctions" that "become an infrastructure—a platform providing for and reproducing life in the city."[11] We might, following Simone, read the incorporation of biometric surveillance into border policing as a perverse acknowledgment of peoples' infrastructural potential. On the one hand, humans crossing geopolitical boundaries instantiate the border as a site of desire or aspiration. On the other, biometric and electronic surveillance recruit aspects of the human—what Simone, borrowing from Agamben, designates as bare life—in order to provide for and reproduce infrastructures aimed at their exclusion.

The border links migrant bodies to multinational security corporations, information technology firms, and governments around the world. This is not a new concept, of course—innovations in the sorts of force used to control populations have their own dark migration circuits, as critics such as Lisa Lowe, Nikhil Pal Singh, Miriam Ticktin, and Eyal Weizman have shown us.[12] Nor is this phenomenon limited to the border: 80% of US military operations are staffed by workers from the Global South; in 2009, an international agreement between governments and private military contractors delegated the right to take life with impunity to private actors.[13] The midcentury vision of an international arrangement of nation-states, complete with the protections and privileges of national sovereignty, has morphed into new conglomerate bodies. These bodies may bear the insignia of the nation-state, but they are peopled by and operating under global flows of labor and capital. It is perhaps not revelatory to suggest that the border constitutes an ontological threat to human rights insofar as it marks the geographical and legal space where humanity becomes differentially allocated. Drawing attention to the border zone, however, reveals an emergent world order of globally distributed infrastructures. These zones invoke the geopolitical borders of a nation-state in order to allocate or withhold rights of passage but exceed any single state's sovereignty.

I read the border zone as the grotesque inverse of Arendt's space of appearance, which figures centrally in her political thought: she imagines it as an alternative to the nation-state, a public arena that allows individuals to define rights through collective practice and mutual recognition.[14] "Our political life rests on the assumption that we can produce an equality through organization, because man can act and change and build a common world, together with his equals and only with his equals," Arendt contends.[15] Unlike the nation-state, whose protections extend only to its citizens, this "common world" encompasses all of humanity. Judith Butler takes Arendt to task for failing to articulate the space of appearance as a physical space that provides the "material supports" human bodies need to engage in political action.[16] Butler's critique lingers on the circular logic of Arendt's space of appearance: politics produce the space of appearance, but this space needs political interaction in order to emerge. While I embrace Butler's insistence on the bodily supports needed for civic life, in the context of border infrastructure, the unpredictable way Arendt's space of appearance tethers itself to the world becomes evocative. Arendt avoids invoking either the nation-state or the universal, terms that would fetter collective praxis by linking its viability to citizenship or by grounding it in theoretical abstractions. Bound to the physical world while rejecting its geopolitical realities as unproductive, the space of appearance addresses itself to a geopolitics-to-come.

Like the space of appearance, the border zone seeks to instantiate geopolitical realities while being itself patched together out of any number of amorphous or hypothetical spaces.[17] Where Arendt's space of appearance allows the individual to emerge as a protected participant in civic life, however, the border zone tracks in order to restrict or refuse participation in the public it secures. Migrants entering its purview without prior approval are rebuffed or detained, allowed only liminal access to the nation-state—refugee camps, detention centers, the labyrinthine bureaucracy of immigration courts. Holding the formal logic of the border zone alongside that of the space of appearance helps crystallize the divergence in their logics. Sharing public space, Arendt argues, allows individuals to hash out the terms of mutual recognition—a status she later describes as citizenship. Border infrastructures, however, are designed to preclude such collective self-fashioning.[18] If the space of appearance proffers an infrastructure for summoning public responsibility, the border zone operates by eliminating it.

The Narrative Consequences of Vanishing

Contemporary border policing generates its own lexicon, one that proves strangely helpful for describing the narrative crises that such foreclosed recognition can produce. In 2017, the United States government announced plans to expand physical barriers along the border it shares with Mexico. A whirl of publicity, including the unveiling of eight wall prototypes in San Diego, spurred Customs and Border Patrol (CBP) to announce its surveillance philosophy: "A major factor in determining where investments in impedance and denial would be most effective is referred to as 'vanishing time,' which is the distance between the border and the point at which an illegal border crosser could blend into the local populace," the CBP's communications office explained, adding that "vanishing times are often particularly short in urban areas."[19]

In what is likely an unintentional move, CBP invokes the grammar of painting to explicate its surveillance operations. A vanishing point defines the site where all lines converge in perspectival painting. Joseph Slaughter describes the vanishing point as "the result of all that comes before it and the regulatory principle of convergence that brings everything into line," an account that aligns with broader conversations in art criticism on landscape painting as a medium of cultural signification.[20] As a genre, landscape painting announces perspective as power.[21] What constitutes nature and what does not, what is incorporated into the composition or left outside of it becomes the purview of an acquisitive (or ownerly) gaze. It is no coincidence, W. J. T. Mitchell points out, that the emergence of perspectival landscape painting coincides with imperialism, "which conceives of itself precisely (and simultaneously) as . . . an expansion of 'culture' and 'civilization' into a 'natural' space in a progress that is itself narrated as 'natural.'"[22] In announcing its function to be the measuring of "vanishing time," CBP inserts itself into this genealogy. The border zone, seen as a landscape, takes the migrant as the limit of its perspective. The terminological shift from visual art's vanishing point to the border's vanishing time overtly narrativizes landscape, adding a temporal dimension (the amount of time it takes for border security to lose sight of a migrating body) and an implicit telos to the migrant's movement (disappearing on the far side of the wall).

In the novel, the vanishing time of the individual might once have been measured as the time it takes a character to merge into a new social order. In Georg Lukács's sweeping terms, the realist novel "is the story of the soul that goes to find itself, that seeks adventures in order to be proved and tested by them, and, by proving itself, to find its own essence."[23] This arc allows us to witness the concentration of the human person *into* itself, a distillation less existential than social. As Lukács makes clear in his reading of Goethe's *Wilhelm Meister*, the protagonist resolves a crisis of the soul by finding "the profession which is appropriate to his essence."[24] Narrative genres that represent migration, including the immigrant novel, the bildungsroman, autobiography, and memoir, regularly draw upon these conventions, sketching a narrative arc that traverses the fraught space between displacement and arrival. Realism's investment in this arc is largely framed as an ethics of care for the individual. In Angela Naimou's elegant formulation, "Individual political rights depend on giving the abstract figure of the person a human face and voice, and on giving the person its own story of individual development, one that culminates in the full incorporation of the person into civic life."[25] As we have seen, however, interactions on the border zone scramble the players and terms of the drama of incorporation. The CBP's communiqués announce that the disciplinary function of the border ends when migrants are indistinguishable from their surround. Setting aside the ways that this pronouncement obscures the multiple modalities of border policing for a moment, the vision of a migrant dissolving into the urban crowd, a human among other humans, betokens hope. Re-articulating this moment as a vanishing, however, underscores the border zone's investment in producing gradations of civic and political death. In what follows, I trace how *Exit West* and *EXIT* register the tension between these two possibilities as a referendum on narrative's ability to critically engage the new infrastructures of the border.

Exit West

Mohsin Hamid's *Exit West* conjures up a novel world as interconnected and instantaneously available as technology makes it appear. The border zone's "vanishing time" condenses into seconds, a winnowing that does away with both the conventions for narrating refugees' crossings and the infrastructures that once determined the contours of such a journey. Dissolving geopolitical boundaries, however, turns out to be less of a rejection of the border zone than a reconfiguration of its terms. Belonging in the novel is no longer measured by citizenship but by access to infrastructure; as militarized borders fade away, digital surveillance amplifies. The new ease of migration produces a world in constant flux, but, paradoxically, such collective experience precludes the possibility of public affect. Hamid's alternative present thus presents border infrastructure as a formal provocation for the novel: when traditional structures for producing and securing collective experience vanish, what strategies remain for exfoliating new kinds of imagined community?

Exit West follows the repeated displacement of Saeed and Nadia, whose journey plays out against a background of millions of unnamed others also on the move. Its first pages feint at the construction of suitably postnational citizens: Nadia and Saeed meet in a course on corporate identity and product branding, the sort of buzzwordy education that positions them to be ideally integrated participants in global capitalism. Quickly, however, conflict erupts in their country, obliterating the compact between individual and society on which Lukács's realism depends.

Instead of producing collective experience, this violence anonymizes. The war that ricochets through Saeed and Nadia's hometown "reveal[s] itself to be an intimate experience, combatants pressed close together, front lines defined at the level of the street one took to work."[26] Geographies of neighborhoods shift as militia members take over or destroy streets, blocks, and buildings, rendering them dark spaces on the mental maps characters make to move safely through their ever-shrinking worlds. Violence saturates the domestic space: the narrator announces that the "relationship to windows now changed in the city. A window was the border through which death was possibly most likely to come."[27] After the militia executes Saeed's upstairs neighbor, blood drips through floorboard cracks to stain the sitting room ceiling.[28] Confined to the family apartment as blasts rip through the streets, characters brace against armed men who enter the building without warning and "lenses peering down on their city from the sky and from space . . . the eyes of militants, and of informers, who might be anyone, everyone."[29] Migration, like warfare, plays out inside domestic space. Homes become conduits for magical passages across continents; migratory routes that would otherwise contend with complicated networks of checkpoints, boats, planes, tickets, and documents are collapsed here into a network of "in" and "out" doors. Border walls are dispatched from the novel with no more than a snippet overheard on international news: "Rich countries were building walls and fences and strengthening their borders, but seemingly to unsatisfying effect."[30]

Warfare and forced migration generate similar rhythms in the novel: characters register the effects of geopolitical conflict in isolated domestic spaces. Social and political exigencies loom large, but their exact contours remain blurry. Short accounts of border doors pepper the novel, a series of paralleled solitary journeys that allow readers to register the crisis of a "whole planet on the move" but formally isolate such coherent revelations from the characters and narrative voice alike.[31]

The first account of this new mode of migration floats as narrative shard in the first chapter, unconnected to the early romance of the novel's only named characters, Saeed and Nadia. The fragment begins as an ür-scene of nativist hysteria—the horror of a dark man menacing a sleeping white woman—that introduces the fantastical border architecture as a zone in need of policing. A "pale" woman sleeps alone in a large house in Sydney.[32] The narrative ticks through the contents of the woman's bedroom, the items on her nightstand, the accumulation of circumstances that result in a house alarm being switched off, a bedroom window cracked open, and birth control pills untaken. Her "closet doorway was dark, darker than night, a rectangle of complete darkness—the heart of darkness. And out of this darkness, a man was emerging."[33] In the redundancy of this darkness, the roving eye of the narrative stutters to a halt, tripping over the threadbare language of the racial hysteria it indexes. The initial objectivity of the section's third-person omniscience reveals itself to be a patchwork of the Global North's collective fears. If the imperial centers of the twentieth century were spared the content of Kurtz's horror, its message lost in the distance between the Congo and the Thames, Hamid's rendition at the beginning of the twenty-first century makes avoiding such confrontations impossible. The conjuncture of Global North and South is immediate, intimate—and playing out inside domestic space. *Exit West* reinvokes the threat of sexual violence and miscegenation that Conrad's Marlow works so hard to unsee.[34] A silent drama unfolds in the bedroom's darkness: "His eyes rolled terribly. Yes: terribly. Or perhaps not so terribly. Perhaps they merely glanced about him, at the woman, at the bed, at the room. Growing up in the not infrequently perilous circumstances in which he had grown up, he was aware of the fragility of his own body. He knew how little it took to turn a man into meat."[35]

Narrative sympathies, if they can be said to exist in this passage, play out in the pivot away from racial stereotypes of rolling eyes and straining muscles to a recognition of precarity. The narrative voice questions and then corrects itself: where the repetition of "darkness" a paragraph earlier serves only to consolidate meaning, the three uses of "terribly" modulate from a stereotype to a hypothetical before falling away completely. In the absence of received phrasing, the narrative can clear space to accommodate a different kind of focalization—namely, the perspective of the newly arrived migrant. Inverting the gaze of the passage, the narrator moves away from omniscient surveillance to witnessing with the man the comparative risks of the situation. His poverty contrasts with the woman's comfort, his fearful watching glances off her somnolence, and his placelessness offsets her domestic repose. These differences amplify as he slips out the window, vanishing into a new darkness.

Indeed, the unnamed man disappears from the novel entirely. This fact comes as no surprise to readers of *Exit West*: Nadia and Saeed are the only named characters. We never learn their surnames; the city and country of their origin remain stubbornly unlocatable. Such ambiguity bucks the accumulating conventions of humanitarian and human rights narratives that emphasize the singularity of an individual's experience: as Debjani Ganguly argues, even when the contemporary novel registers friction with the human rights imagination, its "focus on the very singularity of suffering bodies foregrounds the inextricability of an economy of vulnerability with that of an economy of militarized protection."[36] The human rights framework is a recent iteration of a longer-standing dynamic: Benedict Anderson's canonical account of the novel roots its world in the ideational space of the nation; Alex Woloch sees the novel as a "distributional matrix" of characters jostling for space in the novel's world.[37] In these accounts, singularity is the narrative work of distinguishing a character within her context. The shifting sociopolitical contexts occasioned by repeated dislocations, however, deprive the novel of its repertoire for carving out nuanced characters. This has consequences for *Exit West*'s ability to link character to scene and, by extension, to political action: Saeed and Nadia's movements generate insular accounts of Mykonos, London, and Marin, their horizons contracted by the containment strategies of various sorts of refugee camps. The thinning of the characterological field is consonant with the absence of stable contexts in which to place human action and interaction. Provisional collectives emerge in shared houses and on temporary worksites, only to be undone when characters move yet again.

It becomes clear that the central figure in *Exit West* is not a character but a vast, networked architectural space—an "inside" to counter the construction of a similarly networked international border zone producing, over and over, an "outside" to safety, community, and belonging. Softening border infrastructure untethers the novel from geographic constraints. Like its characters, the novel makes abrupt journeys into unknown worlds. Saeed and Nadia's narrative intersects with other possibilities: unnamed people traverse doors that lead them to new landscapes and personal plot twists. The "who" of character or the "where" of the door becomes less resonant than what the characters move toward or away from—depression, isolation, the possibility of love.

In an article on the dangers of turning the migrant into universal figure, Yogita Goyal takes Hamid to task for naturalizing "the fact of migration in a way that evacuates the specific historical experience that generates it, rendering banal what must remain historical."[38] The critique doubles as an condemnation of *Exit West* as a novel that lends itself to the human rights imagination by framing "the refugee as an emblem of the universal human . . . indeed, as a figure of the future of all humanity."[39] I am sensitive to Goyal's plea for historical particularity, which she frames as a necessary precursor to developing cultural forms that can recognize both universalism and difference. My sense, however, is that this critique presupposes the novel's investment in developing the sorts of fully realized subjects that traditionally populate the novel in the first place.

Whether or not Nadia and Saeed are universalized sketches of characters seems less central to the gambit of the novel than the fact that their selves, like the nation-states that once secured the borders they cross, are unmoored, on the brink of dissolution. The thinning of both character and context is figured as the compounded effects of a newly omnipresent border infrastructure that compensates for its relaxed physical barriers with heightened digital surveillance. "It seemed that as everyone was coming together everyone was also moving apart," Nadia reflects. "The nation was like a person with multiple personalities, some insisting on union and some on disintegration, and that this person with multiple personalities was furthermore a person whose skin appeared to be dissolving as they swam in a soup full of people whose skins were also dissolving."[40] Metaphorically contracting the nation into a single figure works, paradoxically, against the fantasies of wholeness that often accompany such nationalist personifications. Refiguring borders as epithelium emphasizes nations' permeability even in ordinary times; the magical infrastructure of doors only amplifies this tendency.

Even as the nation-state dissolves under the pressure of large-scale migration, movement reconfigures the terms of personhood. Time and again, Saeed and Nadia migrate to escape violence, economic hardship, or the sterile conditions of migrant labor camps. Constant relocation causes them to adapt away from each other. Nadia figures the dissolution of love as a problem of perspectives that alter as landscapes shift: "Personalities are not a single immutable color, like white or blue, but rather illuminated screens, and the shades we reflect depend much on what is around us."[41]

Traditional techniques of representation in the novel—how characters come to see and know themselves and others—are now consonant with the technologies surveillance states employ to see and patrol their populations. The light touch of surveillance never explicitly conditions characters' movement, but it does saturate the novel's construction of both infrastructure and the human figure. Nadia's vocabulary for reflecting on her fraying relationship registers a dynamic that characters and narrator alike take for granted: concrete borders may have ceased to constrain, but characters exist "under the drone-crossed sky and in the invisible network of surveillance that radiated out from their phones, recording and capturing and logging everything."[42]

Slippage between the drone's-eye view, the lover's view, and self-reflection becomes increasingly frequent as the novel progresses. In London, Nadia is seized with the certainty that the news she is reading on her phone contains an image of herself, at that moment, reading the news on a phone. Shocked, "she almost felt that if she got up and walked home at this moment there would be two Nadias, that she would split into two Nadias, and one would stay on the steps reading and one would walk home, and two different lives would unfold for these two different selves."[43] Tanks and an army detachment nearby tip the uncanny moment into dysphoria: although Nadia eventually realizes that the picture is not of her, seen from a drone's-eye view, two women in burkas might well be interchangeable. Saeed and Nadia's last act as a couple is to bury a dead drone in their backyard, a wryly sentimental metaphor for the end of their romance. Their gesture points up an extranarrative counterpart to the story unfolding on the page: data gathered by the drones' disciplinary gaze produces records of the characters' relationship catalogued in an unnamed elsewhere by unacknowledged others.

On offer in *Exit West* is not resolution but dissolution—a détente between natives and migrants, between border infrastructures and the bodies that contend with them. Doors present a "rēlease" to the pressure valves of a system of nation-states that no longer functions, but governance of a mobile humanity bypasses collective consensus in favor of an unidentified militarized presence. If the door network is the novel's utopian gesture, surveillance is its unacknowledged dystopia.

As the geographies of cities and nation-states unravel, the danger of diminished public spaces of appearance emerges. The elegance of the novel's architecture for migration is offset by an affective clunkiness that seems to be a consequence of the foreshortened character field. After all, how does the novel register shared sentiment without articulating multiple characters? Early twentieth-century novels used shared public space to weave together collective consciousness, tracing a narrative thread between members of the crowd observing a freewheeling airplane in *Mrs. Dalloway*'s Hyde Park or strolling the afternoon streets of *Ulysses*'s Dublin. In *Exit West*'s early twenty-first century, the portal network exfoliates the narrative, opening a door onto the Namibian coast for a suicidal Londoner or bringing a new lover onto the balcony of a lonely elderly man in Amsterdam. Readers are left with feeling for infrastructure but not a sense of public feeling.[44] This is particularly apparent in moments when consequences of the events described ramify for many of the newly stateless. Much like the fears of the Global North emerging via *Heart of Darkness*, the novel regularly invokes literary or historical tropes to conjure a sense of the collective feeling that *might* accompany significant moments. So, for example, London splits into "light London" and "dark London," an apartheid system of access to the electrical grid. As tensions normalize, refugees in "dark London" purchase the right to a future in the United Kingdom by constructing infrastructures to sustain the swollen populations of urban centers. In case readers are at all likely to miss the way that "light" and "dark" London coincide with racial designators, Hamid cribs from an international lexicon for infrastructural racism, invoking America's failed promise to freed slaves: "Migrants were promised forty acres and a pipe: a home on forty square meters of land and a connection to all the utilities of modernity."[45]

In Hamid's alternative present, affect cannot be derived from collective experiences, for these no longer exist. Like the drones that monitor them, characters are networked—cell phones and Internet access remain coveted commodities—but largely isolated, their ties undone first by the breakdown of civil society in their countries of origin and then by the containment zones constructed in countries like the United Kingdom and the United States. The sorts of fellow feeling that underwrite civic and social life exist as a formal proposition: readers can join the narrative eye as it roves across paralleled lives on the move, but such unencumbered watching tips perilously close to the drone's-eye view that Saeed and Nadia acknowledge as the third participant in their lives. The novel's most grandiose fantasy may well be the characters' ability to leave behind aspects of what Arendt identifies as the "human condition"—circumstances of geography or corporeality that constrain our ability to participate in the making of shared political life. And yet this shared political life seems nonetheless elusive. Imagining away the spread of geography, the stubborn persistence of bodies in physical space, *Exit West* finds freedom within the dilation of the border zone, a sort of *living with* surveillance that takes the place of living *in* the nation-state.

EXIT

If *Exit West*'s resolution regularizes immigration by undoing the constraints of militarized borders, *EXIT* draws upon the kinds of data produced by digital surveillance to refute the notion that an empathetic account of human migration requires us to imagine individual human lives. In so doing, it too develops narrative mechanisms that depart from realism's investment in using the human to secure public affect.

EXIT integrates fifteen years of data on migration patterns into an immersive video installation that debuted at the Fondation Cartier pour l'Art Contemporain. Epigraphs drawn from the 1951 Geneva Convention Relating to the Status of Refugees announce the work's depiction of forced migration as a referendum on our collective commitment to human rights, a set of obligations nation-states seem remarkably ill-equipped to manage. *EXIT* invokes the notion of a world order of nation-states in order to destabilize its coherence. A thin yellow line cuts an uneven "new equator" between Global North and South. As the industrialized world settles onto the globe, disasters follow. Rising seas displace the inhabitants of overpopulated cities;

deforestation and fires carve up habitable space. In response to these crises, migration occurs at a scale that competes with and ultimately overwhelms the capacities of national border zones, militarized or otherwise.

Paul Virilio's initial prompt—to capture the scale of contemporary migration—seems to have been taken up by Diller Scofidio + Renfro as a formal provocation. Virilio polemicizes against the digital landscape, arguing that it makes apathy a pervasive condition. Digital technology compresses and fragments time, allowing us to access mediated accounts of events with a sense of immediacy instead of entering into a space of action. Modernity plays out in the no-time of an always-catastrophe, an "acceleration of reality" that evacuates political life. The vanishing time of migrants, for Virilio, is not the time needed to cross geographical terrain but the digital arena of an expansive perpetual now. To draw upon Debjani Ganguly's helpful formulation, "The narrative grammar of the human in the novel form in this age of spectator capitalism" has changed.[46] When information technology makes accounts of crises around the world accessible at any moment, aesthetic works enter a media landscape of "exorbitant witnessing and scopophilic omniscience."[47] In this context, aesthetic works all too easily become benign excursions into digital surveillance. Sheer excess of mediated information aligns witnessing with insomnia, a dulled continuous functioning that produces ever-diminishing returns.[48]

The dangers of overmediation amplify when a work represents widespread phenomena such as mass migration. In *Antinomies of Realism*, Fredric Jameson argues that works that reference large-scale atrocities are often beleaguered by the notion that they are "ultimately unrepresentable."[49] Analyzing the often protracted and diffuse violence of war, Jameson contends that "atrocities might seem to us today to belong rather to the malignant properties of evil or cursed landscape than to the savagery of an individual actor; and it is as though with this and our other later plot-types we pass from a world of acts and characters to that of space itself—scene, landscape, geography . . . a heterogenous element that is of *Stimmung* or affect as fully as much as of some mere stage or 'context' for human gestures."[50] For Jameson, at this juncture, the problem is largely one of scale: as casualties spread across a landscape, the narrative eye has to choose between drawing up and back to grasp its totality or zooming in close enough to capture the sensory experience of individuals. To register the scale of violence's carnage, its historical and geopolitical sweep, we must lose sight of its participants. (We might think here, once again, of *Exit West*'s struggle to articulate both character and scene.)

In Diller Scofidio + Renfro's hands, however, migration reports offer a rejoinder to the notions that technology produces only apathy or that scalar representation dissociates. *EXIT* turns statistics into a communal requiem for a world population besieged. The firm, whose portfolio includes the High Line, the revamped Museum of Modern Art, and the Shed in Manhattan, has a history of engendering flexible public spaces out of surprising materials. Drawing on data sets from UNESCO, the World Bank, the UN, and geologists at Columbia University, the piece frames migration as a human rights crisis by narrativizing the exigencies causing forced displacement between 1990 and 2014.

A 360-degree screen creates a panoramic theater; audience members stand in the middle. A spinning globe operates as the piece's narrative engine, orbiting the room and printing two-dimensional maps in its wake. As the exhibition catalog explains, "The maps are made from data collected from a variety of sources, geocoded, processed through a programming language, and translated visually. The presentation is divided into narratives concerning population shift, remittances, political refugees, natural disaster, and sea level rise."[51] Viewers have the uncanny sense of experiencing a two- and three-dimensional work at the same time. Diller imagines the position of the viewer as a form of magical inversion, "turning the world inside out, standing in the middle of it, impossibly, and understanding everything all at once."[52] Like *Exit West*'s fantastical border architecture, which condenses the journey from one country to another into the physical struggle of a body crossing a door's threshold, *EXIT* incorporates humans as infrastructure. Overlapping maps shape complex international economic, environmental, and political patterns into images that can be held together within the viewer's field of vision. Instead of producing the absorption Virilio fears, *EXIT*'s flexible perspectives beg interaction (distinguishing it, perhaps, from the border zone's control of the visual field). The 360-degree screen incorporates the body into the viewing experience: in order to achieve the "impossible" sensation of omniscience, viewers have to engage the data, moving around the room and turning to enlarge their fields of vision. The panoramic screens mimic digital surveillance's omnipresence while inverting its terms: where digital surveillance processes the body's information as infrastructural substrate—the data needed to track or detain—*EXIT* encourages viewers to consider how their privileged perspective emerges from ways their body participates in producing and managing the work itself.

The formal repertoire of *EXIT* repeatedly works against the grain of the "diffuse attentiveness" and "semiautonomatism" produced by digital culture.[53] Unlike Ai Weiwei's *Human Flow* (2017), with its saturated landscapes and luscious panoramas of bodies in motion, *EXIT*'s representation of migration at scale is spatially expansive but visually thin. Its line-drawn graphics are a throwback to early MS-DOS; captions recuperate the whirring clack of electronic typewriters. White text ticks across the black screen in OCR-A font (one of the first fonts designed to be read by humans as well as computers), positioning the work at the juncture of human experience and technological knowledge. Human voices only emerge as a garbled chorus of lost or dying languages. Spoken word gives way to an aural narrative of cash registers clinking, chainsaws cutting, and a steady background hum of unidentifiable machines. Deprived of human focalization and a realistic visual field, viewers sense that habitual modes of engagement with migration narratives cannot apply.

This is particularly apparent in *EXIT*'s approach to representing the human person. Migrants are represented as a ratio: "One pixel moving across the screen represents ten people in the database. The pixels draw paths from one country's centerpoint to the next."[54] A digital calendar flips through decades as colors pour from sites of conflict or economic collapse, swirling across nearby borders or tracing flight maps across oceans. At one point, the entirety of the world's population coalesces into a vibrating grayscale swarm, its motion generating the static hum of an old television set between channels. People migrate for all sorts of reasons, and *EXIT* demonstrates no investment in highlighting one over another. Rather, holding often isolated data sets together in a visual field allows viewers to recognize a range of causes for migration as globalized phenomena. Internal and external displacement, usually catalogued as distinct patterns of movement, spill across the same screen. To be clear, relying on data to tell the story of migration does produce aporias: displacement in *EXIT* always corresponds with some sort of arrival, a perhaps unintended consequence of rendering pixels that move from the center of one country to another. The vanishing point imagined by border officials is sidestepped here as ancillary to the global narrative of forced displacement, but so too are the sorts of failed crossing that generate no data: the boats that founder, the bodies that vanish.

Elizabeth Diller explains the choice to bypass human experience as a necessary reconfiguration of realism: "We wanted to expose these issues without resorting to narrative media—whose familiarity and realism is often desensitizing. So, we challenged ourselves to use only data—the driest and most abstract information—to create an immersive experience."[55] Focus on the human, Diller contends, obscures the conditions making human migration necessary. Perhaps more provocatively, realism, in her account, dulls the sympathy of viewers. The resultant work upends common wisdom about narrative's capacity to bear witness to precarity. Literary criticism tends to privilege fiction's contract with realism, the sorts of sympathies that attend the novel's ability to produce what Sidonie Smith and Kay Schaffer describe as "narrated lives."[56] *EXIT* shifts focus away from humans in motion to the collapse of environments that once sustained them. Urging us to see that "consequences transgress borders," the piece replaces human figures with pixels whose movements are not acts but consequences, the ineluctable result of torched forests and unstable economies. In resisting figuration, *EXIT* re-poses the question of forced migration in order to assert a different vocabulary for collective engagement. Borrowing Ariella Azoulay's generative formulation, we might describe the embodied viewership *EXIT* solicits as an exploration of "watching as a civil act and a rehabilitation of the political."[57]

Conclusion

As border zones amplify, contemporary aesthetic accounts of forced migration find the notion of holding border infrastructure, migration, and the individual human together under a compact with realism unproductive or impossible. Self-actualization seems to be off the table. After all, the human today is the human surveilled, a fact that *EXIT* and *Exit West* register to different ends. Perhaps, heeding their terms, we might find letting go of representing the individual human person in favor of representing infrastructures that support, track, or thwart movement to be provisionally necessary—relinquishing singularity in order to articulate what Jameson might call the "unrepresentable" large-scale disaster.

Notes

1. Hannah Arendt, *The Origins of Totalitarianism* (New York: Harcourt, 1973), 14.

2. United Nations High Commissioner on Refugees, *Global Trends: Forced Displacement in 2020* (Copenhagen: UNHCR), June 18, 2021.

3. Seyla Benhabib, *Exile, Statelessness, and Migration* (Princeton, NJ: Princeton University Press, 2018), 103.

4. Wendy Brown, *Walled States, Waning Sovereignty* (New York: Zone Books, 2017).

5. Atossa Abrahamian, "Beyond the Wall: A Q&A with Wendy Brown," *Nation*, January 9, 2019.

6. Michael Rubenstein, *Public Works: Infrastructure, Irish Modernism, and the Postcolonial* (South Bend, IN: University of Notre Dame Press, 2010); Michael Rubenstein et al., "Infrastructuralism: An Introduction," *MFS Modern Fiction Studies* 61, no. 4 (December 2015): 575–86.

7. Susan Leigh Star, "The Ethnography of Infrastructure," *American Behavioral Scientist* 43, no. 3 (November 1999): 377–91.

8. Brian Larkin, "The Politics and Poetics of Infrastructure," *Annual Review of Anthropology* 42, no. 1 (October 2013): 329.

9. Trevor Paglen, "NSA-Tapped Undersea Cables, North Pacific Ocean," photograph (New York: Metro Pictures; and San Francisco: Altman Siegel Gallery, 2016).

10. Debarati Sanyal, "Calais's 'Jungle' Refugees, Biopolitics, and the Arts of Resistance," *Representations* 139, no. (August 2017): 1–33, 14–18.

11. AbdouMaliq Simone, "People as Infrastructure: Intersecting Fragments in Johannesburg," *Public Culture* 16, no. 3 (September 2004): 424.

12. Lisa Lowe, *The Intimacies of Four Continents* (Durham, NC: Duke University Press, 2015); Eyal Weizman, *Hollow Land: Israel's Architecture of Occupation* (New York: Verso, 2017); Nikhil Pal Singh, *Race and America's Long War* (Berkeley: University of California, 2017); Miriam Ticktin, "Invasive Others: Toward a Contaminated World," *Social Research: An International Quarterly* 84, no. 1 (May 2017): xxi–xxxiv.

13. Adam Moore, *Empire's Labor: The Global Army That Supports U.S. Wars* (Ithaca, NY: Cornell University Press, 2019); International Committee of the Red Cross, *The Montreux Document on Pertinent International Legal Obligations*

and Good Practices for States Related to Operations of Private Military and Security Companies During Armed Conflict (Geneva: ICRC, August 2009).

14. I draw here upon Seyla Benhabib and Lindsay Stonebridge's work on statelessness in Arendt's theory in *Placeless People: Writings, Rights, and Refugees* (New York: Oxford, 2018).

15. Arendt, *The Origins of Totalitarianism*, 301.

16. Judith Butler, *Notes toward a Performative Theory of Assembly* (Cambridge, MA: Harvard University Press, 2015), 73.

17. See Étienne Balibar's influential account of the border as a "tautological absurdity" in *Politics and the Other Scene* (London: Verso, 2002), 77.

18. I am indebted to Sandro Mezzadra and Brett Neilson's *Border as Method; or, The Multiplication of Labor* (Durham, NC: Duke University Press, 2013) for theorizing the border as the production and circulation of difference.

19. Balibar, *Politics and the Other Scene*, 78.

20. Joseph R. Slaughter, "Vanishing Points: When Narrative Is Not Simply There," *Journal of Human Rights* 9, no. 2 (May 2010): 217. Slaughter ties the vanishing point of Brueghel's *Landscape with the Fall of Icarus* to the suffering that organizes the painting's world, arguing that the landscape "with" suffering is actually a landscape "because of" suffering, an introduction of causation that marks the transition to narrative. I am indebted to Slaughter's framework here, but CBP's "vanishing time" is unique in *announcing* itself as the operative logic of border infrastructure.

21. See John Berger, *Ways of Seeing* (London: Penguin, 1990).

22. W. J. T. Mitchell, *Landscape and Power* (Chicago: University of Chicago Press, 2002), 17.

23. Georg Lukács, *The Theory of the Novel: A Historico-Philosophical Essay on the Forms of Great Epic Literature* (Cambridge, MA: MIT Press, 1993), 89.

24. Lukács, *The Theory of the Novel*, 82.

25. Angela Naimou, *Salvage Work: U.S. and Caribbean Literatures amid the Debris of Legal Personhood* (New York: Fordham, 2015).

26. Mohsin Hamid, *Exit West* (New York: Riverhead, 2017), 68.

27. Hamid, *Exit West*, 71.

28. Hamid, *Exit West*, 85.

29. Hamid, *Exit West*, 93.

30. Hamid, *Exit West*, 73.

31. Hamid, *Exit West*, 169.

32. Hamid, *Exit West*, 7.

33. Hamid, *Exit West*, 8.

34. Marlow, the teller of Kurtz's tale, famously misrepresents Kurtz's last words. When asked by Kurtz's "intended" what her fiancé's last words were, Marlow prevaricates to save her "pale visage" from a truth that would have been "too dark—too dark altogether." The story he cannot tell is one of forced labor, exploitation, and violence, featuring an unnamed African woman whose screams follow the boat carrying Kurtz back up the Congo. See Joseph Conrad, *The Heart of Darkness* (Oxford: Oxford University Press, 2008), 183, 186.

35. Hamid, *Exit West*, 9.

36. Debjani Ganguly, *This Thing Called the World: The Contemporary Novel as Global Form* (Durham, NC: Duke University Press, 2016), 27–28.

37. Benedict Anderson, *Imagined Communities: Reflections on the Origins and Spread of Nationalism* (New York: Verso, 1983); Alex Woloch, *The One vs. the Many: Minor Characters and the Space of the Protagonist in the Novel* (Princeton, NJ: Princeton University Press, 2003).

38. Yogita Goyal, "'We Are All Migrants': The Refugee Novel and the Claims of Universalism," *MFS Modern Fiction Studies* 66, no. 2 (2020): 241.

39. Goyal, "'We Are All Migrants,'" 244.

40. Hamid, *Exit West,* 158.

41. Hamid, *Exit West,* 186.

42. Hamid, *Exit West,* 188.

43. Hamid, *Exit West,* 157.

44. See Ann Cvetkovich, "Public Feelings," *South Atlantic Quarterly* 106, no. 3 (July 2007): 459–68.

45. Hamid, *Exit West*, 170.

46. Ganguly, *This Thing Called the World*, 156.

47. Ganguly, *This Thing Called the World*, 32.

48. Jonathan Crary, *24/7: Late Capitalism and the Ends of Sleep* (London: Verso, 2014).

49. Fredric Jameson, *The Antinomies of Realism* (London and New York: Verso, 2015), 233.

50. Jameson, *Antinomies of Realism,* 240.

51. Paul Virilio and Diller Scofidio + Renfro, *EXIT* (London: Thames & Hudson, 2020).

52. Elizabeth Diller, "EXIT—Entretien avec Elizabeth Diller et Ricardo Scofidio," December 28, 2015, Fondation Cartier pour l'art contemporain, https://www.youtube.com/watch?v=6i83tje_H8w.

53. Crary, *24/7*, 88.

54. Virilio and Diller Scofidio + Renfro, *EXIT*, 52.

55. Diller, "EXIT."

56. K. Schaffer and Sidonie Smith, *Human Rights and Narrated Lives: The Ethics of Recognition* (New York: Palgrave, 2004), 5.

57. Ariella Azoulay, *The Civil Contract of Photography* (New York: Zone, 2008), 23.

Chapter 8

✦

An "Elastic Severalty"

Distributive Infrastructuralism in Namwali Serpell's *The Old Drift*

Jeannie Im

Namwali Serpell's *The Old Drift* (2019) is a novel that refuses to be a national epic. It certainly has the historical scope: beginning with the peregrinations of a hapless British opportunist at the start of the twentieth century, the novel proceeds through British settlement and colonial administration, into Zambia's independence and the present day, before flinging ahead to the just plausible, near future of the year 2025 and beyond. The novel's expansive story line encompasses major infrastructural developments, from the Kariba Dam project of the 1950s to Zambia's postcolonial development state to its implication in global neoliberal networks. But these projects do not fit neatly into linear narratives of nation building, development, and modernization. Instead, infrastructure emerges as an ever-mutating and unruly assemblage of social forms, technologies, affects, and materialities, which mediate, in Arjun Appadurai's words, a "range of vitalities, energies, and agencies that bind the human order to other natural orders."[1]

In this essay, I explore how the novel's formal innovations constitute an infrastructural poetics that, following Caroline Levine's definition of infrastructuralism, brings into view "a vast variety of chaotically overlapping, repetitive social forms that extend from multiple pasts and replicate themselves, indefinitely, into unpredictable and distant futures."[2] The most significant of the novel's formal innovations is the use of choral interludes uttered by an unspecified "we" who interrupt the narrative to place their caustic gloss on an episode. Like the chorus of ancient Greek drama, the novel's chorus occasionally insert themselves into the story, as when they claim to be a pesky swarm of mosquitoes spreading misery and malaria among the characters; but more frequently, the chorus provide commentary from the perspective of a collective, although the public that this collective represents is not clearly defined. Rather, the chorus are an *elastic severalty*: their classification is variable but not particularized, and their number is multiple but not enumerated. Defying classification, the chorus declare that they are "*neither gods nor ghosts nor spirits nor sprites*," but simply an agency distributed across an ever-mutating net or web of entities whose composition remains heterogeneous and indeterminable.[3]

The novel's formal innovation of the swarm as an elastic severalty amplifies narrative gaps and multiplies focal possibilities in surprising ways. The choral swarm serves an important metadiegetic function by invoking perspectives unfocalized in the narrative, drawing out resonances with historical figures marginalized or repressed by official histories, offering alternative representations of events within the story, and indicating experiences and agencies that remain outside the storytelling conventions of the narrative. In so doing, I argue, the swarm constitutes a network of what Jane Bennett calls "distributive agency," whereby "efficacy or agency always depends on the collaboration, cooperation, or interactive interference of many bodies and forces" at multiple scales of matter.[4] Thus, the swarm enables a reading of the novel itself as a distributive agential network, an aesthetic infrastructure that enables the interplay between narrative functions shared across narrative chapters and the swarm's choral interludes. Through this distributive infrastructuralism, the novel figures how infrastructures coalesce historically specific assemblages of power and affect, as well as how these assemblages overlap, mutate, endure, and decay.

The essay that follows is divided into two sections. In the first section, I explore how the choral interludes destabilize infrastructure as signifier of developmental colonialism and national developmentalism. The choral interludes produce rhetorical effects that bring into view agencies and materialities, both human and nonhuman, that undermine monolithic developmental narratives. In the next section, I demonstrate how the choral swarm shifts from the built infrastructural megaprojects of the past to more contemporary modes of neoliberal speculation and control enabled by advances in information technology and the life sciences. As the novel's timeline converges on the present and moves into the future, the choral interlude orients its infrastructural aesthetic to anticipate the possibilities of what Lauren Berlant has called "affective infrastructures," which she describes as an "aesthetic structure of affective expectation, an institution or formation . . . allowing for complex audience identifications."[5] By way of conclusion, I explore the novel's catastrophic ending as a paradoxical but necessary gesture toward the lively possibilities within the distributed play of infrastructural mediations.

Infrastructure, Modernization, and Developmental Project Time

The first two sections of *The Old Drift* take place against the backdrop of major infrastructural developments, from the emergence of colonial outposts on the Zambezi to the founding of Lusaka to the Kariba Dam project of the 1950s and the ambitious, postindependence national projects that further built up energy, transportation, and social welfare infrastructures in the 1960s and 1970s. Motivating these projects was a developmental narrative positing an idea of modernity—economic, political, cultural, technological—as the defining telos of the nation. As James Ferguson explains, developmentalism assumed that "things like industrial economy and modern transportation and communications necessarily brought with them political democracy."[6] In the case of colonial megaprojects such as the Kariba Dam, it was also assumed that development would lead to the political maturity of subject peoples viewed as emerging from a backward, tribal state, preparing them for independence at the same time that this independence was premised on their continued exploitation and openness to predatory international investment. The Kariba Dam project, for example, was prioritized over more incremental measures because it provided a spectacle of "exterior modernization done perforce" in terms of its geographical impact and technological sophistication.[7] The dam radically altered the landscape of the Gwembe valley, creating what was then the largest man-made lake in the world: it displaced thousands of Tonga and decimated their habitat and livelihoods. The dam thus instantiated what Brian Larkin has called the "colonial sublime," the use of infrastructure as both exercise and representation of colonial power as "the terrifying ability to remake landscapes and force the natural world to conform to these technological projects."[8]

The Old Drift ironizes this model of megaproject as modernization by interrupting what Ashley Carse and David Kneas call the "project time" of infrastructural projects, which they define as "a linear succession of phases or stages oriented toward meeting pre-defined objectives" that also implicate "the ideological positions that presuppose the materialization of blueprint plans in physical form," including the ideology of modernization that structurally mirrors its temporality.[9] The classic sequence of project time is "plan, budget, procure, build, complete": the execution of this sequence is not reliant on merely rational calculation but also on the presumption of material conditions for the project's completion, such as predictable and malleable natural resources, consistent funding, reliable technologies, availability of construction materials and technical expertise, political stability, and compliant labor. As Carse and Kneas point out, however, construction can often be unpredictable, encompassing statuses as diverse as "proposed, planned, funded, underway, delayed, failed, abandoned, and so on."[10] In the delays and failures that get in the way of translating blueprints into built structures, project time reveals its fictiveness, exposing the ideological underpinnings and unforeseen variables that give the lie to its calculus; at the same time, in moments of incompleteness, deferral, or breakdown, possibilities for other social imaginaries or affective infrastructures can emerge. Infrastructural projects expose the gap between an idealized project time and social, material, and environmental realities, but this gap also makes visible "imagined orders and realities," promised but not produced, "affective states from hope to anxiety and practices from speculation to protest."[11]

In the novel, the swarm helps make such affective infrastructures legible by doubling and refiguring moments when project time is suspended or jammed within the narrative, especially when it comes to the Kariba Dam, which looms large in the novel as the megaproject par excellence in terms of its significance to colonial and postcolonial Zambia and which is ultimately a target of sabotage at the end of the novel. Primarily developed between 1955 and 1959, the Kariba Dam project was beset with accidents and construction delays.[12] Rather than presenting the dam as a triumph of modern engineering and colonial administration, the novel instead highlights a spectacular moment of disrupted project time. The character Smith, a British colonial officer in charge of the works, becomes increasingly frustrated at the failure of the dam to have its intended sublime impact on the Tonga, who resist rather than express awe and subservience. Smith still believes in the power of the colonial sublime: he arranges a tour of the dam works because he thinks "it might help if they could set eyes on it."[13] This attempt at publicity and control is a massive failure. In the final scene of one section, the Tonga arrive at the dam just as it is about to crumble due to river outflow: what they witness is a breakdown of colonial reason and modernizing hubris in the face of the Zambezi River's natural power. The section ends abruptly on the edge of the incomplete dam with the turbulent waters of the Zambezi looming, "raising its red hackles."[14]

At this point, the choral swarm intervenes with a reframing of the same scene that disassembles the monolithic megaproject into an assemblage of multiple, heterogeneous agencies. While the colonial administration views the river as a force to be channeled into its own narratives of development and modernization, the swarm offers a way to acknowledge the river as an agential vector and, by extension, the different forms of life that shape the composite of agencies that make up the Gwembe River valley ecosystem. Whereas in the story the actions of the Tonga are focalized through the European characters—Sibilla, Gavuzzi, Smith—the swarm continues the story beyond the section break from the perspective of the Tonga. For the Tonga, the swarm elaborates, the spirit of the Zambezi is a god named Nyami Nyami, "*a god with the head of a fish and the tail of a snake*."[15] To dam up the Zambezi is to disrupt both an ecosystem and a cosmology, a way of life that revolves around the seasonal patterns of the Zambezi and relies on Nyami Nyami's generosity. The swarm inserts itself into the scene, directly addressing the colonial administrators and engineers: "*You can't trap a river . . . much less the mighty Zambezi, which is ruled by a god with the head of a fish and the tail of a snake. Nyami Nyami will undo your work*." While the narrative breaks before the unfinished dam is destroyed, the swarm continues the story through the Tonga spectators, who witness "*the feckless* buzungu"—a term for the white man that literally means "one who wanders"—as the river "*plastered them to the dam like insects.*"

By inserting the Tongan perspective back into the narrative, the swarm folds back into the preceding scene, where the Zambezi had been troped as a kind of animal, "raising its red hackles." Within the narrative, the phrase "red hackles" is a descriptive metaphor; the swarm's interlude, however, gives the phrase a different status. Animalistic metaphors are consistent within the Tongan worldview, which considers the dynamics of the river as a spirit composed of multiple animal parts—a fish's head, a serpent's tail. In its commentary on the foregoing chapter, the swarm invites, metaleptically, a rereading, collapsing the metaphorical "red hackles" onto "red hackles" as synecdoche for Nyami Nyami's body and thus for other agential vectors. Nyami Nyami names here both the Tongan river spirit and the fracturing of colonial project time at the nexus of a host of heterogeneous effectivities, from the Tongas' resistance to the incalculability of the river's fluid dynamics and from the engineers' faulty calculations, which produced the mistake that made the disaster possible, to the material composition of the incomplete dam itself.

As the novel moves to postcolonial Zambia, the swarm draws out congruities between the colonial sublime, instantiated in monumental infrastructure projects as a spectacularization of colonial power, and the developmental sublime of a nationalist ideology promoting infrastructure as the expression of Zambia's postcolonial modernization. Flush with the revenue from the copper mining industry in its initial decade, Kenneth Kaunda's government was able to fund an impressive number of extensive infrastructural projects, including public utilities and expanded educational and health care systems.[16] Yet, as the choral swarm will make clear, these benefits were unevenly distributed across genders, creating a masculinist ("*Man*-centered") model of development that is emblematized in Kaunda's self-representation as benevolent father of the nation.[17] This contradiction is explored in the novel through a story line that fictionalizes the experiences of Matha Mwamba, the sole female astronaut in Zambia's National Academy of Science, Space Research, and Philosophy. At this moment of postindependence euphoria, the forces that Nyami Nyami names seem to be harnessed to Edward Mukuka Nkoloso's idea of "turbulent propulsion," which, according to Nkoloso, was an African technological innovation for generating velocity far more advanced than anything scientists in the West had discovered.[18] Despite Nkoloso's grand claims, Nkoloso's space program was ridiculed by the international press as turbulent propulsion appeared to be generated by vigorously swinging from a tree. At least one journalist, however, viewed the program as anti-imperialist political satire, satirizing the exorbitant sums the United States and the Soviet Union were pouring into the space race in order to establish their global prestige while Zambia was devoting its funds to building up its infrastructure.[19]

Yet, as the choral interludes that bookend the "Matha" chapter show, Nkoloso's infrastructuralist theater, as synecdoche for Kaunda's developmental policies as a whole, excluded women from the promises of anticolonial nationalism and postcolonial development. In the interlude that precedes the chapter, the chorus offer an extended address to Alice Lenshina, the charismatic leader of the Lumpa church, an evangelical movement in northern Zambia that had been brutally suppressed by the United Nationalist Independence Party (UNIP) for its apolitical stance.[20] The swarm bemoans the patriarchal violence unleashed against Lenshina: "*They send the White Father to call you the devil, to mock little Alice in Wonderland. They send chiefs and* kapusas *to demand your taxes. . . . They send Kaunda's men to denounce you as savage*."[21] This interlude then gives way to the story lines of Matha Mwamba and her mother as they intersect with Nkoloso's.[22] Matha perceives her activist mother as the promise of gender equality in Nkoloso's and, by extension, UNIP's vision of modern Zambia. But as Ilse Schuster explains, "Attitudes toward the political activities of women reflected a deep ambivalence in Zambian society," where a strict moral conservatism and suspicion of "morally suspect modern educated sub-elite women" predominated.[23] Matha experiences this contradiction between egalitarian rhetoric and gendered development through her involvement with Nkoloso's space program. When the United States lands Apollo 11 on the moon, leading to the disbandment of the Zambian space program, Nkoloso places the blame for the failure of his project on Matha, who is unmarried and pregnant: "We could not face our sponsors with a pregnant girl!" he claims. "The rumours have squashed us."[24] For Matha, Nkoloso's rejection results in the realization that "to be a woman was always, somehow, to be a banishable witch."[25]

In the interlude following the "Matha" chapter, the swarm acknowledges Nkoloso as a kindred aesthetic, as "*one of [their] own*," a "*needler of convention and rules*" like the swarm itself, but chides him as one who "*succumbed to custom*."[26] The swarm's criticism of the constraints of patriarchal custom resonates with its interlude invoking Lenshina at the start of Matha's story: like Lenshina, Matha embodies a dangerous femininity that must be expurgated in order to further a patriarchal narrative of postcolonial transition into national autonomy. Nkoloso's rejection of Matha reveals how his appeals to an "unbending dedication to freedom and justice"[27] depend on women's political labor at the same time that it throws up barriers to women's visible participation: in pregnancy, Matha's body is not a symbol of women's power but of women's vulnerability and impropriety in a public, masculine arena. By accepting and insisting on the boundaries of political life dictated by custom, Nkoloso's exclusion of women sparks an autoimmune reaction within the postcolonial developmental narrative that rejects while implicitly acknowledging the necessity of women. *The Old Drift* undermines such autoimmune narratives not only by reinscribing women's work in the historical record but also by aggregating their work as future possibilities for agency and resistance. While the indigenous agencies of the Gwembe valley were figured as Nyami Nyami, here, women's agency is figured as bodily infection or genetic deviation, manifesting in the fantastically hyperbolic capabilities of Sibilla's and Matha's bodies: Sibilla's entire body is covered by long tendrils of rapidly growing hair, and Matha weeps copiously and without interruption for years. In both cases, their extraordinary corporeal capacities sustain communities of women, whether it is the family members Sibilla supports through the sale of her hair for wigs or the cult of wailing women that develops around Matha. Through the swarm's mediation and contextualization, these extraordinary bodies emerge as a politics as well. Both Nkoloso's political theater and Sibilla's and Matha's embodied poetics persist in succeeding generations, offering an epigenetic heritage of resistance and an archive of unrealized futures as the historical setting of the novel shifts from postcolonial developmentalism to the more contemporary context of neoliberal speculation.

Neoliberal Speculation and Speculative Futures

Through the interplay between narrative and choral interlude, the first two parts of the novel detached infrastructural megaprojects from narratives of developmentalism and modernity, as well as the implied subject of those narratives, whether it is the colonial subject developing into modern citizenship or the postcolonial subject as patriarchal hero. The novel's bifurcated structure offers an infrastructural counteraesthetic, revealing the lively composite of agencies, ideologies, institutions, materialities, and communities that produced and were mediated by infrastructural formations. In the third and final section of the novel, Sibilla's and Matha's grandchildren attempt to translate the subversive histories and embodied poetics of their grandmothers into action, and their methods seem to mirror the swarm's distributive modality, deploying forms of resistance that attempt to radically decentralize and pluralize the institutions of political and economic power. Yet as the story line moves into the future and the realm of speculative science fiction, their final act of sabotage results in a catastrophe that reduces Lusaka to a village, and the swarm's commentary is stripped of the exuberant wordplay of previous interludes. In this final section of my essay, I examine the necessity of the characters' failure in the context of the novel's aesthetic of distributive infrastructuralism.

The characters' activism, which they name "SOTP" after a misspelled traffic sign, takes place in the contemporary context of global neoliberalism, which marks a departure from the massive built infrastructural projects of both the colonial and postcolonial development state. As James Ferguson has explained, a new form of "extractive neoliberalism" emerged in many African states, including Zambia, in the 1980s, with national revenue flowing into the endless repayment of international debt rather than domestic infrastructure.[28] "The capitalists replaced the colonialists. And now these foreigners take our minerals away and even shoot our miners," bemoans one character as he mourns the collapse of Kaunda's socialist vision of a "society for the people."[29] Concomitantly, advances in genetic and information technologies have enabled new modes of extraction that do not require the "thick" infrastructural investments of the past. Instead, neoliberalism tends toward a "socially thin model of enclave extraction,"[30] through forms of resource extraction, such as isolated offshore oil platforms, that do not require investment in infrastructures that sustain and promote social welfare, such as housing, roads, health care, and education.

The novel places a particular emphasis on genetic and information technologies as socially thin modes of enclave extraction, where genetic and biometric data about users culled through "technics of algorithmic governmentality" become sources of capitalistic value.[31] Kaushik Sunder Rajan terms this transformation at the confluence of information technologies and biomedical research "biocapital": biotic matter becomes "conceived and represented in informational terms" that render it monetizable. Subjects are valued as aggregates of subindividual components and properties that can produce surplus value to be inserted into late capitalist circuits of accumulation and exchange.[32] In *The Old Drift*, the technics of neoliberal biocapital are encapsulated in the Digit-All Bead, a chip implanted into a finger that serves as a multifunctional, prosthetic smartphone. It is a device designed specifically for markets in developing countries, powered by melanin, distributed widely and cheaply through the cooperation of local governments. The character Naila, visiting India, contemplates the utility of her Digit-All Bead with irony: "The Third World had been ripe for them. Power cut? A torch in your finger. Poor schools? Google in the palm of your hand. Slow communication? A photo beats a thousand words: a Bead was also an eye."[33] Naila's thought juxtaposes the monetizable functionalities of the Digit-All Bead with the thick social infrastructures it has displaced. The Digit-All Bead enables new forms of government surveillance, which include monitoring its subjects' HIV status and culling user data that can be sold to multinational pharmaceutical companies, while infrastructures such as clinics and qualified health care professionals are neglected. The character Sylvia, for example, is exploited by her scientist lover for her genetic material, which makes her immune to most strains of HIV; once infected by a strain of HIV that she is vulnerable to, however, she dies in a Lusaka slum, unable to access or afford the health care she needs.

The Digit-All Bead indexes how subindividual units—genetic material, bodily processes, affects—have become part of a global technoscientific infrastructure that has expanded the scales at which matter can be manipulated and monetized. As Patricia Clough explains, technologies such as quantum computing and genetic engineering have enabled an "intensification of control at every scale of matter," extending to the modulation of substance at a molecular, even subatomic level. This intensification of control leads to an ever-increasing "preemption" of the traditional humanist subject by manufacturing control at a material and subindividual level, leading to a "smoothening of the space of civil society institutions, capitalizing on their increasing reluctance or inability to socialize, to interpellate individuals to the ideals of the nation-state."[34] In the novel, this intensification of control is exemplified when a large crowd is vaccinated en masse by a swarm of government drones: the mass vaccination happens so quickly that the crowd is barely aware that their capacity to consent has been preempted. The logic of preemption is at the heart what Shir Alon calls "neoliberal speculation," which attempts to forestall an unpredictable and incalculable future by shifting from the more socially thick structures of the welfare state to generating "flexible," mobile, transient, and therefore more vulnerable populations.[35] But neoliberal speculation is inherently contradictory, oriented by the catastrophic possibility of capitalism's collapse at the same time that it overlooks the actual enormity of capitalism's effects on economies, societies, and environments, which the novel simply refers to as "the Change," a term that refers both to climate change and its attendant and wide-ranging consequences.

It is against the backdrop of the Change that the novel follows the last generation of characters—Joseph, Jacob, and Naila—as their characters' technosocial imaginaries begin to converge with the choral swarm. Instead of the hydropower assemblages of the colonial or nationalist sublime, the characters experiment with more mutable and temporary networks that distribute agency across human and nonhuman actors, just as the principle of elastic severalty animates the swarm. And instead of accepting the developmental emplotment of heroic modernization, the characters play with opportunities for mistakes, errancy, and breakdown that have been amplified by the choral swarm in earlier interludes: the characters attempt to devise technologies and modes of social action that emboss the smoothness of neoliberal control with the uneven and the frictional. Both Joseph and Jacob seek to create technologies outside the circuits of neoliberal speculation, discovering generative models in nature. Joseph is inspired by the biological phenomenon of commensalism, whereby "one organism benefits from another without affecting it, like the lice that eat human skin flakes or the vultures that trail lions for carcasses."[36] Jacob, a self-taught inventor, continues the legacy of the Zambian Afronaut program through Matha, his grandmother, in devising a microdrone system: called "Moskeetoze," the drones are designed to mimic the behavior of mosquito swarms. A self-regulating, distributed information system, Jacob's Moskeetoze hive is able to make choices as a collective about which drone to sacrifice for fuel without Jacob's intervention. Both inventions, however, are appropriated by the more powerful corporate entities that financed their work: Joseph's genetic research is poached by a Chinese multinational corporation; Jacob's, by a Zambian general for trafficking black market goods.

Although their technologies have been appropriated by others, the characters attempt to develop a politics built on the same distributive dynamic at the core of their innovations. Naila theorizes their political intervention as a kind of virus modeled on Joseph's genetic research: "Insert mistakes into our genetic code so The Virus can't get inside our cells. We have to insert the errors into the system. Not with activism but with the inactive: the loiterers, the shitters, the unemployed—the idlers who jam the circulation of money and goods and information."[37]

Here Naila's politics hinges on what Susan Leigh Star calls a "paradox of infrastructure"[38]: because of the way it conjoins a broad range of actants, it can be susceptible to relatively minor interventions. As Star puts it, "Nobody is really in charge of infrastructure.[39] For example, the Internet is a vast, global communications infrastructure that can be disrupted by a single hacker or rogue server. But the Internet's expansiveness is also the source of its resilience—it is never offline for long. The characters' successive protests bear this out: their attempt to jam Lusaka's traffic is ignored by commuters as just another instance of "slo-go," and while a social media blitz attracts masses of spectators to their next protest, their event only enables the government to mass vaccinate the population more easily through tiny drones modeled on Jacob's designs.

In a mirroring back to the beginning of the novel, the characters embark on their final act: disabling the Kariba Dam long enough so that they can bring down AFRINET and set up an alternative wireless Internet with Jacob's drone system. These events take place in the near future—too close to the present to be completely fantastical, but still too far ahead to be anticipated with certainty. While their earlier attempts were ineffective, their attack on the dam results in the dam's total collapse, and the choral swarm picks up the narrative in the aftermath: "*The bodies of water spilled their banks within days and soon the whole country was drowned. The gorges and valleys were rivers and lakes, the escarpments were lost under waterfalls. Electric grids failed, people fled from their homes. The flood flowed broad and washed out the roads, making streams and canals of the tarmac. Traffic slowed down, then stopped altogether. Passengers waded, then swam.*"[40] By bringing down the Kariba Dam, the characters have unleashed the same catastrophic landscaping of the colonial sublime. What may be most haunting, however, is the swarm's gliding over the mass mortalities required to reduce Lusaka to "*a small community, egalitarian, humble*": the narrative doesn't explicitly number or address the fatalities. Mieke Bal has noted that "where descriptions appear orphaned of diegetic focalization, it is best to look more keenly for traces of the repressed focalizer."[41] Throughout the novel, the swarm has performed the narrative function of refocalizing the events of the story and by doing so has served a metadiegetic function exploring the limits and possibilities of narrativization. But the paragraphs cited above are stripped of the exuberant verbal play and editorializing that characterized previous choral interludes. In a final silencing, the swarm's last words are not its own, but channel all of the characters throughout the novel, who are themselves reduced to a decontextualized "we": "*And so we roil in the oldest of drifts—a slow, slant spin at the pit of the void, the darkest heart of them all.*"[42] Invoking Joseph Conrad's *Heart of Darkness* seems to consign all effort to what Chinua Achebe has called, in his famous critique of the novel, the "mindless frenzy of the first beginnings."[43] Subdued to the point of self-extinction, the swarm seems to have been rendered mute by a devastation that it cannot bring itself to acknowledge or enumerate.

This near future seems to actualize the catastrophic collapse of the late capitalist world system that neoliberal speculation presumed in order to assert its preemptive control. But the characters' project foundered, according to the swarm, because they hadn't accounted for the Change and its unpredictable climatic effects: "*They'd made no concessions to chance. Indeed, their mistake—their Error of Errors—was simply forgetting the weather.*"[44] The characters also, in a crucial way, closed off the possibility of general change through their destructive actions: the opportunity for the public to express a preference or political will; the possibility for errancy, deviation, and agencies that are incalculable and unpredictable; and the space for inventing, reimagining, and adapting infrastructures—material, social, affective—that might mediate those possibilities. The swarm's phrase "*the weather*" in fact puns on Tweather, another technology in the novel that suggests what such infrastructures might look like. Because of the Change, conventional meteorological methods no longer work: Tweather depends on the live tweets of its users to create a crowdsourced data map to generate a more flexible, updated, and finely grained weather forecast. For Joseph, Tweather is an example of how a swarm exhibits a kind of consciousness: the app is the "consciousness of the Change"; however, Tweather's slogan implies that it is also a kind of consciousness of change in general, "A Hive for Change."[45] Tweather enables the kind of decentralized, mass consciousness as hive mind that Naila, Jacob, and Joseph had attempted to model in their SOTP activism, but it is also a model for the possibility of sustaining a platform for mass engagement in "fractious systematicity."[46] Thus, SOTP's final subversive act was bound to fail because they had neglected to take into account the mass consciousness enabled by Tweather ("*the weather*").

Due to SOTP's catastrophic sabotage of the Kariba Dam, the possibilities for mass engagement that Tweather intimates are closed off within the novel. But the swarm's pun on Tweather at the end gestures toward another way to read the ending: as an opening to anticipate differently, to ask "what kinds of desirable accountabilities to and kinship with the future might be fostered through such work."[47] And this is also why the ending is consistent with *The Old Drift*'s aesthetic of distributive infrastructuralism: a novelistic form that accumulates the swerves and detours, that expands more capacious fields of actants and relationalities both within and aslant institutions and infrastructures, enacting without predicting or promising more elastic social forms in its narratological play. As Rob Nixon recently observed of the "spirit of anticipatory memory" in speculative fiction and nonfiction, these works "encourage us to feel our way forward into the emergent worlds that our current actions are precipitating. They encourage us to break out of our temporal silos and—from our diverse Anthropocene positions—face the challenges that shadow the path ahead."[48] If the swarm self-effaces in the end, it is because, as it says, "*The best kind of tale tells you* you *in the end, unveils the unsolvable riddle.*"[49] Ultimately, *The Old Drift* must refuse our desire for a utopian ending, if only to provoke us to "feel our way forward" and find ways of anticipating different futures and the infrastructures that might sustain their flourishing.

Notes

1. Arjun Appadurai, "Mediants, Materiality, Normativity" *Public Culture* 27, no. 2 (2015): 224.

2. Caroline Levine, "Infrastructuralism, or The Tempo of Institutions," chap. 2 in *On Periodization: Selected Essays from the English Institute*, ed. Virginia Jackson (Cambridge: English Institute in collaboration with the American Council of Learned Societies, 2010).

3. Namwali Serpell, *The Old Drift* (New York: Hogarth/Crown Publishing, 2019), 19. I follow the novel's convention of italicizing the choral interludes.

4. Jane Bennett, *Vibrant Mattter: A Political Ecology of Things* (Durham, NC: Duke University Press, 2010), 21.

5. Lauren Berlant, *The Female Complaint: The Unfinished Business of Sentimentality in American Culture* (Durham, NC: Duke University Press, 2008), 4.

6. James Ferguson, *Global Shadows: Africa in the Neoliberal World Order* (Durham, NC: Duke University Press, 2006),183. For studies of infrastructural megaprojects as statecraft, see Christopher Sneddon, *Concrete Revolution: Large Dams, Cold War Geopolitics, and the US Bureau of Reclamation* (Chicago: University of Chicago Press, 2015); and Grant M. Gutierrez, Sarah Kelly, Joshua J. Cousins, and Chistopher Sneddon, "What Makes a Megaproject? A Review of Global Hydropower Assemblages," *Environment and Society: Advances in Research* 10 (2019): 101–21.

7. Julia Tischler, "Negotiating Modernization: The Kariba Dam Project in the Central African Federation, ca. 1954–60," in *Modernization as Spectacle in Africa*, ed. Peter J. Bloom, Stephen F. Miescher, and Takyiwwa Manuh (Indianapolis: Indiana University Press, 2014), 160.

8. Brian Larkin, *Signal and Noise: Media, Infrastructure, and Urban Culture in Nigeria* (Durham, NC: Duke University Press, 2008), 36. For the sublime as a quality of megaprojects more generally, see Brent Flyvberg, "What You Should Know about Megaprojects and Why: An Overview," *Project Management Journal* 45 (2014): 6–19.

9. Ashley Carse and David Kneas, "Unbuilt and Unfinished: The Temporalities of Infrastructure," *Environment and Society: Advances in Research* 10 (2019): 11.

10. Carse and Kneas, "Unbuilt and Unfinished," 13.

11. Carse and Kneas, "Unbuilt and Unfinished," 15.

12. Joseph Chikozho, Tapuwa Raymond Mubaya, and Munyaradzi Mawere, "Nyaminyama, 'The Tonga River-God': The Place and Role of the Nyaminyami in the Tonga People's Cosmology and Environmental Conservation Practices," in *Harnessing Cultural Capital for Sustainability*, ed. Munyaradzi Mawere and Samuel Awuah-Nyamekye (Bamenda: Langaa RPCIG, 2015), 255.

13. Serpell, *The Old Drift*, 72.

14. Serpell, *The Old Drift*, 76.

15. Serpell, *The Old Drift*, 78, 77. On the Tonga myth of the vengeful Nyami Nyami disrupting the Kariba Dam construction, see Chikozho, Mubaya, and Mawere, "Nyaminyama, 'The Tonga River-God,' " 254–57.

16. Marcia M. Burdette, *Zambia: Between Two Worlds* (Boulder, CO: Westview Press, 1988), 90, 67–68.

17. On Kaunda's "presidentialism," see Burdette, *Zambia*, 75–77.

18. Serpell, *The Old Drift*, 167. Nkoloso was a historical figure, an active member of UNIP, guerilla fighter, and political provocateur who made international headlines by inaugurating the National Academy of Science, Space Research and Philosophy with the ambition of besting both the United States and the Soviet Union by sending Zambian astronauts into space. See Namwali Serpell, "The Zambian 'Afronaut' Who Wanted to Join the Space Race," *New Yorker*, March 11, 2017.

19. Serpell, "The Zambian 'Afronaut.' "

20. On UNIP's brutal tactics against the Lumpa church, see David Gordon, "Rebellion or Massacre? The UNIP-Lumpa Conflict Revisited," in *One Zambia, Many Histories: Towards a History of Post-colonial Zambia* (Leiden: Brill, 2008), 45–76. On the Lumpa church and its feminist and regionalist significance, see Iris Berger, *Women in Twentieth-Century Africa* (Cambridge: Cambridge University Press, 2016), 64.

21. Serpell, *The Old Drift*, 139.

22. In Serpell's *New Yorker* article, Matha Mwamba gets a few brief mentions as the sole female astronaut-trainee, a sixteen-year-old who "eventually got pregnant and dropped out," a member of the UNIP Youth Brigade who spread propaganda during the Cha-Cha-Cha guerilla campaign of the 1960s. In the novel, a whole chapter is devoted to writing Matha's counterhistory, and she appears periodically as the novel moves into ensuing decades. Matha's trajectory in *The Old Drift* contrasts with another treatment of Matha's story mentioned in Serpell's *New Yorker* article; in Frances Bodomo's short film *Afronauts*, Matha dies in a rocket explosion.

23. "Constraints and Opportunities in Political Participation: The Case of Zambian Women," *Genève-Afrique* 21, no. 2 (1983): 19–21. In the massive infrastructural projects of Kaunda's First Development Plan, women were excluded from training programs and access to land and credit, with "women's projects" relegated to the underfunded Home Economics Section of the Department of Agriculture. See also Berger, *Women in Twentieth-Century Africa*, 94.

24. Serpell, *The Old Drift*, 180.

25. Serpell, *The Old Drift*, 199.

26. Serpell, *The Old Drift*, 200.

27. Serpell, *The Old Drift*, 178.

28. Ferguson, *Global Shadows*, 210.

29. Serpell, *The Old Drift*, 420.

30. Ferguson, *Global Shadows*, 203.

31. Sharae Deckard, "Trains, Stone, and Energetics: African Resource Culture in the Neoliberal World-Ecology," in *World Literature, Neoliberalism, and the Culture of Discontent*, ed. Sharae Deckard and Stephen Shapiro (New York: Springer, 2019), 243. This does not mean that global infrastructural megaprojects are on the wane, however, as neoliberal institutions have found ways to finance and accelerate their production. See, for example, Peter Bosshard, "The World Bank is bringing back big, bad dams," *Guardian*, July 16, 2013, https://www.theguardian.com/environment/blog/2013/jul/16/world-bank-dams-africa.

32. Kaushik Sunder Rajan, "Two Tales of Genomics: Capital, Epistemology, and the Global Constitutions of the Biomedical Subject," in *Reframing Rights: Bioconstitutionalism in the Genetic Age*, ed. Sheila Jasanoff (Cambridge, MA: MIT Press, 2011), 194.

33. Serpell, *The Old Drift*, 496.

34. Patricia Clough, "The Digital, Labor and Measure beyond Biopolitics," in *Digital Labor: The Internet as Playground and Factory*, ed. Trebor Scholz (New York: Routledge, 2019), 120.

35. Shir Alon, "Neoliberal Riskscapes and Preemptive Poetics in Orly Castel-Bloom's *Dolly City*," *Comparative Literature* 71, no. 1 (2019): 7.

36. Serpell, *The Old Drift*, 402.

37. Serpell, *The Old Drift*, 526.

38. Susan Leigh Star, "The Ethnography of Infrastructure," *American Behavioral Scientist* 43, no. 3 (1999): 483.

39. Star, "The Ethnography of Infrastructure," 478.

40. Serpell, *The Old Drift*, 562.

41. Mieke Bal, "Over-writing as Un-writing: Descriptions, World-Making, and Novelistic Time," in *The Novel: Volume 2, Forms and Themes*, ed. Franco Moretti (Princeton, NJ: Princeton University Press, 2006), 604.

42. Serpell, *The Old Drift*, 563.

43. Chinua Achebe, "An Image of Africa," in Joseph Conrad, *Heart of Darkness*, ed. Paul Armstrong (New York: Norton, 2006), 338.

44. Serpell, *The Old Drift*, 562.

45. Serpell, *The Old Drift*, 511.

46. Jane Bennett, "Systems and Things," in *The Non-Human Turn*, ed. Richard Grusin (Minneapolis: University of Minnesota Press, 2015), 229.

47. Vincanne Adams, Michelle Murphy, and Adele E. Clarke, "Anticipation: Technoscience, Life, Affect, Temporality," *Subjectivity* 28 (2009): 260.

48. Rob Nixon, "All Tomorrow's Warnings." *Public Books*, August 13, 2020, https://www.publicbooks.org/all-tomorrows-warnings/.

49. Serpell, *The Old Drift*, 563.

Part Three

✦

Energy, Environment, Extraction

Chapter 9

Poetic Ultrasound

Atmosphere, Photography, and the Natural Aesthetics of Wind Power

Georgiana Banita

The shift from coal, oil, and natural gas to solar and wind energy is one of the defining events of our era. In large part due to the sheer scale of its infrastructure, wind has become the most iconic among renewable resources, drawing support and skepticism in equal measure. Hailed on the one hand for stimulating an energy revolution, modern wind power is also accused of marring landscapes, obscuring clear skies, and destabilizing animal habitats with each of the thousands of new turbines being erected every year. Conservation groups criticize the impact of noise pollution linked to offshore wind parks on ocean mammals, birds, bats, and insects. The fact that wind parks occupy pristine areas such as coastal territories and forests further dampens public acceptance of wind power as a key driver of energy transition. In addition, studies on the human health effects of wind turbine ultrasound remain inconclusive, which in turn fuels resistance to the wind farms engulfing rural areas, inching closer and closer to homes. The sounds produced by modern wind turbines include audible and ultrasonic frequencies generated either by the gear box inside the nacelle or by the whooshing rotation of the blades through air.[1] I will return to the issue of noise emissions momentarily. The initial impetus of this essay concerns the aesthetics of wind power, specifically of the material and symbolic worlds conjured up by advanced forms of wind energy infrastructure.

Aesthetics as a theory of the beautiful cannot, of course, be reduced to a single definition of the visually pleasing, since sensory experiences and representations reflect subjective perceptions of reality. And yet the semantic field of aesthetics entails a completeness and harmony, an unaffected naturalness and integrity that can easily be seen to clash with the jagged infrastructure of wind power. The question of how wind turbines modify natural landscapes makes visible one of the most virulent psychosocial and cultural challenges of the clean energy transition. Do the optics of modern wind parks satisfy expectations about what is natural and aesthetically pleasing? What does it mean to contemplate nature and savor this experience as a form of aesthetic pleasure? To be sure, impressions of wind power land- and seascapes defy objective categorization, running the gamut from abhorrence to delight. Some observers are alienated by enormous wind farms that appear to disturb an untouched, harmonious natural view. Others regard wind power as the only alternative to the unsustainable regime of fossil fuels, a standpoint that renders issues of environmental disfigurement moot. Many supporters relish the rhythmic rotations and simple aesthetics of wind turbines, not least because the sedate demeanor of wind farms dovetails with the growing popularity of bucolic, minimalist, and decelerated lifestyles. At this point in the history of energy modernity, in the words of Harmut Rosa, it appears that "the call for deceleration and the nostalgic desire for the lost 'slow world,' whose slowness first becomes a distinct quality in retrospect, outweighs the excitement about gains in speed."[2] Despite this polarization of opinion, images of majestic rotor blades partly submerged in fog, or set off by striking cloud cover, stimulate an abiding fascination. Aerial photographers have eagerly drawn on the semitechnic, semiorganic appeal of these insect-like figures—reminiscent of the gangly shape of the crane fly or daddy longlegs—and been transfixed by their elegant, instinctive choreography. It is these images that inform my interest in wind power arts and advertising.

By cutting a wide swath and taking a transnational view of how photography and wind power intersect, I aim to give a preliminary outline of the transformations heralded by the renewable energy transition. Two interrelated questions animate this study, and for the sake of clarity I will address them in sequence. The first is, What rhythms and temporalities separate wind power infrastructures from the scaffolding of oil culture? And the second is, What can we glean, from photographic depictions of these new object-sites, about the impact of clean energy on the human realm of sensation and its affect world? In looking at wind power photography, I want to draw attention to the optical and practical aesthetics of wind energy infrastructure by asking which desires, affects, and consumption styles are produced or queried in the visual archive on the subject.[3]

My investigation rests on two presuppositions that are central to recent conceptual work on infrastructure and affect theory. Wind power is as much about assembling towers and turbines as it is about forging an aesthetic imagination of the atmosphere as an energy resource and about staging an ecstatic dissolution into the inexhaustible force of nature. In foregrounding the symbolic dimension of wind power's industrial framework, I build on Brian Larkin's "poetics" of infrastructure, which manifests itself when the "form" of infrastructural technologies "is loosened from technical function."[4] The form of wind turbines, disengaged from the specific mechanisms by which they generate electricity, materializes a set of symbolic narratives about the future of the planet as well as the temporality of humankind's industrial experience within geological deep time. Moreover, the poetry of wind energy infrastructure operates at the visual level to mount a convincing rebuttal to the visibility thesis, which states that infrastructure remains undetectable until it fails, malfunctions, or breaks down—as is the case, to be sure, with catastrophically disabled nuclear power plants (Fukushima, Three Mile Island) or compromised oil pipelines (Deepwater Horizon, Exxon Valdez).[5] The form of wind power infrastructure is inextricable from the sensations, attachments, and fantasies—which, with Kathleen Stewart, we might collectively term "ordinary affects"—evoked by wind power technologies.[6] As I aim to show, the intensities generated by these hyperperceptible modes of attention—to landscape, technology, and the self, in short, to life itself—are lodged in quietly resonant camera images of wind power turbines in locations ranging from Palm Springs to Amsterdam.

A different way to configure wind power is to focus on what I call its poetic ultrasound, that is, on its atmosphere and aura as constitutive of the artistry of low-energy living, with its emphasis on the pleasure of knowing that one is doing the right thing to protect the planet and on the comfort that the best way to achieve more is to accomplish less; reduced effort—less traveling, less work, less commuting, and so on—is, in this reading, a source of inspiration rather than guilt. I begin by locating the appeal of wind power photographs in the manifold pleasures they encode, which mark a new stage in the visual history of energy technology. If photos of oil rigs, derricks, and pipelines as scepters of sovereignty over nature materialize a violation of the seas and land surface, images of wind turbines capitalize on phallic fantasies as symbols of sexual desire, that is, of a productive yet deeply reverential communion with nature. To make sense of how this emerging infrastructure might shed new light on nonanthropocentric imaginations of resources, I take a brief stab at an object-oriented ontology of wind power through Heidegger and Timothy Morton. In engaging more deeply with the infrastructure of wind power, the semiotics of the atmosphere offer a helpful path. I want to bring Gernot Böhme's theory of the atmosphere to bear on the photography of wind power because it sharpens the contrast between the factual and the atmospheric power of art. To perceive the photograph of a wind turbine aesthetically, which I suggest is the only way to perceive it, is to open up one's senses to its poetic ultrasound, namely, the sum of sensations related to landscape, acoustics, figurative dynamics, and color intrinsic to the atmosphere generated by wind power. In the second part of the essay, I recruit several photographers, known and obscure, as witnesses to the performative aesthetics of wind energy infrastructure before settling on three key elements of an infrastructural poetics (autonomy, temporality, and sound) that add an ethical dimension to my aesthetically driven argument. It is a circuitous, somewhat eccentric analytical design that seeks to pinpoint guiding questions rather than adjudicate a definitive debate.

Infrastructural Porn: The Erotics of Ironwood

Over a decade after Patricia Yeager's field-founding call to consider literary production in relation to the dominant energy regimes from which it emerged, wind power remains a blind spot of energy humanities.[7] This is surprising if we consider that a critical approach to past and present petrocultures inevitably presupposes at the very least an inchoate understanding of how a postcarbon future might serve as an antidote to the toxicity of oil. While solar energy has recently surfaced in energy scholarship as a central paradigm of technocultural history,[8] much remains to be said about the infrastructure of wind power, especially since wind farms are bulkier and therefore more likely than solar panels to feature in everyday fields of vision.

Importantly, wind turbines are often comforting to look at in a way that sets them far apart from the melancholy, entropic sublime of oil photography.[9] Whereas Mitch Epstein in *American Power* juxtaposes refinery towers with cemetery crosses in the same image,[10] wind energy photographers are invested in selling, not mourning, a product and its quotidian philosophy; in other words, they seek to enlist the viewer as buyer, consumer, and admirer of wind power. To this end, images of wind power challenge perceptions of energy production by foregoing the endemic negativity of energy photography in the period following the OPEC oil embargo of 1973, eschewing the apocalyptic tones of environmental photography after the 1989 Exxon Valdez oil spill, and outshining the aesthetic flatness of photovoltaic parks.

Were we to ask, with W. J. T. Mitchell, what wind power images want, the answer is evident.[11] They want to be kissed, and there is no need for me to comment on the explicitness and obscenity of the phallic fantasy such images invoke. At a more abstract level, in disavowing the ignoble sensorium that attaches to fossil fuels, including abjection, nausea, or disgust—the kind of "ugly feelings" that Sianne Ngai theorized as generative of a "general state of obstructed agency"[12]—wind power photographs exude an overpowering aesthetic of neediness. For, although they aspire to be liked, in the most basic sense, by valorizing a romanticized vision of technonatural symbiosis, they also push for a major rethink of private energy habits. They do so, I suggest, by activating an erotics of technological infrastructure through spectacular shots that embed wind turbine trunks and their canopy of rotor blades into a natural setting to which they seemingly and seamlessly belong and where they can unfold the full drama of their jouissance—a mixed enjoyment in environmental justice, a clear conscience, and a commodified life. Wind art as a genre is becoming increasingly vulnerable to an insatiable public desire for a kind of infrastructural porn that at every level aims to make the viewer rejoice in the virtuous pleasure of guiltless energy production.

Wind power photography achieves its erotics of energy by destabilizing the tension (a foundational one for the genre of fossil fuel photos) between a purportedly pristine nature and the poisoned capillaries of petroleum infrastructure. Specifically, the material form of wind turbines themselves effectively conflates man-made alloys (steel, fiberglass) with natural textures. In reference to the striking metonymy contained in the title of Tom Pendleton's 1966 novel *The Iron Orchard*—a book about oil derricks and the lives of the men who operate them—we might refer to the hybrid object of the natural-looking wind turbine as a species of ironwood, a type of tree or plant known for the dense wood structure that supports it. Applied to the turbines that form a wood "farm" (another term that naturalizes industrial wind power plants), the half-metallic, half-organic construct brings into uneasy conjunction the imaginaries of infrastructure, technology, and the natural world.

An Object-Oriented Ontology of Wind Power

The relation between human beings and the energy obtained from nature is deeply transformed by the shift from subsoil carbons to renewables. If carbon extraction objectifies the world for the benefit of the human subject, turning to readily available resources privileges a less hierarchical relationship that echoes the tenets of object-oriented ontology. Among other things, object-oriented ontology affirms the dignity of all entities, dislodging the human from the center of being. Despite their unmistakably anthropogenic provenance, by using a primitive, noninvasive technology wind turbines force us into a nonanthropocentric thinking of our surrounding life worlds. Much like the hyperobjects theorized by Timothy Morton, wind turbines "can be detected in a space that consists of interrelationships between aesthetic properties of objects"[13]—in this case, the symmetrical power of energy systems and assemblages that dwarf their human operators, look down on them, and seem to merely tolerate maintenance workers' puny presence rather than being subservient to them.

To Heidegger, modern technology "puts to nature the unreasonable demand that it supply energy that can be extracted and stored as such."[14] By not permitting any significant storage of energy, wind power is, in that sense, less demanding, reflecting instead a premodern dependency on nature—unlike, say, subsoil carbon extraction or even hydroelectric dam systems.[15] The moment James Watt patented the steam engine in 1784, he paved the way for the expansion of coal extraction and ushered in the "primitive artificial intelligence"—the conquest of nature through blunt force—of the industrial age.[16] Counterclockwise to the rise of carbonized industrialization, wind power reverses the transition from mechanical to thermal energy, erasing the steam and combustion engine in favor of slow energy from microcurrents in the atmosphere.

And yet the wind farm encodes a paradox. In one sense, rotor blades spinning furiously in the wind substantiate conceptions of nature as an untrammeled force. In another sense, however, the leisurely rotation speed and geometrical harmony of the design appear to withstand the whimsical pressure of the intermittent winds. A similar tension becomes most apparent in the perceptual turmoil brought about by the steamship. "Where sail ships worked with nature and responded to its vicissitudes," John Mack writes in his cultural history of the sea, "by the mid-nineteenth century steam had allowed ships to cut their course directly through the waves. The experience of the sea was to change utterly. . . . Man's relationship to elemental nature was irrevocably changed, or, as some regarded it, 'violated.'"[17] "It is worth remarking," Mack continues, that the idea of sailing with the wind is also entirely consistent with the theological imperative of submitting to God's will."[18]

The Aesthetic Life of Air: Distance, Aura, Ultrasound

We tend to give little thought to the atmosphere, the "thin blue line" that "has transformed our planet from a barren lump of rock into a world full of life."[19] Only sixty-two miles of air separates the earth's surface from the edge of space, yet this deceptively fragile layer is suffused with power. Wind energy systems derive electricity from atmospheric currents at the lower end of the atmosphere, while in its upper region, the ionosphere, electrically charged particles from the sun bounce off Earth's magnetic field. Aside from its meaning in meteorology and climate dynamics, atmosphere understood as an ambient mood or disposition is embedded in aesthetic economies and the language of art.

What the German philosopher Gernot Böhme terms New Aesthetics no longer derives its power from the traditional fields of art and aesthetic discourse. "To the aesthetics of a work of art," Böhme writes, "we can now add with equal right the aesthetics of everyday life, the aesthetics of commodities, and a political aesthetics."[20] To get a better grasp of these new categories, Böhme deploys the concept of the atmosphere; the artwork, he asserts, is no longer merely a form of mimetic representation like a painting or a sculpture, but an atmospheric space or a space tinged with atmosphere. To the extent that it is brought into being by inhaling this atmosphere, the work of art substantiates a performative aesthetics. Central to the atmosphere of wind power is the naturalization of the technologically modified landscape by setting infrastructure apart from nature, on the one hand, and bringing landscape and infrastructure into a harmonious conjunction, on the other. What makes this atmosphere unique and amenable to both artful and everyday aesthetics is its aloofness and distance.

Compared to the "hot" technologies of coal mining, oil drilling, and hydraulic fracturing ("fracking") in shale rock, or the geothermal power derived from Earth's subsurface heat, wind power is a "cold" form of energy, both in the sense that temperatures are lower at the height of a typical rotor and because the design of wind turbines channels an aesthetics of detachment. To invoke another contrastive pair coined by Aristotle, if oil and gasoline are "wet," wind power embodies a "dry" elemental principle, with all the wryness and remoteness the term implies. "I am smart, efficient, and can survive anywhere apart from space," the turbine seems to say. "I move without human prompting, and I'm difficult to take down. Millions of years of heat and pressure on ancient organic materials have produced viscous, foul-smelling hydrocarbons that might be denser in energy than I am, but they can't compete with my smooth body and fresh radiance, or my small footprint on the land; besides, I will outlive them all. I am not held hostage by foreign markets; in fact I can go on producing after the turbines around me have broken down or been made idle."[21]

The atmosphere around a wind turbine as an ordinary work of art emits an ineffable and yet recognizable radiance. Its streamlined, clean design generates what Walter Benjamin would refer to as an "aura" and Adorno as something "more"—a halo, a beyond, a nimbus traced and retraced with each rotation.[22] Benjamin defines the aura as the confluence of the near and the far. To look at a mountain range across the horizon or to behold a branch that throws its shadow onto a resting observer, he explains, is to breathe in the aura of these mountains or of this branch.[23] A wind turbine offers both. Distance (or the appearance of it) and the closeness that comes from knowing that the contraption we're looking at cannot be too far, a mixed experience complicated by the overwhelming multitude effect of a wind park.

To fully become immersed in an aura, Böhme cautions us, requires a state of rest and inactivity, a state of physical relaxation that doesn't irritate the atmosphere of the entity under our gaze. Böhme's imagination of contemplating windmills with the air of someone who's been mesmerized by them intersects intriguingly with my own observation that regimes of renewable energy like wind or solar power gradually stimulate new—more casual, energy-preserving—systems of labor and repose. If energy used to be synonymous with the violence of breaking up rock or chipping at a coalface, renewable energy augurs a societal movement away from intense (physical) labor, as well as from the protestant ethic and spirit of "carboniferous capitalism"[24] that gave it birth, toward more leisurely paths to self-fulfillment.

Aeolian Photography

Much of the early photographic archive of hydrocarbon extraction and processing infrastructures is shot through with the minimalist, static formalism of New Objectivity—the postexpressionist, decidedly unpoetic German art movement that informed Bernd and Hilla Becher's matter-of-fact documentation of mining structures in the 1960s and 1970s. In the Bechers' austere photographs of gas containers, headframes, and other extraction equipment, often on the eve of their demolition, the anonymous forms of energy infrastructure are wrested away both from their natural backdrops and from human control. The banal aesthetics of New Objectivity seeped into the New Topographic movement, a term coined by William Jenkins in 1975 to describe images of natural landscapes that were increasingly eroded by industrial development.[25] It is in this tradition that Richard Misrach and Mitch Epstein have documented energy facilities and equipment, adding bruised, pestilent color schemes to better expose the energy extraction site, with forensic precision and unalloyed condemnation, as an abhorrent crime scene of industrial modernity. Both New Objectivity and New Topographics imagine carbon energy infrastructures on the decline and harness the power of photography to mourn their passing. Antithetical to this lugubrious tone, wind power photography is more forcefully optimistic and more overtly aestheticized, in line with a more palatable version of sublimity than what was common to the techno-Gothic figurations of oil.

The genre of aeolian photography, by which I mean still images of wind parks set against natural environments that visualize the atmosphere as an energetic medium, is more widespread, I would wager, than the entire photographic archive dedicated to hydrocarbons. Partly because wind parks are more easily accessible to drone camera photographers than remote tar sands plants and offshore oil platforms, more energy-themed photographs have been shot over a much shorter span of time than ever before. The shift from a carbon-fueled economy to one powered by the sun and the wind, which only got underway over the last decade, compresses a century of energy representation into just a few years.

It is easy to understand the "serial" appeal shared by photography and wind energy infrastructure if we remember Benjamin's "The Work of Art in the Age of Mechanical Reproduction." More than any other kind of energy infrastructure, be it pump jacks, refineries, dams, or nuclear plants, wind turbines rarely make solo appearances. Their visual strength lies in numbers: 116 in the Rampion offshore wind park (West Sussex), 338 at Shepherds Flat Wind Farm near Arlington, Oregon. Certainly, Edward Burtynsky's photo of an army of pump jacks in Bakersfield, California, also pivots on the sublime of sheer agglomeration, as do other photos he has taken of discarded tires and other detritus of the fossil fuel age. Yet photographs of wind turbines enumerate a mass of objects just as much as they inspire pleasurable states of virtue and benevolence, quite the opposite of Burtynsky's guilt-ridden aesthetics of petrodisgust.

With the sense of culpability about the damage wrought by fossil fuels also comes a tendency to frame extraction photography as an act of revelation, in line with the visibility thesis, which posits that infrastructure comes into view following its malfunction or, in this case, its exorbitant environmental and human cost. In oil photography, petroleum is literally excavated from its submerged location in the collective subconscious like an undetected, untreated hematoma, only after the catastrophic event of a serious rupture. In contrast, the photographic approach to wind turbines is predicated on their immediate visibility, which brings its own set of demands. Above all, the images invite a subliminal reaction of familiarity and affection. For wind turbines are shaped, despite their striking size, like the smallest of toy windmills that the smallest of babies can play with. In addition, the gyroscopic movement of the blades around the rotor hub evokes the motion of a spinning top, one of the most ancient artifacts in human history and a source of primitive pleasure. Through these and other associations, wind turbines perform what Böhme would call essential "aesthetic work."[26] In what follows I propose six categories for navigating the aesthetic work of wind power through the archive I have collected: energy transition, scale and proportions, the art of lighting, the dark romanticism of steel ruins, commercial photography, and a rediscovery of the sea as a result of the sector's offshore expansion.

Energy-themed visual art often capitalizes on the violent attraction of picturing energy regimes side by side, as if caught in a battle between the future and the past. To mark the transition from an agricultural economy to subsoil carbons in the American Midwest, the regionalist painter Thomas Hart Benton (1889–1975) placed ranches and oil derricks in the same frame. In his autobiographical film *A Life on Our Planet* (2020), the British broadcaster and natural historian David Attenborough shows herds of bison roaming underneath gigantic wind turbines. In this idyllic view, wind power landscapes are reconfigured to overlap with cultivated or gardened space, so earthlings can double-crop their land by harvesting electricity while simultaneously grazing cattle or growing corn. The stark iconography of energy transition also informs some of the most striking photographs of wind parks. Most such images document the sudden appearance of individual turbines in unspoiled areas and residential rural landscapes.

Some also dramatize a different kind of shift, namely, the transformative impact of wind energy on the familiar spaces of art. In "The Kite" (fig. 9.1), an image set in the California desert, the Dutch photographer Erwin Olaf outfits a mother and daughter out for a picnic in 1960s clothing and hairstyles but has them gaze across a field of wind turbines that were only built in the 1980s. In an Edward Hopper painting of the 1950s or 1960s, the same figures would have gazed, alienated and lost, into a flat horizon, but here their view is blocked by the thick forest of towers and rotor blades. Setting the models in an anachronistic setting speaks not only to issues of timeliness and belatedness in how energy regimes establish themselves but also to how new infrastructures modify mythic American landscapes by filling up previously empty spaces.

The American Kim Stringfellow applies a similarly contrastive lens in her depiction of a desert wind park overlooking the neighboring boneyard, an index to the bygone fossil fuel era (fig. 9.2). Unusually for a photo of energy

Fig. 9.1. Erwin Olaf, *The Kite*, from the series *Palm Springs*, 2018. © Erwin Olaf, courtesy Edwynn Houk Gallery, New York. Reproduced with permission of the artist.

and transport infrastructure, almost two-thirds of the image consists of nothing but clouds and air. The disproportionate attention to the sky in this photo foregrounds the new visual valence of the atmosphere in a world where it has ceased to be the backdrop to polluting aircraft, spinning instead the sluggardly wheels of the renewables revolution. In a project on energy that shifts between Oildale, Bakersfield, and the San Gorgonio Pass Wind Farm outside Palm Springs, San Francisco photographer David Gardner takes his cue from Burtynsky and Misrach to both condemn the irreparable damage inflicted by oil extraction and illustrate a more reparative stage in the history of the Anthropocene. At Bakersfield, randomly erected oil wells evoke the shameful scrapyard of an outdated energy world; what awaits visitors of the Palm Springs wind park is quite the opposite—neat rows of turbines that foreshadow nothing less than a smart, efficient, expeditious technoreforestation of the planet.

Considering that, aside from hydroelectric dams, the wind turbine is by far the largest energy-harnessing construction, it makes sense that it should pose logistical challenges. Cameras attached to mini drones have provided a handy, fittingly electric instrument in documenting and promoting the transition to sustainable fuels, particularly among German photographers. The Berlin-based photographer Paul Langrock has taken drone camera shots of Brandenburg wind parks for many years, paying unusual attention to the way turbine components are assembled on site, often from the rotor tip perspective, which allows him to capture the nearby landscape from a more unearthly, vertigo-inducing angle (fig. 9.3). Ulrich Mertens, a Hamburg-based

Fig. 9.2. Kim Stringfellow, *The Boneyard with Tehachapi Wind Farm, Mojave, CA*, 2015. © Kim Stringfellow. Reproduced with permission of the artist.

photographer, has also taken pictures from the top of gearboxes, often zooming in on the workers performing maintenance work on the tower underneath. To be sure, the resulting reversal of perspective magnifies construction details and replicates in this sense the strategies of classical industry photography. And yet the sheer height of the towers engenders a boundary aesthetic on the rim of technology and nature that clashes with the dead-tech assemblages favored by Bernd and Hilla Becher and other members of the Düsseldorf School. Simply put, the rotor's-eye view reveals what the transition away from fossil fuels is presumed to protect in the first place: expansive vistas of unspoiled natural beauty, whose aesthetic value as a welcome by-product of sustainable energy is at least implied, and at most forcefully stylized in the bulk of wind power photography. So unabashed is the aestheticizing impetus, that before long the recreational value of wind power landscapes—and the appeal of wind farms themselves as a tourist attraction, a marvel from afar, and a new climbable feature of the landscape—will likely be used on a large scale to boost public acceptance of wind power as a mainstream energy resource.

Since wind turbines can reach over 450 feet tall, weather-dependent lighting conditions largely determine whether the turbine towers and blades shimmer or flash before the camera lens. Over the last decade, photographers working

Fig. 9.3. Paul Langrock, *Aufbau Enercon WEA E126 im Windpark Feldheim*, 2019. © Paul Langrock. Reproduced with permission of the artist.

with light and shadow effects have created a romanticized, melodramatic photo archive of wind energy. In their thoughtfully composed and heavily retouched pictures we recognize various associations triggered by individual towers and rows of turbines, from military formations to ridiculously oversized crossroad signs or snow-covered summit crosses. Photographers like Deon Reynolds and Stephen Penland often pick compositions that fix the viewers' gaze on a full moon or spectacular cloud formations that effectuate a somewhat facile, perhaps unearned, natural aesthetics of wind power. That being said, even this contrived immersion in a pastoral world has the commendable ability to make the viewer pause to consider a more judicious, conservationist approach to the environment, energy, and human needs. Few of us will get the chance to linger under the rotors of a wind turbine for long enough to start wondering whether and why we are driving an electric or a gasoline-powered vehicle, to notice how the landscape has changed—or indeed whether it is the pointy, filigree blade bouquets on the horizon that nudge us to acknowledge the landscape in the first place.

Notably, the wind turbines that feature in the abovementioned photos are in mint condition—newly built, young, or well-preserved. To explore the dark side of wind energy, we must turn to a different group of artists, to motifs and locations that dare ask what happens at the end of these giants' life cycle. Aging turbines can be too costly to maintain and operate, and as many of

Fig. 9.4. Mitch Epstein, *Palm Springs, California III*, 2007, from *American Power* (Göttingen: Steidl, 2009), 46. © Mitch Epstein. Reproduced with permission of the artist.

them approach twenty years of use, they are decommissioned and dismantled into a cumbersome new kind of industrial trash.[27] In Mitch Epstein's *American Power*, derelict wind turbines portend a time when renewable energy infrastructures will visibly and spectacularly fail as well, albeit with far less devastating consequences than a leaking pipeline or nuclear core meltdown. In one picture, a battered turbine in the foreground of a vast wind park foreshadows the fate of all wind power infrastructures (fig. 9.4). For they are no less fragile and at risk of wear and tear than drilling towers and offshore rigs. Epstein's image suggests that disused, rusty wind turbines will soon be no less common in the California desert than abandoned pump jacks, tanks, pipelines, and wells. It also reminds us that in talking about the aesthetic life of infrastructure we must talk about its death, too. Even as we relearn to harness wind energy, the materials we use are far from harmless, and we might, at one point, have to use more energy to maintain the turbine fleet than it will ever be able to produce over its limited lifetime.

Edward Burtynsky, an environmental photographer known mainly for his aerial photos of petroleum infrastructures, took for his 2013 book on water a rare photo of the port of Rotterdam. The image includes not only

Fig. 9.5. Edward Burtynsky, *Flood Control Levee, Maasvlakte, Rotterdam, the Netherlands*, 2011. Photograph © Edward Burtynsky, courtesy Nicholas Metivier Gallery, Toronto. Reproduced with permission of the artist.

the Slofterdam wind farm, a popular subject among wind photo enthusiasts, but also BP refineries and the Maeslant storm surge barrier, a unique flood defense system that protects Rotterdam's low-lying coastal zone from sea levels rising as a result of climate change (fig. 9.5). At first glance, the photo accentuates the urgency of the transition to renewables, which among other things will phase out oil refineries and dams, and singles out the floodgates in particular as a cataclysmic consequence of the damage caused by carbon-driven industries. Seen in the technopessimist context of his work, Burtynsky's photo arguably also puts pressure on the notion that wind energy will solve the problem of resource scarcity and global warming. His photograph makes visible what will soon become "stranded assets," the term used in the energy industry to denote the infrastructural vestiges of a hydrocarbon economy, in this case handling and storing facilities at ports. This, too, is rooted in a noteworthy aesthetic tradition. Out-of-service gasoline stations inspired a memorable visual iconography of energy infrastructures coming into disuse in Eric Tabuchi's *TwentySix Abandoned Gasoline Stations* (2008). As early as 1935, Walker Evans recorded similar detritus in "A Graveyard and Steel Mill in Bethlehem, Pennsylvania," where the chipped, weather-beaten headstones in the foreground adumbrate the ultimate decay of the industrial infrastructure in the distance.

To round off this overview, let's consider advertising campaigns for offshore wind farms, before arriving at my final point about how wind power aesthetics is driving a rediscovery of the sea.[28] Because wind turbine fleets look incongruous far offshore, photographers are tempted to shoot the towers as if they weren't so much industrial objects as natural formations, like a flooded, half-submerged prehistoric forest. A series of photos by the Danish photographer Tristan Stedman for the marketing department of the wind turbine manufacturer Vestas Wind Systems is a fitting case in point. The images aim to familiarize viewers with specific innovations in wind power technology, but they do so by detaching wind energy from the actual function of the turbines and stylizing it instead as a "natural experience." Stedman's camera focuses attention on individual, both organic and technofuturistic, components of the wind turbine. We are not being sold a high-tech form of electricity generation here but an inquisitive, appreciative view of nature and of the nature-like texture and aerodynamic designs of wind turbines.

Ben Harvey's photographs of the Rampion wind farm on the south coast of England (2017), a recently commissioned facility in the English Channel, offer an apt synthesis of the ways in which offshore wind power has launched a rediscovery of the seas as sites of aesthetic gratification. The location of the wind park in a zone of retreat for retirees, near the seaside resort of Brighton, vividly illustrates the controversy around erecting new turbines in wealthy areas that derive their attraction in large measure from the promise of pristine natural views. On the positive side, since the EON wind farm is only thirteen kilometers off the coast, it can easily be explored by boat—in tours kindly provided by the operator—and photographed from the sea level. Harvey's images are flanked by personal impressions of the facility that aim to convey the effects of the turbine towers on spectators at their base. Whether or not he succeeds is debatable; what I want to highlight instead are the aesthetic issues his images only obliquely articulate. How far away do we need to be from a natural terrain before we can regard it as a landscape, with all the ocular delectation the term implies? Are the rotor blades of a wind turbine "aesthetic" only from a certain distance, and much less so when they spin and whistle eerily above one's head?

The Future Is a Ferris Wheel: Slowness, Leisure, and the Moral Sublime

Unlike these intrepid artists, on a daily basis we are far more likely to encounter the photograph of a wind farm than to actually walk or drive past a wind turbine. Indeed, the natural aesthetics of wind power is not fundamentally about a direct experience of nature but about an idea of energy production and consumption within it, an idea that aeolian photographs get across especially well. Put simply, wind power is a technology, an art form, and a lifestyle. And much like Ed Rusha's photographs of gasoline stations in the 1960s, wind farm images epitomize a way of life.[29] If gas stations encapsulated modern mobility, wind turbines are looking down on a quieter, more place-bound world. They also return us to a lifestyle of "milling" (rather than dashing) around, a more pacific way of life that predates the carbon terraforming of the planet.

Photographs of wind parks are not representations of energy infrastructure so much as indexes to the static, sedate experience of wind power embedded in an infrastructure whose central dynamic—the slow rotation around an axis—conveys an aesthetic of idleness, rest, and reassuring permanence. Wind power renders obsolete a set of inherited rituals, including fast mobility and cheap consumption, as well as a body of instinctual knowledge about the surmountability of space-time limitations, for instance, by traveling from London to New York in two hours, and so on. The energy of the atmosphere opens up new views on the vastness of the natural world and its deep time, which in turn require new modes of exploration. The sedate predispositions associated with wind power may in the end be of the same order as—and likely to undo—the habits fostered by gasoline and plastics over the last century and a half.

The photogenic aesthetics of wind power convey an ethics of human restraint and vulnerability, an ethos of humility that honors nature by embracing its moods as a welcome character-building contingency. While systemic instability continues to cast a shadow over the future of wind power, the same feature also signals a closer, less guarded relationship between humanity and the planet. The challenge in speeding up energy transition and preventing climate crisis, the anthropologist David McDermott Hughes writes in the *Boston Review*, is learning to tolerate intermittency and rationing, much the same way the coronavirus pandemic has accustomed us to lockdown, blackout, and pause.[30]

While exhibiting the sublime scale and calming rhythms of wind energy, photography on the subject also removes us from the familiar realm of petro-industrialization (no highways or cities in sight), thus documenting a recent shift in social status symbolism from luxury mobility to local leisure. I will conclude by speculating on how wind turbines illustrate and energize this socioethical transition by transforming three key factors in the relation of self to the world: autonomy, sound, and the perception of time.

First, one emerging answer as to why modern wind power has made such an immediate impact on everyday life, and why indeed it has been embraced so readily by the photographic medium, concerns the self-reliance implicit in its technology. Combining a sense of submission to natural forces with full control over energy-generating infrastructure produces an attractive system of holistic harmony that can be understood without much imaginative effort.

If the turbine on the one hand defies natural order by putting up an obstacle in the path of strong winds, on the other hand it also complies with that order, in that it remains unable to flout the weather by moving higher or lower, rotating counterclockwise, and so on. On the whole, as a decentralized form of energy production, wind carries connotations of energy independence at the end of a century that witnessed several boom-and-bust cycles in global energy markets. With the coronavirus pandemic further weakening the demand for oil, public attention has shifted to resources that are less liable to disruption, require less maintenance, and are therefore at lower risk of collapse as a result of pandemic lockdowns.

Second, wind power serves as a noise-muffling cloak able to absorb the industrial din of combustion engines and resource extraction. We shouldn't, of course, regard wind power as unchanging across its different applications. Dutch paintings of rural windmills amid hushed landscapes couldn't be further from the sound and fury of sailing images in some of the most iconic of Turner's paintings.[31] And yet, even though they operate by harnessing the atmosphere—the medium that acts like a vibrating drum to send sound across space—and emit various sounds themselves, wind turbines appear engulfed in silence. Third, the streamlined design of wind turbines resonates with the images etched on our minds by the bicycle renaissance and its attendant shift to slow mobility. The blades turn in much the same way the spikes on a bicycle wheel do, when contrasted with the wheels of a car: slower, more thoughtfully, cutting a more meandering path.[32] The moods of the photographs discussed above reflect analogous ideals: tranquility, patience, peace of mind. Taken seriously, the knowledge that wind energy production cannot deplete the resources of the atmosphere—much the same way that the laws of physics don't require fuel to set a bicycle in motion—forges a new perception of time—of urgency, dueness, fear of missing out—that pivots on a different durée in both human-psychic and geological terms.

It is impossible not to notice that ideas of slowness and tranquility are invested with moral purpose, particularly after several decades' worth of petrophotography has mourned the damages wrought by the global addiction to hydrocarbons. As the variety of aeolian pictures analyzed here makes clear, it requires little effort to stylize wind power as the source of a new movement for environmental justice and a new wave of virtuous asceticism.[33] Thanks to its most basic principle, wind power places us at a refreshing distance from the dark allure of subsoil carbons and the concerns of Earth's surface. To imagine oneself 450 feet in the air is to occupy a simpler space of discipline and moral clarity. Crucially, then, the natural aesthetic of wind power is entwined with a latent ethical imperative, cofueling a wholesale revolution to which the world seems to be readily converted. Whatever disquiet might reside in some photographs by Epstein or Burtynsky is becalmed by the general sense that wind power images want to be seen—as an occasion for pleasurable wonder—and seen, too, as being or doing something good.

Through their interest in a more rarified experience of energy, sublime images of wind power valorize both aesthetic and ethical principles, obscuring to some degree the challenges of a transition away from stable energy networks toward a more intermittent supply. Some will be tempted to see in the photographic infatuation with the turbines' harmless forms a somewhat naive or sanctimonious approach to renewable energy. After all, part of the infrastructure of wind power is of course concealed underground. To balance intermittent resources like wind and solar, long-distance transmission corridors are needed to run over a wide geography. High-voltage power lines may emit a different, less poetic kind of ultrasound, and buried cables in particular could reaffirm the visibility-through-failure approach to industrial infrastructure. It remains to be seen to what extent the turn to wind power will go beyond, and beneath, the aesthetic rediscovery and ethical inscription of the lower (from our terrestrial viewpoint nonetheless spiritually heightening) atmosphere.

Notes

1. National Research Council, *Environmental Impacts of Wind-Energy Projects* (Washington, DC: National Academies Press, 2007), 97.

2. Harmut Rosa, *Social Acceleration: A New Theory of Modernity* (New York: Columbia University Press, 2013), 41.

3. More so than other media of cultural production around renewable energy regimes, photographic emblems of wind power merit special attention, on two grounds. First, the wind energy sector has benefited in no small measure from the persuasive power of travel, industrial, and commercial photography. Second, underpinning the sublime aerial aesthetics of electricity-producing wind parks are advances in battery technologies and the popularization of the airborne camera as an accessible tool of remote, unmanned image making. On the relation between photographic technology and its impact on the aesthetic of energy photography, see Georgiana Banita, "Photography," in *Fueling Culture: 101 Words for Energy and Environment*, ed. Imre Szeman, Jennifer Wenzel, and Patricia Yaeger (New York: Fordham University Press, 2017), 263–66.

4. Brian Larkin, "The Politics and Poetics of Infrastructure," *Annual Review of Anthropology* 42, no. 1 (2013): 335.

5. See Susan Leigh Star, "The Ethnography of Infrastructure," *American Behavioral Scientist* 43, no. 3 (1999): 377–91.

6. See Kathleen Stewart, *Ordinary Affects* (Durham, NC: Duke University Press, 2007).

7. Patricia Yeager, "Editor's Column: Literature in the Ages of Wood, Tallow, Coal, Whale-Oil, Gasoline, Atomic Power, and Other Energy Sources," *PMLA* 126, no. 2 (2011): 305–26.

8. See, for instance, Gregory Lynall, *Imagining Solar Energy: The Power of the Sun in Literature, Science and Culture* (London: Bloomsbury, 2020).

9. Michael Truscello, *Infrastructural Brutalism: Art and the Necropolitics of Infrastructure* (Cambridge, MA: MIT Press, 2020).

10. Mitch Epstein, *American Power* (Göttingen: Steidl, 2009).

11. See W. J. T. Mitchell, *What Do Pictures Want? The Lives and Loves of Images* (Chicago: University of Chicago Press, 2010).

12. Sianne Ngai, *Ugly Feelings* (Cambridge, MA: Harvard University Press, 2005), 3.

13. Timothy Morton, *Hyperobjects: Philosophy and Ecology after the End of the World* (Minneapolis: University of Minnesota Press, 2013), 1.

14. Martin Heidegger, "The Question concerning Technology," in *The Question concerning Technology and Other Essays* (New York: Garland, 1977), 14. The visibility theory, which dictates that infrastructures function unobtrusively until they break down, seems indebted to Heidegger's distinction between tools (which operate silently while we're occupied with something else) and broken tools, which abruptly become noticeable and nakedly present.

15. See also Karen Pinkus, *Fuel: A Speculative Dictionary* (Minneapolis: University of Minnesota Press, 2016), 108.

16. Morton, *Hyperobjects*, 5.

17. John Mack, *The Sea: A Cultural History* (London: Reaktion Books, 2011), 34.

18. Mack, *The Sea*, 47.

19. Gabrielle Walker, *An Ocean of Air: A Natural History of the Atmosphere* (London: Bloomsbury, 2007), 1.

20. Gernot Böhme, *The Aesthetics of Atmospheres* (London: Routledge, 2018), 23.

21. The reason why some turbines sit idle has to do with the blistering pace of wind farm construction, which has outpaced transmission and grid updates.

22. It is important to note that Benjamin describes the aura as a form of atmosphere or a gas that can be inhaled.

23. Walter Benjamin, "The Work of Art in the Age of Mechanical Reproduction," in *Illuminations: Essays and Reflections* (New York: Schocken Books, 2007), 222–23.

24. Lewis Mumford, *Technics and Civilization* (1934; Chicago: University of Chicago Press, 2010), 158.

25. William Jenkins, *New Topographics: Photographs of a Man-Altered Landscape* (Rochester, NY: George Eastman House, 1975).

26. Böhme, *The Aesthetics of Atmospheres*, 16.

27. The aesthetic aura of wind turbines disguises some serious long-term effects of wind power. Steel towers and rotor blades cannot be easily recycled, nor are the concrete foundations of disused turbines easily crushed without recourse to on-site demolitions. Removing foundation pillars buried in the sea floor is, of course, even more challenging, and underwater detonations are more liable to cause injury and death among marine species. See Sarah K. Henkel, Robert M. Suryan, and Barbara A. Lagerquist, "Baseline Assessments of Seabirds, Marine Mammals, Sea Turtles and Benthic Communities on the Oregon Shelf," in *Marine Renewable Energy Technology and Environmental Interactions*, ed. Mark A. Shields and Andrew I. L. Payne (Heidelberg: Springer, 2014), 101.

28. Regarding wind power through the lens of modern advertising reveals one of its most unusual firsts: it is the first energy industry that advertises with production facilities instead of products. In the 1950s and 1960s, Chevron Oil focused its branding and advertisements on the service station and on cars themselves as

status and sex symbols. Wind energy companies and turbine manufacturers prefer to highlight instead the simple, recognizable design of the "electric windmill," a suitable strategy indeed for an Instagram-driven electronic age when virtually everyone is carrying an electric device at all times, be it a smartphone or a Juul.

29. Ed Ruscha, *Twentysix Gasoline Stations* (Alhambra, CA: Cunningham Press, 1969).

30. David McDermott Hughes, "To Save the Climate, Give Up the Demand for Constant Electricity," *Boston Review* (October 2020): 5. See also McDermott Hughes, *Energy without Conscience: Oil, Climate Change, and Complicity* (Durham, NC: Duke University Press, 2017).

31. Mack, *The Sea*, 32.

32. The blades of newer turbines turn more slowly than those of earlier models, partly to prevent avian deaths. See Lester Brown, *The Great Transition: Shifting from Fossil Fuels to Solar and Wind Energy* (New York: W. W. Norton, 2015), 89.

33. There is also an implication that wind power can atone for the past sins of a racist extraction economy. Given their wealth of wind, problematic zones of energy extraction such as Native American reservations are providing thousands of megawatts of generating capacity.

Chapter 10

✦

To Be Addressed by Nuclear Reactors

Radiation Exposure and the Aesthetics of Life Itself

Rahul Mukherjee

This essay surveys the aesthetic address of nuclear infrastructures in a wide range of media forms and genres. Brian Larkin has argued that there is an aesthetics to the way infrastructures address people who design and use them. This infrastructural address shapes sensory perceptions of humans and nudges them to make connections between their experiences and wider social arrangements.[1] To Larkin's point, I would add that mediation of infrastructures through documentaries, journalistic feature reports, fictional films, and television shows inflects the poetics of such an address by infrastructures. My goal is to relate infrastructural aesthetics with media aesthetics, where focusing on aesthetics is understood to be both (1) "a theory of culturally and historically embedded sensation and perception" and (2) the study of genre-based stylistic tendencies.[2] Particular media genres and forms emerge laden with specific aesthetic qualities, and such genre-based aesthetics influence the different ways in which nuclear reactors are represented.

Infrastructures like nuclear reactors do not just serve instrumental functions of nuclear energy production; they also have formal characteristics designed into them to perform discursive and political functions. The giant domes of nuclear reactors make them monumental infrastructures and sublime objects that hold out the promise of an energy-secure future for a nation on its way to development. The giant domes and the "clean emissions" (at the surface level in terms of white-colored water vapor emanating from chimneys) appear to a media person as objects and phenomena to be photographed and filmed so that they can be stored and represented as "the promise of infrastructure making that promise—as mode of political rationality—emotionally real."[3] The aesthetic address of infrastructures, their formal qualities, encourage particular ways of depicting them. For example, filmmakers might choose to use camera tilts to emphasize the height of the giant domes of a nuclear power plant, or intrigued by the secrecy of atomic reactors, some investigative journalists might decide to expose the precarious working conditions of nuclear workers inside the plant. These are different styles of infrastructural visibility performed by varied technopolitical regimes.

The question of the visibility and invisibility of infrastructures has been a crucial way of theorizing infrastructures. Geoffrey Bowker and Susan Leigh Star note that exaggerated displays of the monumentality of infrastructures is one kind of infrastructural visibility; to show intricate details that explain how infrastructures work on a day-to-day basis would be a demonstration of another kind of infrastructural visibility.[4] Therefore, it is important to study the depictions of nuclear reactors in a wide variety of fictional and nonfictional formats and genres to account for differing infrastructural (in) visibilities, including the invisibilities of nuclear radiations (alpha and beta particles, gamma rays) emitted by atomic plants.

In exploring mediations of nuclear reactors, this essay focuses on how laborers working every day in an atomic power plant apprehend their bodily exposure to radiation doses. In doing so, I draw from the emerging literature on "critical infrastructure studies," which has called for foregrounding people's phenomenological encounters with infrastructures in terms of occupational hazard and public health.[5] Gabrielle Hecht has noted that it is not just radiation or nuclear waste, which is imperceptible, but that the plight of nuclear workers, especially subcontract employees, has been made invisible in dominant mainstream media narratives.[6]

I analyze fiction films like *Silkwood* (dir. Mike Nichols, 1983) and *Grand Central* (dir. Rebecca Zlotowski, 2013), as well as a short film, *Nuclear Waste*, by Ukrainian filmmaker Miroslav Slaboshpitsky (2012), that demonstrate how working in a nuclear reactor makes radiogenic injury a part (or possibility) of life itself. These films, through innovative use of stylistic techniques, present the bodily encounters of workers with nuclear infrastructures. They create a corporeal cinema of body and senses that instigates visceral viewing experiences and makes audiences pay attention to aspects of relationality, affect, scale, labor, and maintenance in the mundane workings of infrastructures. This essay argues for studying the aesthetics of infrastructures and the aesthetics of various media forms and genres as a way to understand the aesthetic life of nuclear workers and, put another way, the aesthetics of life itself.

By "life itself," I not only mean the everyday life of workers at the nuclear plant but also gesture to the biopolitics of self-management the workers participate in (by walking in protective hazmat suites, carrying dosimeters, and taking showers to self-regulate radiation exposures) and the governance of their risky lives (including calculating workers' radioactive contamination) that atomic power plant authorities undertake. In conceptualizing "aesthetics of life itself," I borrow from Nikolas Rose's assertion that neoliberal regimes of governmentality have created conditions where the biological existence of human beings has become political in new ways.[7] Rose terms this biopolitics as the "politics of life itself," where governmentality is constructed around risk and security of human life rather than property and rights. Focusing on the "politics of life itself" in an atomic plant requires attending to the working conditions of laborers inside the reactor because radiation exposure (and hence risk) varies depending on which section of the plant (from the reactor core to the control room) the laborer is situated in. Aesthetics understood here as "forms determining what presents itself to experience" is related to politics understood as "what can be seen and what can be said about it."[8] Both nuclear radiation and the working conditions of nuclear laborers often remain invisible, and I argue that certain aesthetic practices can make perceptible (and palpable) sensory experiences that are kept hidden as constitutive of a nuclear politics that tries to manage the risks of a nuclear reactor.

In this essay, I move from mainstream journalistic representations of nuclear reactors to how narrative films mediate such infrastructural spaces. Secrecy protocols around atomic plants give rise to the figure of the whistleblower in Hollywood films of the 1970s and 1980s who transgresses regulatory protocols and leaks information about nuclear emissions, accidents, and faulty plant equipment. Examining the representations of nuclear workers in experimental documentaries and fictional films, I relate the political aesthetics of nuclear reactors to the aesthetics of (in)visibilities/secrecies of information, radiation, and precarious labor conditions prevailing within atomic power plants. Nuclear fallouts are massive infrastructural breakdowns that release very slowly disintegrating radioactive particles. Such an aesthetics of decay accompanies the mediation of nuclear reactors.

Secrecy Protocols and Whistleblowers

When the nuclear energy sector in India faces a credibility crisis owing to public apprehension about risks from nuclear reactors, the nuclear establishment tries to shift public opinion back in its favor by revealing some information. One such occasion happened post-Fukushima (after March 2011), when concerns were raised about the reactors being built at Koodankulam (in Tamil Nadu, in southern India) and journalist Pallava Bagla was allowed entry into the plant. Bagla has on earlier occasions been allowed entry into nuclear facilities. When I asked Bagla to explain his movements inside those facilities, he mentioned that there are restrictions: "When I am being led into a facility, if I am told that 'please, on the left side of the room we have stuff which we don't want to be shown, on the right side [stuff which] we want to be shown, so don't shoot left because left is national security issue,' that boundary you respect."[9] The unwritten protocols of "national security" continue to shape the movements of Bagla and his crew, making "right sides" transparent and leaving "left sides" opaque. The restriction on the movement of journalists importantly gestures to the negotiated act of access.[10] Such public relations campaigns where some select group of journalists are chosen to be given guided and restricted tours around the nuclear reactor premises is not limited to India. In 2018, seven years after the Fukushima disaster, TEPCO, which runs the atomic plants in Japan, expanded the power station tours for journalists and the general public to win back the goodwill lost soon after the nuclear fallout of 2011.[11]

National Geographic has also incorporated stories from inside nuclear power plants. The episode from the *Inside* series of National Geographic "Tarapur Nuclear Power Plant: Unlock Power" systematically takes viewers through the different parts of the reactor site based in Tarapur, India. Spectators first see the control room (where different factors/inputs are monitored to ensure they are within safety levels) and then the nuclear fuel loading area, after which the tour moves to the spent fuel storage tank and the turbine engine where electricity is produced and then finally the location where equipment is maintained. Whether it is Pallava Bagla for NDTV or the National Geographic reporter, both show us confident, elite nuclear engineers who are emphatic that they love their jobs and find their working conditions to be safe. However, these journalists do not converse with contract workers, the most vulnerable group in the nuclear industry.[12] In these feature reports, audiences get to hear expert opinions celebrating the safety features of nuclear power plants, but precarious nuclear workers remain voiceless.

Oftentimes, given the culture of secrecy, journalists are too beholden to experts for access to the nuclear facility site and information about nuclear power plants. Hence their reliance on official explanations from experts about nuclear matters. This privileging of the expert opinion is not to be found in Michael Madsen's sci-fi documentary *Into Eternity* (2010), where experts discussing the waste storage and treatment facility at Onkalo, Finland, do not seem to be sure or certain about what will happen to the nuclear waste in various futuristic scenarios. Madsen heightens that uncertainty in expert interviews as he lets the experts speak in halting pauses, refusing to cut away when the expert has stopped speaking, as if waiting for more clarification. A. Bowdoin Van Riper explains how the camera created bodily uncertainties of expert interviewees: "Madsen frequently holds the camera on the subject's [expert's] face, waiting—like a patient but disappointed teacher—for something more substantive."[13]

The experiences of an actual nuclear worker, Karen Silkwood, are the focus of the 1983 fictional film *Silkwood*. Silkwood worked in the Kerr-McGee nuclear power plant in Oklahoma. The film offers close-ups of Karen (played by Meryl Streep) and her friends' everyday work of manufacturing plutonium pellets to be used in reactors at Hanford, Washington. The film not only delves into the difficult working conditions and the exhausting hours of work and extra shifts that laborers have to endure but also explores the complexities of Karen's willingness to join the workers' union and later to espouse the role of a whistleblower when she decides to share information with a *New York Times* reporter regarding malpractices in the nuclear facility.

The Kerr-McGee Cimarron Fuel Fabrication Site creates what Scott Kirsch has called "geographies of unknowing."[14] Such geographies of unknowing generate a perpetual regime of imperceptibility, where nuclear workers do not fully know about the harmful bodily effects of handling plutonium. Karen is unhappy about the way the company's managers are handling the cases of workers who get contaminated while working in the plant. She is worried about her own health after she gets "cooked," the company lingo for when workers are contaminated. Furthermore, Karen discovers that some of the fuel rods produced for the breeder reactor are faulty. To cover up the inferior quality of the fuel rods, managers are retouching the negatives of X-rays of these rods. These worries and discoveries not only act as triggering events but also gradually firm up Karen's resolve to become a whistleblower.

In another Hollywood film, *China Syndrome* (1979, dir. James Bridges), audiences witness similar incidents of whistleblowing by an insider and then a cover-up by the plant officials, with the difference that this time the insider who tries to reveal the secrets of a nuclear facility is not a blue-collar worker but a manager, a nuclear scientist. Here Jack Godell (played by Jack Lemmon) is a shift supervisor who initially is shown to firmly believe in the safety protocols of the plant. Later Jack uncovers evidence that in order to save money, X-rays of welds in the nuclear reactor have been falsified. With the help of journalist Kimberly Wells (Jane Fonda) and cameraperson Richard (Michael Douglas), Jack is about to reveal to the general public the risks in the nuclear reactor, but he does not succeed in his endeavors.

Around the mid-1970s, the act of whistleblowing gained a lot of attention in the US mainstream media and politics, thanks to the popularization of the term "whistleblower" by Ralph Nader and the public praise of Daniel Ellsberg, who leaked top-secret Pentagon papers about the US intervention in Vietnam. The whistleblowers in both *China Syndrome* and *Silkwood* do not fully succeed in leaking secrets (via journalists) about the organizations they work for to the wider public. This might be because both *China Syndrome* and *Silkwood* were inspired by the real-life story of labor union activist Karen Silkwood, who did not get to share evidentiary documents with the *NYT* reporter because she tragically died in a car accident on November 13, 1974, on her way to meet the journalist.[15] Whether it is a disgruntled nuclear worker (and labor activist) in *Silkwood* or a dissident scientist in *China Syndrome*, what we find is that whistleblowing becomes a key practice in films about nuclear reactors. Through close-ups on Karen or Jack, who play the roles of the whistleblowers, the films ask audiences to viscerally empathize with the characters, their bodily experiences, and their ethical struggles.[16]

These films suggest that another formal quality of nuclear reactor designs, beyond the monumental domes, is their internal components, which remain hidden. Since they remain hidden, there is also a desire to know more, to reveal. It not surprising that the act of whistleblowing becomes a trope in several fiction films and TV shows that depict nuclear reactors (or accidents in nuclear facilities). Nuclear reactors incite a curiosity in some people that there is much more to know and find out. Secrecy protocols and their transgression by whistleblowers become a part of the aesthetic address of nuclear infrastructures.

The HBO miniseries *Chernobyl* (2019) portrays the nuclear fallout of the Chernobyl-based nuclear reactor and responses of the Soviet scientists and government functionaries. The Soviet scientists are not exactly depicted as whistleblowers in the show, but some of them are shown to challenge government and corporate practices for the sake of public interest. HBO is often associated with "quality TV" aesthetics, and *Chernobyl* not only embraced high production standards but also represented with almost flawless accuracy the material culture of the former Soviet Union. It was able to recreate with precision the physical surroundings and the affective atmosphere within which the Soviet people lived.[17] The show depicts the hierarchies of bureaucrats and scientists well, but given the history of fictional films connecting nuclear reactors and whistleblowers, *Chernobyl*, in its willingness to have dissident scientists standing up to the Communist establishment and acting as whistleblowers, mischaracterizes (to some extent) the behavior of Soviet scientists. Masha Gessen finds the scenes of heroic scientists confronting rigid bureaucrats by explicitly criticizing the Soviet system of decision-making to be "ridiculous and repetitive."[18] That said, these heroic acts of dissidence propel the narrative and provide a melodramatic air. In *Chernobyl*, like *Silkwood* and *China Syndrome*, the audience is made to identify with the figure of the dissident/whistleblower.

Going beyond whistleblowers and secrecy protocols, this essay focuses on the affective encounters of nuclear laborers with infrastructures. Investigating such embodied encounters with radiation is crucial to the aesthetic address of nuclear infrastructures as the worker's body becomes the site where the invisibility of nuclear radiation is mapped.

Embodied Encounters with Radiation

The Greek sense of the term "aesthetics" is "aesthesis," or sense perception.[19] Brian Larkin finds not just art objects but also infrastructures participating in what French philosopher Jacques Ranciere calls "*aisthesis*": "how it is those things produce modes of felt experience."[20] In this section, I examine films that depict the felt experiences of workers inside a nuclear reactor: how they walk with dosimeters through different zones of radiation intensities within the facility, how they dress in their protective clothes and then undress and take showers, what kind of care they have to take in their movements to evade high amounts of radiation exposure, and finally how they react when an alarm goes off and they know that a particular zone or one of their fellow worker's bodies has been contaminated. The design of the nuclear reactor, its various components and spaces, thus generates an address to the nuclear worker that calls forth affective states of alertness, attention, fear, dread, and apprehension.

In addition to *Silkwood*, I examine two other films, *Grand Central* and *Nuclear Waste*, in order to draw connections between the aesthetic address of nuclear reactors and the aesthetic strategies of filmmaking. Both these films have a tendency to engage with the medium of cinema not at the level of plot or narrative but as an "object of perception."[21] Doing away with elaborate plotlines, both these films focus on the texture of the image and draw audiences in to feel the tonalities of the film. There is an explicit attention to the bodies of characters, and it is simply impossible for the audiences to not notice the care with which the bodies are framed and lit in these films. In adopting these audiovisual strategies, *Grand Central* and *Nuclear Waste* invite spectators to open themselves to sensory awareness. This kind of corporeal and textural style makes these films particularly suitable for exploring the aesthetic address of nuclear reactors to the workers who toil inside the plant and for probing the rhythms and felt experiences of nuclear workers as they make their bodies susceptible to radiation exposure. This twin focus on infrastructural aesthetics and the aesthetics of the body in the corporeal cinema of *Grand Central* and *Nuclear Waste* leads me to explore an aesthetics of life itself conditioned by the nuclear reactor.

I begin with *Silkwood*, even though it is more narratively driven than *Grand Central* and *Nuclear Waste*, because I did find the influence of some of the viscerally affecting body-related scenes in *Silkwood* on these latter films. Consider, for example, the iconic scenes in *Silkwood* of nuclear workers, including Karen, receiving the "shower" after being "cooked" (contaminated by radiation), often referred to as the "Silkwood shower." Initially, Karen is horrified to see her friend and coworker, Thelma, get a shower after being contaminated. Thelma is stripped naked and brutally and thoroughly scrubbed by employees wearing hazmat suits. This first shower scene foreshadows the next set of shower scenes in the film involving Karen herself. Conveyed in swift economical shots, the scene begins with Karen placing her hands on the Geiger tube before leaving her section. Karen's action triggers the alarm, and she takes her hands to her head in disbelief. A steady camera depicts medical employees rushing through the narrow corridor to reach her. The next shot cuts to a close-up of Karen's side face and hand, which is being scrubbed, with her lineaments suggesting the humiliation she is being subjected to (see fig. 10.1).

Reminiscent of these shower scenes in *Silkwood*, the 2013 French film *Grand Central*, which portrays the lives of decontamination subcontractors working in a reactor, has the character of Géraldine (played by Camille Lellouche) undergo a similar shower after the alarm goes off and she is found to be contaminated by radiation. Instead of a close-up of Géraldine's face (akin to Karen Silkwood's in *Silkwood*), director Rebecca Zlotowski and cinematographer Georges Lechaptois present a starker scene amplifying the

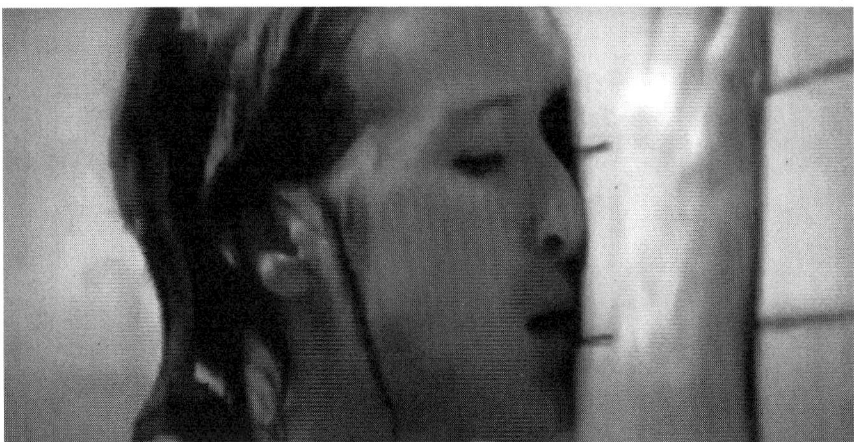

Fig. 10.1. Karen's shower scene. Still from *Silkwood*. © American Broadcasting Companies, Inc.

estrangement that Géraldine feels: the camera takes in the whole shower room, with Géraldine's naked back to the audience and to the two medical officials in the room who are fully clothed in protective gear. Even after the shower, the medical workers continue to monitor her body dosage level with the Geiger counter, which, when brought to her hair, indicates a high radioactive dose. Géraldine is then subjected to further humiliation. To reduce her body's radioactive contamination levels, her long hair is shaved off, and the camera alternates between her tense feet and sobbing face. Occurring simultaneously in the aural register, Géraldine's cries and the buzzing of the electric hair trimmer create an affective atmosphere of anguish and dread.

The gender politics of laboring bodies in these shower scenes is explicit. The shower scenes, as portrayed in *Silkwood* and *Grand Central*, are acts of bodily violation, and it is women who are subjected to them. *Silkwood* has no such shower scenes involving men, and in *Grand Central*, while men are disinfected/cleansed at times through showers (although mostly they shower themselves), those scenes are not presented in a sensually stark manner. J. W. Whitehead notes that the sonic and visual tropes of shower scenes in *Silkwood* are borrowed from the horror genre, particularly from *Psycho* (dir. Alfred Hitchcock, 1960). These scenes seem to suggest Karen and Géraldine's victimhood, but they also act as pivotal moments (of transcendence) when they realize their bodies and their labor are being extracted by the nuclear company, which is subjecting them to relentless radioactive exposure. Whitehead, citing director Mike Nichols, calls it Karen's reified "awakening."[22]

Compared to *Silkwood*, Zlotowski's *Grand Central* relies less on plot and more on creating the milieu, where characters playing itinerant workers live out of trailers next to a nuclear plant in the countryside and carry out the dangerous operations of decontamination inside the plant. The film begins with Gary (Tahar Rahim), an unskilled worker, looking for work. He soon finds himself in a small town in the Rhone valley doing the lower-grade (but well paid) dangerous work of nuclear decontamination. Gary starts socializing with the local community of power plant workers there and befriends Toni (Denis Menochet) and his fiancée Karole (Lea Seydoux). Without courtship or much explanation, an immediate attraction develops between Gary and Karole, and they begin a fervent romance. There is no respite for Gary, as Zlotowski puts this character either in the hazardous working conditions inside the nuclear plant or in the frenzied love triangle with Karole and Toni outside the reactor.

Every two years or so nuclear reactors are taken offline for repairs, and that is when the decontamination operatives, like the ones portrayed in *Grand Central*, come into the plants to clean and repair valves and pipes, remove spent fuel from the core, and add new fuel. Gabrielle Hecht notes that in France, these subcontracted decontamination operatives, often dubbed "nuclear nomads," move from one nuclear reactor to another depending on when and where their services are required.[23] Due to this migratory lifestyle, they stay in trailer parks.[24] While the radioactive dose they are exposed to is recorded for a specific nuclear plant, Hecht notes that there is no centralized archive that systematically compiles the collective (cumulative) radioactive dose received by each of these migratory workers as they move across nuclear reactors.

Two clear settings emerge in *Grand Central*, the interior of the nuclear reactor and the outside bucolic space where nuclear workers live and socialize. In an interview, Zlotowski explained that she wanted to maintain a contrast between these two spaces. She achieves that by shooting the nuclear reactor scenes in a digital medium, thereby obtaining sharp images under artificial lights, and by shooting the exterior scenes using 35 mm film to capture the warm tones of the workers' lives in the countryside and the natural light of Gary and Karole's trysts on a secluded island.[25] These differences are emphasized sonically as well: audiences hear leaves rustling and birds chirping in the exterior shots, while the sound in the hermetically sealed closed space of the nuclear reactor is composed of metallic percussion beats and the occasional muffled sounds of breathing from within a gas mask. Even as the interior and exterior spaces are contrasted, the nuclear reactor does make its presence felt outside, for its alarms and sirens screech out and reach Gary and Karole, disturbing their mutual embrace on the island outside.

The feeling that he is irradiated never leaves Gary after he is exposed to high doses, once when a radioactive substance spills from a tank and another time when he takes off his glove while trying to help Toni when they are both working close to the nuclear fuel rod area. In one telling scene, Gary faces the mirror and scrubs the back of his neck hard, as if he is trying to clean all radiation from his body (see fig. 10.2). He is not sure how much he has

Fig 10.2. Gary scrubbing while facing mirror. Still from *Grand Central*. Reproduced with permission by UniFrance.

been internally contaminated by radiation by this time, and scrubbing at the surface does not tell him what radiation is doing inside his body. Gary's frustration with radioactive exposure, conveyed through his restless scrubbing, suggests that once radioactive isotopes are inside the body, it becomes difficult to differentiate the inside and outside of bodies.

Another reason Gary relentlessly scrubs is because he desperately wants his bodily contamination levels to be low so that he can continue to work at the plant, and in sensitive areas of the plant no less, for which the pay is higher. In another scene, as a way to prolong his employment, Gary tries to fudge his radiation readings by leaving behind the dosimeter and going inside the plant without them.

While shooting inside the plant, Zlotowski constructs scenes of work that bring audiences closer to experiencing the care and attention with which workers have to move inside the plant so as not to expose themselves to radiogenic injury.[26] One scene shows Toni in the heart of the nuclear reactor doing some maintenance work. We, as the audience, see Toni down at the reactor core (where the nuclear fuel is present) from Gary's perspective, who is observing him from above, behind a glass window (see fig. 10.3). Toni is meticulously stepping around the fuel rods trying to find a part that has broken loose. Even as this image offers a significant depth of field, it remains sharp enough. This is a scene of heightened anticipation because both Gary and the audience know that one wrong step by Toni and he will be severely contaminated. Here the audience can witness just how the formal qualities of the nuclear reactor condition particular kinds of movement and structure specific modes of embodiment.

Fig 10.3. Gary observes Tony working in reactor core. Still from *Grand Central*. Reproduced with permission by UniFrance.

While the abovementioned scene is a dramatic one, *Grand Central* has many scenes of habitual routinized work as laborers do their repair work tethered to ropes, dress and undress, take showers, discuss their dosimeter readings, and carry containers full of radioactive material. Even while depicting these banal work routines, the cinematographer, editor, and sound designer are able to lend the film a sense of delirium, a dream-like quality, perhaps imitating the uncanny quality of ionizing nuclear radiation, which can sneak up from anywhere.

Espousing a slow cinema aesthetics, the film *Nuclear Waste* (2012) by Ukrainian director Miroslav Slaboshpitsky presents the routine life of two workers, Sergiy and Sveta, in Chernobyl's nuclear waste management department. The twenty-four-minute film depicts the lives of nuclear workers in even more stark detail than *Grand Central*. In the establishing shot of the film, a steady camera waits for trucks to move over roads as audiences take in the ice-filled landscape with snowflakes falling. Through minimal slow pans, the camera follows a red truck carrying a container of nuclear waste. Audiences wait (for what seems like an excruciatingly long time) as the protagonist Sergiy waits in his truck while the radioactive container is lifted from the truck and the heavy machinery performs this part computerized and part mechanical job. Then Sergiy drives, and spectators get their first glance at Sergiy from inside the truck. After finishing this task, Sergiy and one of his coworkers undress next to lockers in a slow, deliberate manner: we watch as each coat, jacket, shirt, pair of pants, and undergarment is taken off. Then they shower and pass through a door with a Geiger counter locking system.

These shots of the dressing room and showers, like the ones of the landscape outside, are tightly controlled, very composed shots at a dilated pace. Unlike in *Silkwood* or *Grand Central*, where one saw a group of workers and their camaraderie, and there was a bustling, kinetic, and lively movement to characters and their conversations, the slow cinema aesthetics in *Nuclear Waste* render character interactions in a deadpan manner. The film then continues following Sveta, who works at the plant's launderette. She carries clothes in a cart to a washing machine. And then Sveta carries some cleaned and ironed clothes to where Sergiy is eating food and resting.

The Zone: Uncertainty, Decay, and Catastrophe

Slaboshpitsky's film, *Nuclear Waste*, takes place in the Chernobyl exclusion zone of northern Ukraine. On April 26, 1986, reactor number 4 exploded in the Chernobyl nuclear plant, and the radioactive isotopes scattered widely. While the radioactive ash spread across Eastern Europe and Scandinavia and even affected Cumbrian sheep farmers in Wales, the three nations of Russia, Belarus, and Ukraine (then part of the Soviet Union) were deeply affected. Thousands of their citizens and significant parts of their agricultural land were lost to radioactivity. The thirty-square-kilometer area in and around Chernobyl, called the "exclusion zone" or "red zone," was depopulated and considered uninhabitable because of the high amounts of radioactivity that prevailed over the landscape. The "sarcophagus," a massive shelter structure made of steel and concrete, was built to contain the spread of radioactivity, but with radiation, nothing is leakproof, and seepage continues. Since then, some displaced people have returned to the zone. There are some formal and informal tour guides who take tourists to the zone.[27] There are workers like Sergiy and Sveta who continue the work of radiation monitoring and nuclear waste management in the zone.

Some of the radioactive isotopes that were leaked by the Chernobyl nuclear plant decay very slowly, having half-lives of a thousand years and more. This is such a slow disintegration process that the Chernobyl zone might remain uninhabitable for a thousand years, and there will have to be people like Sergiy and Sveta who will need to do the required cleanups. But who can say anything about what is going to happen in a thousand years? The Chernobyl catastrophe invites realist and apocalyptic readings at the same time. Photographing the landscape of industrial ruin and lush wildlife is one way to "realistically" depict the closest approximation of what a nuclear apocalypse looks like. However, photographing landscapes and making documentaries about the Chernobyl zone hardly represent the theater of decay that the invisible radioactive isotopes are enacting, for they remain invisible, eluding the camera's capture. These radioactive isotopes will continue to decay for thousands of years, and this slow disintegration can be conceptualized in the blown-out scale of deep time. The aesthetics of nuclear reactors entails not only an aesthetics of bodily exposure to invisible radiation but also an aesthetics of decaying radioactivity, which in turn is associated with an aesthetics of deep time.

While the camera cannot represent radioactive isotopes, decaying radioactive particles do leave their traces on photographs and irradiated film stock. Vladmir Shevchenko led the first film crew into the exclusion zone. On the surface of the documentary film *Chernobyl: Chronicle of Difficult Weeks* (dir. Vladmir Shevchenko, 1987) that this crew shot, audiences can see myriad tiny pops and scratches. These distortions did not indicate defective film stock but were the impressions created by decaying particles as they passed through the camera.[28] Historian Kate Brown writes about Alexander Kupny, who in his quest to understand nuclear energy returns again and again to shoot inside the sarcophagus.[29] He seems to be hailed back by the enigma of the fallen reactor. Some of his photographs are shots of wrecked machinery and rusted equipment in almost complete darkness, with tiny orange flecks lighting up one of the corners. Brown explains that these flashing lights are radioactive isotopes imposing themselves on the image: "These points of light are not representations. They are energy embodied. The specks are none other than cesium, plutonium, and uranium self-portraits."[30] Brown likens Kupny's work to that of geologists who dig to uncover the inscriptions of deep time. Kupny inaugurates a novel visual aesthetics of nuclear deep time by using decaying isotopes as raw material for his photography.

Having seen the images of a post–nuclear fallout in Fukushima and Chernobyl, having heard stories of people affected by these disasters, it is difficult to imagine standing next to a presently online (working) nuclear reactor and not thinking that another nuclear accident is not only possible but is part of the everyday life of the reactor. Risk scenarios proposed by nuclear energy proponents could not account for the Chernobyl or Fukushima or Three Mile Island incidents or predict the effects of the slowly decaying radioactive isotopes released during these nuclear fallouts. Peter van Wyck has noted that the potential dangers and hazards from "ecological threats" like nuclear disasters cannot be confined within the rubrics of quantifiable probability, that is, risk.[31] At one level, Slaboshpitsky's *Nuclear Waste* is a sarcastic take on nuclear risk scenarios of the past. At another level, the film suggests that life in the midst of a landscape of nuclear waste is still, well, life, and that one way to understand nuclear waste is to comprehend that (irradiated) people go about their routines and continue to survive amid nuclear waste. Maybe surviving amid radical uncertainties is a way of understanding nuclear waste.

Nuclear Waste does not explicitly engage with the sociopolitics of the disaster and its aftermath. By contrast, the Ukrainian Soviet film *Rozpad/Raspad* (1990) by Mikhail Belikov projects social and political meanings into the Chernobyl incident. It portrays the crumbling of the familial and social ties of the main protagonist, journalist Aleksandr Zhuravlev, who, after making a (heroic) trip to the exclusion zone (involving taking pictures and reporting from there), seems to regain his wife and friends. The title of the film, *Rozpad*, translates into English as "disintegration" and could point to atomic disintegration, that is, the decay of radioactive isotopes. It could also gesture toward the disintegration of the Soviet Union as many believe that the Chernobyl incident hastened the fall of that country. The film also allegorically points to the rebirth of Ukraine after the breakdown of the Soviet Union. Just like Zhuravlev reclaims his familial and social life after a trip to the exclusion zone, Ukraine is able to assert its sovereignty with respect to the former Soviet Union by attempting to responsibly take care of its citizens who were affected by the disaster allegedly brought about by a corrupt Soviet administration.[32] An infrastructural breakdown, that is, a nuclear fallout, and the consequent atomic disintegration in *Rozpad/Raspad* are linked to individual, familial, and national decay and rebirth.

Coda

The films I have discussed emerge out of varied temporal and geographical contexts. Hollywood films like *China Syndrome* and *Silkwood*, produced as they were in late 1970s and early 1980s, are part of the whistleblower genre. Less driven by narrative than these Hollywood productions, *Grand Central* and *Nuclear Waste* are more poetic and experimental films, providing a sensuality to the aesthetics of inhabiting the nuclear reactor as experienced by workers. *Raspad* was being produced and released as a new nation-state was forming out of a larger disintegrating nation whose indelible and tragic legacy would remain in the form of a decaying nuclear reactor: this partly explains the film's allegorical bent, merging the personal and the political, the citizen and the nation.

Studying the aesthetic life of nuclear reactors needs to account for the aesthetic life of nuclear workers as nuclear infrastructures condition embodied perception. Ionizing radiation strips electrons from atoms or molecules, and once inside the bodies, the kind of mutagenic theater they will unleash on living tissues remains unpredictable. Soon after the Chernobyl incident, some "liquidators" who were sent to quench fires, dig up earth, trees, and houses, and bury the nuclear waste died immediately. However, some of these liquidators, as Keith Gessen writes in his translator's preface to Svetlana Alexievich's *Voices from Chernobyl*, "wouldn't break down until weeks or months later, at which point they'd die horribly."[33] One such story of a firefighter, Vasily Ignatenko, is present in Alexievich's oral history accounts and also depicted in the TV miniseries *Chernobyl*. Lyudmilla Ignatenko's story about the transformations of her husband Vasily's body as radioactive particles decayed inside is an unfathomable experience. Lyudmilla recalls her husband's skin cracking on his arms and legs and a nurse telling her: "This is not your husband anymore, not a beloved person, but a radioactive object with a strong density of poisoning."[34] Such are the estranging qualities of radioactive decay where bodies and ecologies can no longer be separated. At another time, Lyudmilla is told that Vasily got a dose of 1,600 roentgens and that she is "sitting next to a nuclear reactor": her husband's body is compared to a nuclear reactor. This aesthetics of decay is also the aesthetics of life itself.

Notes

Thanks to the volume editors, and to Meta Mazaj, Svitlana Matviyenko, and Masha Shpolberg for suggestions and conversations.

1. Brian Larkin, "Promising Forms: The Political Aesthetics of Infrastructure," in *The Promise of Infrastructure*, ed. Hannah Appel, Nikhil Anand, and Akhil Gupta (Durham, NC: Duke University Press, 2018), 175–202.

2. Liv Hausken, *Thinking Media Aesthetics: Media Studies, Film Studies, and the Arts* (Berlin: Peter Lang, 2013), 30.

3. Larkin, "Promising Forms," 193.

4. Geoffrey Bowker and Susan Leigh Star, *Sorting Things Out: Classification and Its Consequences* (Cambridge, MA: MIT Press, 1999).

5. See Olga Kuchinskaya, *The Politics of Invisibility: Public Knowledge about Radiation Health Effects after Chernobyl* (Cambridge, MA: MIT Press, 2014); and Lisa Parks and Nicole Starosielski, eds., *Signal Traffic: Critical Studies of Media Infrastructures* (Champaign: University of Illinois Press, 2015).

6. Gabrielle Hecht, "Nuclear Nomads: A Look at the Subcontracted Heroes," *Bulletin of Atomic Scientists*, January 9, 2012.

7. Nikolas Rose, "The Politics of Life Itself," *Theory, Culture and Society* 18, no. 6 (2001): 1–30.

8. Jacques Ranciere, *The Politics of Aesthetics: The Distribution of the Sensible*, ed. and trans. Gabriel Rockhill (New York: Bloomsbury, 2013), 13.

9. Personal interview with Pallava Bagla, New Delhi, October 8, 2012.

10. Rahul Mukherjee, *Radiant Infrastructures: Media, Environment, and Cultures of Uncertainty* (Durham, NC: Duke University Press, 2020).

11. Andrew Deck, "Touching from a Distance: The Workers of Fukushima Daiichi," *Metropolis*, September 28, 2018.

12. Mukherjee, *Radiant Infrastructures*, 115.

13. A. Bowdoin Van Riper, "Into Eternity," *Film and History* 43, no. 1 (2013): 101.

14. Scott Kirsch, "Harold Knapp and the Geography of Normal Controversy: Radioiodine in the Historical Environment," *Osiris* 19 (2004): 167–81.

15. The circumstances of Karen Silkwood's death remain mysterious, and the film portrays the "accident" as Silkwood's car being rear ended by another car (whose ominous and approaching headlights are shown in an earlier shot). Both intent and mystery are added to the accident as the folder containing documents incriminating Kerr-McGee authorities goes missing and the door of Silkwood's car is shown to be slightly ajar. Following Silkwood's death in 1974, actress Jane Fonda wanted to make a film about her but was refused the rights to fictionalize the story by Silkwood's heirs. Some elements of the whistleblower aspect of Karen Silkwood's story were retained in *China Syndrome*, a film that Fonda's IPC

Productions coproduced with Michael Douglas. *China Syndrome* was released on March 16, 1979, foreshadowing the nuclear accident that occurred at Three Mile Island on March 28, 1979. Refer to Aljean Harmetz, "Fallout from 'China Syndrome' Has Already Begun," *New York Times*, March 11, 1979.

16. Alexa Weik von Mossner, "The Stuff of Fear: Emotion, Ethics, and the Materiality of Nuclear Risk in *Silkwood* and *The China Syndrome*," in *The Anticipation of Catastrophe: Environmental Risk in North American Literature and Culture*, ed. Sylvia Mayer and Alexa Weik von Mossner (Heidelberg: Universitätsverlag, 2014), 101–17; Kyle Stevens, *Mike Nichols: Sex, Language, and the Reinvention of Psychological Realism* (Oxford: Oxford University Press, 2015).

17. Masha Gessen, "What HBO's 'Chernobyl' Got Right and What It Got Terribly Wrong," *New Yorker*, June 4, 2019.

18. Masha Gessen, "HBO's 'Chernobyl.' "

19. Hausken, *Thinking Media Aesthetics*.

20. Larkin, "Promising Forms," 176.

21. *Grand Central* might be seen as a continuance of a trend set by contemporary French films since 2000, which, as Martine Beugnet notes, have betrayed "a characteristic sensibility to and awareness of cinema's sensuous impact and transgressive nature." Martine Beugnet, *Cinema and Sensation: French Film and the Art of Transgression* (Edinburg: Edinburg University Press, 2007), 14.

22. J. W.Whitehead, *Mike Nichols and the Cinema of Transformation* (Jefferson, NC: McFarland, 2014), 123.

23. Hecht, "Nuclear Nomads."

24. This kind of dangerous maintenance work is a regular feature of the nuclear reactor industry (because of the nuclear fuel cycle) and needs to be differentiated from the cleanup and decontamination required when there is apocalyptic nuclear fallout like in Chernobyl and Fukushima.

25. Zlotowski's interview with Nicholas Elliot in *Film Comment*, March 7, 2014. https://www.filmcomment.com/blog/interview-rebecca-zlotowski-grand-central/.

26. Zlotowski's film is indeed fictional, but through painstaking research and shooting in an actual nuclear reactor (the Zwentendorf plant in Austria), she is able to convey the felt experiences of workers living these itinerant lives. Their lives remain invisible to the general public, but they play a key role in the functioning of France's large nuclear energy industry.

27. Adrian Ivakhiv, "Chernobyl, Risk, and the Inter-zone of the Anthropocene," in *The Routledge Companion to Media and Risk*, ed. Bishnupriya Ghosh and Bhaskar Sarkar (London: Routledge, 2020), 209–31.

28. Peter C. van Wyck, *Signs of Danger: Waste, Trauma, and Nuclear Threat* (Minneapolis: University of Minnesota Press, 2004), 96.

29. Kate Brown, "Marie Curie's Fingerprint: Nuclear Spelunking in the Chernobyl Zone," in *Arts of Living on a Damaged Planet: Ghosts and Monsters of the Anthropocene*, ed. Anna Tsing (Minneapolis: University of Minnesota Press, 2017), G35–G50.

30. Brown, "Marie Curie's Fingerprint," G41.

31. Van Wyck, *Signs of Danger*, 116.

32. Johanna Lindbladh, "Representations of the Chernobyl Catastrophe in Soviet and Post-Soviet Cinema: The Narratives of Apocalypse," *Studies in Eastern European Cinema*, 10, no. 3 (2019): 240–56; Olga Briukhovetska, "Nuclear

Belonging: "Chernobyl" in Belarusian, Ukrainian (and Russian) Films," in *Contested Interpretations of the Past in Polish, Russian, and Ukrainian Film: Screen as Battlefield*, ed. Sander Brouwer (Leiden and Boston: Brill Rodopi, 2016), 95–122. The government in Ukraine set up an infrastructure to provide health care and welfare to those affected by the Chernobyl nuclear accident by including a 12 percent Chernobyl tax. This provision has helped some patients and populations resettled from the former Chernobyl plant. However, with Ukraine's economy not doing well, this scheme has been a mixed success. For more, see Adriana Petryna, *Life Exposed: Biological Citizens after Chernobyl* (Princeton, NJ: Princeton University Press, 2003).

33. Keith Gessen, preface to Svetlana Alexievich, *Voices from Chernobyl: The Oral History of a Nuclear Disaster*, trans. and preface by Keith Gessen (New York: Picador, 2005), xii.

34. Alexievich, *Voices from Chernobyl*, 16.

Chapter 11

✦

Cocaine Logistics and the Neoliberal Art of Credibility

Susan Zieger

Frozen sharks. Canned asparagus. Butt implants. Moisturizer. Balloons. Carpets. Diapers. Fake pineapples.

These items have nothing in common—except that cocaine has been smuggled in each of them.[1] They represent a shift in the transportation medium, from the bodies of drug mules on brief commercial flights to shipping containers that carry vast quantities over much longer, transoceanic distances. Mules still operate and indeed train themselves to ingest cocaine capsules that, if they rupture in their intestines, will subject them to agonizing deaths. But the real money—and from the point of view of the smugglers, less risk—lies in the shipping containers. Their larger scale maximizes profit by securing the supply chain: massive shipments reduce the risk of seizure posed by more numerous, smaller operations to transport the same amount. Like other twenty-first-century globalized economies, cocaine distribution has scaled up, becoming a logistical enterprise. And, like all modern logistics, it colonizes infrastructure, turning ports, container ships, building materials, and even the bloodstreams of workers into silent servants of capital, not the commons. One logistician spoke of an operation in which even the customs official did not know what was passing under his nose as "a masterpiece."[2] Taking its cue from such aesthetic language, this essay will read two disparate nonfiction novels about cocaine smuggling to trace their contrasting approaches to the defining aesthetic, and criminal strategy, of infrastructure in the neoliberal era: that of credibility. Smuggling cocaine is an art of deception that succeeds by presenting cheap goods as believably mundane cargo while secretly glazing them with what may be the world's most highly valued substance. Likewise, its infrastructures appear to operate credibly for both free trade and the public good, when they truly only serve global capitalism's criminally extractive activities.

Logistics is the art and science of moving goods, people, and information efficiently to maximize profit. Its icon is the shipping container, that intermodal technology that, since the 1970s, has been craned off of ships and onto truck beds for faster distribution of goods around the world. Logistics transpires through the channels and frameworks of infrastructure; as a technique of capital, it can even be said to bring infrastructure into being, as when a company lobbies the state for a new road to speed the flow of goods.[3] Logistics, as a management science, is an instrument of global capitalism; the state serves as the intermediary between it and the people who might additionally benefit from the infrastructure it proposes. Where the state abdicates its democratic role, logistics—whether criminal or legitimate—takes it up. As Ned Rossiter writes of our neoliberal era, "Infrastructure makes worlds. Logistics governs them."[4] Cocaine smuggling operations are managed by logisticians known as a *sistematistas*, using infrastructure like ports that can be controlled by criminal organizations; for example, the port of Gioia Tauro by the Calabrian group known as the 'Ndrangheta. The sistematista has become as important a figure to the criminal organization as its boss; his services are so valuable that he can name his price. As one smuggler put it, "People like me were of great value because we were the ones that put the product where the money was. The smuggle is . . . the toughest part of the business."[5] Cocaine logisticians—rather than the government—quietly manage infrastructure, turning ports, airports, and roads to their own ends.

In this, they demonstrate the fundamentally extractive character of legitimately managed infrastructure, from the ancient period to the present. Keller Easterling, describing free zones as examples of infrastructural space, calls them "a means by which both state and non-state actors cooperate at someone else's expense—usually the expense of labor."[6] The more a state in thrall to neoliberal economic policies fails to mediate between capital and human interests, the more clearly its infrastructural projects operate as machines for transferring money to elites. The Asian Infrastructure Bank and the Canadian Infrastructure Bank, which subsidize financiers to hold monopolies over essential infrastructure and rent it to the public, make this relation obvious.[7] That cocaine abuse occurs even in states with comparatively better labor protection, health infrastructure, and living wages suggests that even these standards are not meeting human needs. As portrayed in two novels, cocaine smuggling, a plainly lawless enterprise, vividly illustrates a specific twenty-first-century permutation of the criminal spirit of imperialist, capitalist extraction.

Reading the literature that relates cocaine, logistics, and infrastructure, this essay makes two main interventions. First, it disables the visibility thesis, which holds that infrastructure only becomes visible upon collapse. While it may seem that cocaine smuggling is the breakdown in legitimate trade that suddenly makes the infrastructure of ports and shipping containers visible—the cliché of cops breaking open container seals, crates, and goods to reveal the drugs hidden inside—this story is the easy one of propaganda. For such moments of exposure serve to conceal the original breakdown that happened when the port and its machinery were constructed and licensed and that has been continuing with every "clean" shipment. Even when infrastructure appears operational, it works primarily for capital and only incidentally for people. As China Miéville acerbically reframed the pious discourse of "conflict diamonds," "Every toilet-roll procured legitimately in a Toronto suburb is Conflict Tissue. Every branny breakfast item in a New York Starbucks is a fucking Blood Muffin."[8] The impossibility that any scandalous exposure of drug trafficking could ever be the final one is not due to an intrinsic human need for cocaine; it is a structural effect of logistics' and infrastructure's service to capital. Because formal and informal economies cannot be fully separated, the apparent scandal of finding cocaine in a shipment of footwear only points to the other, ongoing scandal of the putatively legitimate apparel industry. Only the spectacular violence and illegal exploits of the trade in cocaine and other drugs make the slow, "legitimate" industrial violence against people and the environment unremarkable.

For suggestive evidence of these claims, I examine Italian journalist Luca Rastello's *I Am the Market: How to Smuggle Cocaine by the Ton, in Five Easy Lessons* (2009). Narrated by a sistematista who is an amalgam of Rastello's underworld contacts and describing deceptive smuggling techniques, *I Am the Market* sketches an abstract, postmodern, financialized surface of undifferentiated global trade. But the paradoxical genre of "the nonfiction novel" is capacious enough to feature an almost opposing strategy, one that relies in equal parts on realism and allegory. Here, in Roberto Saviano's *ZeroZeroZero* (2013) and *Gomorrah* (2006), resides a faith in exposure missing from Rastello's book and going against the grain of my theoretical claim: bring the truth to light, and the state will punish the crime and correct the flaw. Saviano's technique of exposing the sensing, thinking, and laboring human body is an effort to purify a social body as energized and sickened by cocaine as its infrastructure is ultimately owned and managed by capital. Hector Amaya, using the catastrophic drug-related and paramilitary violence in Mexico to revise theories of the public sphere, calls such publicness and transparency "broken tools created by the West."[9] This essay acts in part as a barometer of the credence its readers give to this statement or of their continued faith in the state's capacity to defend the people against capital predation. It also describes the disparate uses of the nonfiction novel to intervene in its political moment under its own shamelessly flimsy covering of truth with the veneer of fiction. Whichever literary technique you prefer, Rastello's or Saviano's, and whatever position you take on infrastructure's inextricability from private investment, I hope at least to convince you of infrastructure's extractive effect on laboring bodies. To make this point, before taking each novel in turn, I will first interpret cocaine itself as a global infrastructure supplying energy for human labor.

Cocaine as Infrastructure

"There are plenty of corners of the planet where people live without hospitals, without the web, without running water. But not without cocaine" (*ZeroZeroZero*, 72). Found everywhere humans live, cocaine is a global commodity—and something more. It is also a form of infrastructure, supporting human life in the absence or inadequacy of more conventional examples such as access to hospitals, internet connectivity, and clean drinking water. Logistics distributes cocaine far, wide, and deep: one shipping container can disperse it into millions of bloodstreams. There, it realizes its true infrastructural purpose: to support the working body. Every day, food is harvested and packed, trucks are driven, hotels are built and cleaned, paperwork is filed, surgeries are performed, and children are taught in schools and universities, all on cocaine, which scaffolds every variety of labor.[10] Cocaine operates as soft infrastructure because it provides short-term energy for work: vigor that is not being otherwise conditioned by states in the form of labor protection, adequate health and nutrition, and living wages.[11] It bears emphasizing that this apparent energy is addictive and depleting and that it is not limited to cocaine. Various habit-forming substances have always been used to alleviate the stress and injury of hard and coerced labor, from opium on southeast Asian plantations, to gin, beer, and sugar in industrializing Britain, to OxyContin and black tar heroin in the twenty-first-century United States.[12] For office work, we might count coffee and cigarette breaks, not to mention antidepressants and Ritalin; for unpaid domestic childcare (and, during the pandemic, education), wine and cannabis; and for everything, ubiquitous sugar. Because they help workers overlook injuries, endure long shifts, and function effectively, such substances assist capital in extracting labor. While this essay focuses on cocaine—which the opioid crisis has now made to seem passé—the critical intervention is relevant to all labor-managing substances.

My idea that cocaine operates as infrastructure builds on the recent turn in scholarship that inspires this volume, away from infrastructure's conventional meaning of public works like roads and electrical networks and toward laboring, circulating, and speaking human bodies. Pointing out that infrastructure "is not identical to system or structure," Lauren Berlant defines it as "the living mediation of what organizes life: the lifeworld of structure."[13] AbdouMaliq Simone proposes "people as infrastructure": the flexible, contingent interactions between residents that "become a platform providing for and reproducing life in the city."[14] I too reframe infrastructure to foreground collective life and to emphasize life's energetic aspect. Yet this broadening of infrastructure from its conventional understanding as public works risks its critical stakes if it loses focus on political economy. In this essay, infrastructure is lifelike or energetic human and environmental assemblages that produce profit for capital. This definition connects humans, natural and built environments, and political economies, recognizing their complex interdependencies.

Similar work by Stephanie Graetner, Michelle Murphy, and Rahul Mukherjee relocates infrastructure within human bodies that process industrial and nuclear waste.[15] Reinterpreting cocaine as infrastructure likewise reframes its overdetermined status as a plant derivative that is harvested, processed, and integrated into human physiologies, and once there, a substance that facilitates the legitimate global economy. When we attend to cocaine's extraction of labor, we reverse its status as a figure in the global economy's ground. If cocaine is not the scandalous spectacle but instead the abiding infrastructure that supports human labor, then all the consumer effluvia—the balloons, the fake pineapples—sliding around the ocean and crawling along roads emerge as the truly surreal, monstrous parasite feeding on it. Performing this aesthetic and political operation, we expose the limits of the conventional visibility thesis, which is blind to the inequities built into infrastructure as an effect of global capital.

As with infrastructure, this line of reasoning expands the referents of extraction, which is more than just the exploitation of natural resources like logging and fracking. Once again, I follow the lead of other theorists who reposition it in relation to human and environmental life. Macarena Gomez-Barris reframes extraction through visual and embodied knowledges, transfeminist and Indigenous formations that perceive "the proliferation of life," countering extractive state and corporate maps of territories-as-commodities.[16] Anna Tsing observes how the supply chain of the matsutake mushroom industry makes commensurable wildly diverse forms of work and nature, connecting different modes of extraction and accumulation.[17] Sandro Mezzadra and Brett Neilson deploy a diffuse sense of extraction that, triangulated with logistics and financialization, enacts capital through operations that implicate gender, race, sexuality, and other identifications by which individuals make sense of their everyday lives.[18] And Kalindi Vora resituates extraction as the transmission of vitality and energy from working to consuming bodies.[19] Such theories helps us see the role cocaine plays in an expanded political-economic field that includes the lives, habits, and bodies of workers, as well as the natural environment where coca plants are grown and harvested. The increasing brutalization of workers in neoliberal economies around the world ensures continued demand for illegal drugs simply in order to survive. Accordingly, their continued illegality is the state's technique for helping capital keep them docile. Oswaldo Zavala demonstrates how the neoliberal Mexican state's militarization, ostensibly against drug-trafficking organizations, stages massacres to perpetuate the mythology of the vicious cartel as an alibi to support the corporate plunder of oil, natural gas, and minerals on communal lands.[20] The ensuing violence—wreaked by the state's war on drugs—has led to massive internal displacement of people in forced migration, their unoccupied lands now vulnerable to unregulated traditional extraction. In this way, workers' use of cocaine and other drugs forms only one piece of infrastructural extraction, tied to more traditional methods and new strategies of power alike. Although my priority here is to defamiliarize infrastructure rather than to dismantle the "narco narrative," my account of cocaine infrastructure resounds beyond the bloodstreams and heartbeats of working people, to their land and right to live free from all forms of violence.

The Art of Darkness

How to Smuggle Cocaine by the Ton, in Five Easy Lessons. The subtitle of Luca Rastello's *I Am the Market* signals its perverse, darkly comic business start-up advice for the would-be drug logistician. "Important: when asking for an advance . . . make sure you get your estimate right because you can't go back to a big-time narco and tell him a little problem has arisen" (124). And: "To stuff a ship full of cocaine, you need mathematical precision, sweat, and good luck. Marble is always a good material because it's easy to cut" (135). And: drug-sniffing dogs can be distracted with ketchup and McDonald's bags, but "should you find yourself in that kind of situation, remember that mustard is much better" (79). Here is a fine satire of the entrepreneurial worker, looking for side-hustles, cultivating contacts, and learning on the job in a postorganization economy. The title *I Am the Market* signals this new environment in do-it-yourself language: "Look at me. I am the market. I am the world as it is. By the end, if you've followed me attentively, you'll be able to set up in business yourself." In a labor market in which formal credentials count for less and less, one needs to convince backers of one's competence. Rastello's logistical underworld thrives on this improvisatory credibility. The essence of all this manipulation of appearances—hiding the cocaine, selling one's own ability to smuggle it, moving it around the world without anyone else knowing—is what Rastello calls "the darkness." The darkness is credibility, or a semblance of reality that is just plausible enough to not provoke a longer look. It depends on the background noise of familiar commodities and brands—all the canned food, toys, clothes, toiletries—but also on the unseen and unheard quality of material. The sistematista becomes an expert on materials—their weights, composition, performance at different temperatures, and thus their capacity for sheltering drugs. Such instrumentality goes all the way down, conjuring a material world already tailored to technical specifications. Material becomes the infrastructure of infrastructure. Its uses already inherent, it is the antimatter of human society, apparently without aesthetics or politics. But, like ordinary infrastructure, material is overwhelmingly visible in its operations, as Rastello's text exemplifies.

"The darkness" signals an aesthetic shift, from a modernist sense of deception that relies on hidden depth to a lighthearted, postmodern play of surfaces and simulation. Rastello's narrator explains the difference like this: "If you carry a box, there will almost always be someone who opens it to see what's inside. But it's rarer for them to take the box to pieces" (131). That means cocaine is best smuggled on the surfaces of containers, inside things that are themselves materials, and in the company of like materials. He hides it in marble, granite, wood, glass, and parquet flooring, often drilling into these infrastructural substances and even ordering them to specification from quarries, or in the case of sheets of glass, coating them in coca paste. As an extra layer of security, he recommends shipping legitimate items made of the same material as the cover material, so that, for example, if you're hiding cocaine from port security scanners with graphite, you ship pencils along with it. The narrator imagines impregnating the tarpaulin used to cover eucalyptus wood with virtually undetectable liquid cocaine; and one wonders if sistematistas have by now coated the shipping containers and ships themselves with it. Spurning anything like a container that could be opened, the narrator even cites the nineteenth-century text that became a stalwart of poststructuralism, Edgar Allan Poe's "The Purloined Letter," quoting its maxim, "Nothing is better hidden than what is in full view" (132). In this Baudrillardian simulacrum, containers are turned inside out, interior becomes surface, and ground and figure are reversed. As in ordinary management science, the emphasis is on innovation rather than invention, cleverness rather than inspiration. Take for example Malcom MacLean, who merely noticed that the shipping container could be craned onto a truck bed to make transportation more efficient, proving that technical feats of deception only improve an existing system.[21] As Saviano notes, "No business in the world is so dynamic, so relentlessly innovative, so loyal to the pure free market spirit as the global cocaine business" (310). The sistematista is the logistician's logistician, optimizing profit by rearranging the packaging and the materials. Fittingly, the narrator's name is that of a material: "They called me Piastrella, 'Tile,' because of my official job—marble" (111).

A second aspect of "the darkness" is the art of fake invoicing, which allows the sistematista to move cocaine inside the shipments of reputable firms. The cocaine-dosed shipment of marble is invoiced to a well-known corporation, but with the logistician's name on the delivery order. He goes to the customs house to receive the shipment and pays all the fees. But then he explains that after he shipped the marble, the reputable firm withdrew its order. He tells the customs officer he will lose all his money if he can't buy it back himself; if the official can amend the invoice to release the goods to him, he will gift him 10 percent. In this way, Tile describes shipping cocaine through the respectable Venezuelan marble firm Zanon, who sold it to a well-known Italian brand, Marazzi; no one at either company ever knew that Tile was using them. "The art of delivery in the dark relies on this fact; it's a cynical art. It implicates people who have nothing to do with it. It's a form of vampirism: you don't suck their blood, you suck their names" (145–46). A cynical art requires a cynical method: the cocaine hiding in Fiat cars or Dole pineapples exposes the extent to which recognizable brands form a brittle veneer of credibility on the exploitations of ordinary global trade.

Cynicism also pervades the long-standing connection between conventional infrastructure, the construction industry, and organized crime: infrastructural projects have long served as fronts for money laundering. As Tile explains, "Often the institutions, whether knowingly or not, play the game too, especially when they need to legitimize themselves. 'Development of the territory,' they call it, and they pay our bills partly by promoting approved building projects. A real washing machine for us" (126). The result is a landscape full of cocaine capital lying in plain sight, as shopping centers and parking garages made with laundered money and the sweat of cheap labor. This is no aberration or failure; rather, it exposes the naivete of liberal faith in clean construction and legitimate business. Rastello's cynical logistician reveals that what is true of organized crime is true of putatively legitimate corporations: the infrastructural projects in which they invest benefit themselves, not the public to whom they're sold. Tile jokes about the fortunes to be made through this cynicism: "What a laugh. It's a gambling table where you bet on the obvious" (137). The criminal's brazenness succeeds because everyone else at the table is zealously overanalyzing—the same way the detectives in "The Purloined Letter" take apart every stick of furniture, rather than notice the stolen letter sitting in the card rack.

Because it dwells only in material's usefulness rather than in its sensuous and realist details—its human interface, so to speak—the sistematista's aesthetic develops into abstraction. Of his cocaine parcels, Rastello's narrator parenthetically muses, "Isn't it beautiful, the geometrical dance of the cakes? Sometimes I see a world made up of little cubes, disks, tips of pyramids, and cones, all dancing against a dark background, every one made of coca, every one opalescent and beautiful" (131). Here cocaine becomes abstract, elemental geometrical shapes that can be made to look like anything. If this seems like artistic freedom, especially since Tile can name his price to his patron, and his "art" has a ready audience, it is artistic license taken to a criminal, antisocial, noncommunicative extreme. Moreover, the cocaine's purity signals its abstraction: "I'm talking about pure substance," says Tile, "an abstraction. What reaches the nostrils of customers is cut with substances of all kinds" (128). The identity and interchangeability of units of pure cocaine make them abstract. Jeff Kinkle and Alberto Toscano have described this fetishization of abstraction in the vogue for visual art that represents logistics. Foregrounding the colorful modularity of shipping containers, they have noted how much artists appreciate them for their "seriality, repetition, and modularity."[22] But this abstract aesthetic of control also signifies the circulation of capital. Alan Sekula has likened the containers to stacked banknotes—emphasizing their signification of financialization.[23] One can always make the obvious bet on cocaine because it operates like currency, a fact underscored by suppliers' practice of paying transporters with it. As currency, cocaine is also part of global finance.

That cocaine, and the profits it generates, grounds the lawful global economy became headline news in 2009.[24] During the financial crisis, drug money came to the rescue, sustaining banks with massive cash infusions before they were bailed out. Antonio Maria Costa, head of the United Nations Office on Drugs and Crime, estimated that $352 billion of drug profits "was the only liquid investment capital" available to keep some banks from failing and was absorbed into the economy as a result.[25] If neoliberal financial policies brought the banking system to the edge of collapse by overvaluing assets as thin as air, then the cocaine economy gave it roots, through merchandisers who deal in a tangible good and demand immediate cash payments. As an asset impervious to resource shortages and market inflation, cocaine—minus the violence incurred by its illegality—is a safe investment. Its vast and deep market penetration, as infrastructure for everyday life, helps maintain the real darkness of inequity in the so-called legitimate economy, which shows no signs of dispersal.

The Work of Cocaine

If Rastello's nonfiction novel confronts the spectacular violence of the cocaine economy with satire, Saviano's *ZeroZeroZero* takes a journalistic approach at once more straightforward and more eclectic, combining highly optionable vignettes of colorful narcos and the shifting fortunes of their organizations with theories of historical materialism. He meditates briefly on cocaine as a substance, including in a terrible poem. And he recounts his own experiences as a writer exiled from his hometown, Naples, for his exposure of the Camorra and 'Ndrangheta. Formally, his books resemble similar accounts by journalists, such as Sam Quinones's *Dreamland* (2015) and Michael Slater's *Wolf Boys* (2016), with more experimentation around the edges, and a more complex autobiographical investment.[26]

One of the more compelling passages in which Saviano excavates the political economy of cocaine infrastructure is the rambling, two-page précis of *ZeroZeroZero*, titled "Coke #1," which requires a slightly lengthy quotation to convey its exhaustive tone:

> The guy sitting next to you on the train uses cocaine, he took it to get himself going this morning; or the driver of the bus you're taking home, he wants to put in some overtime without feeling the cramps in his neck. The people closest to you use coke. . . . And if they don't, the truck driver delivering tons of coffee to cafés around town does; he wouldn't be able to hack those long hours on the road without it. And if he doesn't, the nurse who's changing your grandfather's catheter does. Coke makes everything seem so much easier, even the night shift. And if she doesn't, the painter redoing your girlfriend's room does; he was just curious at first but wound up deep in debt. The people who use cocaine are right here, right next to you. The police

> officer who's about to pull you over has been snorting for years, and everyone knows it, and they write anonymous letters to his chief hoping he'll be suspended before he screws up big time. Or the surgeon who's just waking up and will soon operate on your aunt. Cocaine helps him cut open six people a day. Or your divorce lawyer. Or the judge presiding over your lawsuit . . . the carpenter who's installing the cabinets that cost you a month's salary. Or the workman who came to put together the IKEA closet you couldn't figure out how to assemble on your own. (1)

Saviano's list, which continues in this vein for two pages, describes a Western middle- and working-class society of which cocaine is the lifeblood. The riff answers the question of where the tons upon tons of cocaine in the sistematistas' shipments go. Cocaine makes everyday life happen, especially when labor is tedious and leisure is unfulfilling. Its pervasiveness suggests a culture enshrouded in its own kind of darkness, composed of alienation and lassitude temporarily enlivened by cocaine's energetic bump. Elsewhere in the book he defines cocaine as "a carburant. Cocaine is a devastating, terrible, deadly energy" (375). It is "life, cubed" (36). Although this paradoxically life-giving, death-dealing substance fuels work, the addressee of "Coke #1" is pointedly middle class, someone who owns multiple homes, supports a family and a mistress, has ample discretionary income, hires workers, and reads books at bedtime. The long list winds up with an accusation for this sort of person: "But if, after you think about it, you're still convinced none of these people could possibly snort cocaine, you're either blind or you're lying. Or the one who uses it is you" (4). The point of the book that follows, then, is to reveal to the unethical consumer the real cost of their consumption: primarily of cocaine, but also, Saviano hints, of everything else. Interspersed with such experimental vignettes, the book proceeds mainly through the more traditional mode of storytelling, to narrate the political economy of cocaine-as-infrastructure.

One such story is of an elderly Mexican *campesino* named Don Arturo, who recalls how one day soldiers came and burned down the poppy fields in his village. They were following government orders to stop the drug trade. None of the poor poppy farmers, or *gomeros*, would attempt to rescue their fellows, who had been sleeping in the field and were burning to death. Then a dog, all skin and bones, ran into the fire to rescue "two, three, finally six puppies, rolling each one on the ground to put out the flames" (17). Arturo thus learned at an early age that "beasts have courage, and know what it means to defend life. Men boast about courage, but all they know how to do is obey, crawl, get by" (18). The observation opens onto the further irony that one day twenty years later, more soldiers return to the field and instruct the peasants, who had been growing grain, to start growing poppies again. These are for morphine, because "the United States was preparing for war, and before the guns, before the bullets, tanks, planes, and aircraft carriers, before the uniforms and boots, before everything else, the United States needed morphine. You don't go to war without morphine" (18). Saviano lets Don Arturo's voice tell the story of the US empire, with its hypocritical, ambivalent dependence on Mexican drug production—and its military reliance on pharmacological logistics—and it acquires the force of a parable. Beginning with the realist detail of the dog, the story expands to its novelistic reversal, of the about-face in US policy, then delivers its message as a maxim. The *gomeros*' silence and overdetermination by US military and economic force reveals their labor as processual, systematic, and infrastructural. They become allegorical figures, passive and one-dimensional, cocaine-saturated tools of capital rather than human defenders of life. Shaylih Muehlmann describes a similar romanticization of the Cucapá people of Baja California and Sonora by the narcos who employ them to smuggle drugs.[27] In *ZeroZeroZero*, a compilation of such linked, true-but-embellished stories, with characters such as Arturo passing in and out of the narrative, construes the text as a nonfiction novel.[28] While many of Saviano's stories present grisly narco violence, aligning them with the narco narrative that propagandizes for state militarization against the people, this story at least reminds readers that, as the biggest narco thug of them all, the US government's command of infrastructure is vast and deep.

Gomorrah, as full of grisly violence enacted upon workers as *ZeroZeroZero*, uses story to craft a realism so heightened that it verges on surrealism. It opens with the tale of a Neapolitan port crane operator who is lifting a container when its hatches spring open midair and the contents start falling out. To avoid resensationalizing this literary spectacle of racialized death, I will not reproduce the quote; it involves the operator at first observing mannequins and then realizing they are frozen human corpses. These were Chinese migrant workers who had saved money for their remains to be returned to their hometowns. Here Saviano's literary-visual excess illustrates capital's obscene equivalence between people and goods. The passage evokes Conrad's famous slow-developing image from *Heart of Darkness*, another novel about supply chains, in which Marlow sees "round knobs [that] were not ornamental but symbolic; they were expressive and puzzling, striking and disturbing—food for thought and also for vultures if there had been any looking down from the sky."[29] And like Conrad's, the passage's spectacle is racialized. The crane operator, Saviano writes, "covered his face with his hands as he told me about it, eyeing me through his fingers. As if the mask of his hands might give him the courage to speak" (3). The story inaugurates Saviano's account of the port of Naples, where the Chinese shipping company Cosco brings goods to Europe. Like the sleeping *gomeros*, the Chinese laborers become allegorical figures: although they were in the right place at the right time to supply labor, their lives—exhausted by that role—reach such a negative value that even their dead bodies cannot be properly buried. The spectacle of their fall compresses production and consumption, capital and labor, logistics and infrastructure, extraction and plenitude. The story figures workers' bodies as the origin of the neoliberal world, and their abstraction as its apocalyptic end. By representing logistical infrastructure's desecrating impact on human bodies, Saviano makes its ordinary criminal operationality visible to readers: the very interchangeability of the ubiquitous shipping containers levels the distinction between formal and informal economies.

As interesting to Saviano as workers' bodies is the material of their work. While Rastello's sistematista's dancing geometrical shapes of cocaine erase its sensuous materiality to emphasize its instrumentality to capital, Saviano accentuates the sensuous perceptibility of its material effects. In *Gomorrah*, working construction several summers, and "getting my hands and nose near cement" was "the only way I knew to understand what power—real power—was built on," he writes.[30] In this death world, demands for fast construction lead to fifteen-hour shifts, the elimination of all safety measures, numerous fatalities, and afterward, the well-practiced art of covering them up by stuffing the corpse in a car and faking a crash—another scene of credibility. Describing young, impoverished, anonymous men working long shifts on construction sites for a pittance, he suggests that cocaine helps them perform this backbreaking labor (217). Saviano's work with cement and cocaine allows him to see past ordinary social spaces to the labor and material that created them. He cannot see stairs or floors, only the cement of which they are made: "Materials are not perceived in the same way everywhere. I believe that in Qatar the smell of petroleum and gas evokes sensations of mansions, sunglasses, and limousines. The same acid smell of fossil fuel in Minsk evokes darkened faces, gas leaks, and smoking cities" (214). When he describes "the odor of lime and cement" wafting off the socks, cuff links, and bookshelves of successful Italian businessmen, the sensory detail shows how capital becomes a political actor that is haunted by the violence of extraction (218). Although this includes conventional environmental extraction,—for example, the toxic waste the Camorra buries throughout southern Italy—Saviano always remains focused on the extraction of energy from workers. His most arresting example of cement is its use by the Camorra to eliminate workers who threaten the supply chain: when they fill their victims' noses and mouths with sand, mucus hardens it in a process similar to cement mixing, causing suffocation. The worker's cocaine-tinged flesh and mucus become the excess material of infrastructural construction itself, as much as those workers fabled to be entombed in the concrete of the Brooklyn Bridge or the Hoover Dam.

Written by the Body

The embodiment of labor governs Saviano's literary theory. In contrast to Rastello's performative cynical detachment, *Gomorrah* and *ZeroZeroZero* elucidate a theory that is embodied, sensual, and living. This theory is inseparable from the question of Saviano's survival that arose with the death threats issued at *Gomorrah*'s publication. In the preface to the book, Saviano insists on writing's status as the physical activity of a sensing and perceiving individual, who produces "words which before they were ink on paper were thoughts and feelings, life itself" (preface). Words "rise from your chest and begin to resonate," he tells readers in *ZeroZeroZero* (79). Moreover, this physical writing is itself a violent weapon—not only against the Camorra and 'Ndrangheta—but against an equally sensuous, embodied material world. "I wanted to cut into the flesh of reality," he said of writing *Gomorrah*. "I wanted with my very being to change the reality around me, a reality that disgusted me" (preface). Writing is the intervention of a whole person. Just so, Saviano the living individual defends his published texts, "body and soul. With daily commitment, even after these words were physically removed from me" (preface). In this way, he sees his survival under police protection as a guarantee of his writing. He insists on its veracity, not merely as an assemblage of evidentiary facts but as truths both experienced and made—both factual and artifactual: "The proofs are irrefutable *because they are partial*, recorded with my eyes, recounted with words, and tempered with emotions that have echoed off iron and wood. I see, hear, look, talk, and in this way I testify. . . . I know and I can prove it" (213; emphasis added). As he writes in *ZeroZeroZero*, like a "mosaic" or a "fresco," writing—which in its embodiment and partiality becomes story—"stop[s] the consumption of news and begin[s] the digestion of mechanisms" (1). Digestion, the work of a living body, uses the sensual to make information real and to connect it to its historical context. In all this, Saviano echoes Walter Benjamin's argument in his essay "The Storyteller": that stories, unlike news, seem to come from experience, are told in a language close to speech, possess a practical purpose for the communities in which they are told, and most significantly, are eroding with the acceleration of news cycles and the fetishization of information.[31]

For Benjamin, the story stood opposed to the novel, which, being dependent on the technology of the published book, necessarily disconnected its author from its audience. "The novelist has isolated himself. The birthplace of the novel is the solitary individual, who is no longer able to express himself by giving examples of his most important concerns, is himself uncounseled, and cannot counsel others."[32] This description suggests that Saviano, who is bursting with important concerns, is instead writing stories. *Gomorrah* is subtitled *A Personal Journey into the Violent International Empire of Naples' Organized Crime System* because Saviano narrates his own sorrow and rage at what the Camorra has done to his city. Saviano is so embodied a storyteller that his tales have put a price on his head. Here the death of the author is a material question: although publication has sent his words abroad, his life remains tethered to them. Saviano's self-image, of cutting through reality with words, rings romantic, naive, brimming with white, masculine, middle-class bravado and saviorism. But to Italians nauseated by the criminal infiltration of a democratic state, and the rise of a violent economic system predicated on credible appearances rather than concrete truths, Saviano's willingness to back his writing with his life has made him a national hero. Their faith in Saviano's integrity represents the credit they are still willing to extend to the state, liberally conceived, as capable of protecting and defending them against capital predation once it is made aware of injustice. In this paradigm Saviano, who remains protected by the carabinieri, and who dedicated *ZeroZeroZero* to them, fulfills a classic liberal role of the state writer.

Saviano has since set aside the story-dominated nonfiction novel, publishing *Piranhas: The Boy Bosses of Naples: A Novel.* This bourgeois move, like his Hollywood deals, mirrors the state's constant seduction by capital; yet we might also say that Saviano has performed heroic service and deserves a retirement of sorts. In *Piranhas*, his creation of a Neapolitan criminal underworld run by teenagers, the realism, surrealism, and impressionism of his nonfiction novels tilt toward naturalism.[33] Appropriately, Zola is one of his favorite authors, in a group of social realists that includes Melville, Balzac, and Tolstoy. A creaturely view of humans suits a world hemmed in by addictive substances and capital violence on their bodies, which become barometers of extraction, registering alternately energy and exhaustion. Determinism by large economic and political forces channels the fatalism of his nonfiction stories. Of novel genres, naturalism may be the closest to story, because it is tied historically to reformist journalism, a blend of empiricism and activism. Naturalism, story, and allegory cannot slow the logistical pace of profit, regulate capital's control of infrastructure and material, palliate the pain of extracted labor, or realize the state's protective purpose. Is the story complex enough to convey the relations of infrastructure, logistics, cocaine and other drugs, globalized economies, and organized crime? Criticizing narco narratives' romanticization of lethal violence, Zavala calls on them to "abandon the exhausted myths of drug lords and their fantastic kingdoms and stop objectifying drug trafficking as a problem external to official power in Mexico and the U.S."[34] By this metric, Saviano's highly optionable tales only occasionally succeed. Yet both he and Zavala share a belief in narrative. Ten years after writing *Gomorrah*, Saviano wrote, "I lost . . . all faith in social change, but I continue to nourish an almost dogmatic hope: that telling a story can still rescue whatever is human in man" (preface). Story is older than the state, capital, and infrastructure. In spite of its susceptibility to romanticization, it may be the last tool left to us to critique their criminal relations.[35]

I have emphasized the differences between Rastello's and Saviano's uses of the nonfiction novel, between the former's satire and the latter's sincerity. Their common trait, however, suggests that the genre performs cultural work that ordinary fiction, straightforward journalism, and nonfiction cannot. For the credibility that they must cultivate is that of the individual human voice, the origin of story in the truth of narratable experience. This singular credibility anchors and makes relevant to readers all the anonymous violence of infrastructure and global trade that they do not otherwise see.

Notes

1. Roberto Saviano, *ZeroZeroZero: Look at Cocaine and All You See Is Powder: Look through Cocaine and You See the World*, trans. Virginia Jewiss (New York: Penguin, 2015), 326–35 (originally published in Italian in 2013). Further citations to this novel appear in parentheses in the text.

2. Luca Rastello, *I Am the Market: How to Smuggle Cocaine by the Ton, in Five Easy Lessons*, trans. Jonathan Hunt (New York: Farrar, Straus and Giroux, 2009), 147. Further citations to this novel appear in parentheses in the text.

3. See my forthcoming "'Back on the Chain Gang': Logistics, Labor, and the Threat of Infrastructure," in "Making Ground: Infrastructure and Environment," ed. Adriana Johnson and Daniel Nemser, special issue, *Social Text* 40, no. 4 (December 2022).

4. Ned Rossiter, *Software, Infrastructure, Labor: A Media Theory of Logistical Nightmares* (London: Routledge, 2016), 5.

5. Jesse Fink and Luis Nava, *Pure Narco: One Man's True Story of 25 Years inside the Colombian and Mexican Cartels* (London: John Blake, 2020), xlix.

6. Keller Easterling, *Extrastatecraft: The Power of Infrastructure Space* (London: Verso, 2014).

7. See Deborah Cowen and Winona LaDuke, "Wiindigo Infrastructures," *South Atlantic Quarterly* 119, no. 2 (April 2020): 250; and Anna Stanley, "Aligning against Indigenous Jurisdiction: Worker Savings, Colonial Capital, and the Canadian Infrastructure Bank," *Environment and Planning D: Society and Space* 37, no. 6 (2019): 1138–56.

8. China Miéville, "Blood & Ice," *Rejectamentalist Manifesto*, August 6, 2010.

9. Hector Amaya, *Trafficking: Narcoculture in Mexico and the United States* (Durham, NC: Duke University Press, 2020), 217.

10. In 2018, 2 percent of the US population or 5.5 million people reported using cocaine, and common sense suggests the actual figure, including unreported use, is higher. "Drug Abuse Statistics," National Center for Drug Abuse Statistics, 2020, https://drugabusestatistics.org/. See also National Institute on Drug Abuse, "Cocaine Research Report" (Bethesda, MD: NIDA, May 2016). In 2012, the European Monitoring Centre for Drugs and Drug Addiction found that 15.5 million Europeans had used cocaine at least once in the previous year; that report also suggests a decrease in cocaine use since 2008, which accords with a rise in opioid use in both the United States and Europe. European Monitoring Centre for Drugs and Drug Addiction, *Annual Report 2012* (Luxembourg: Publications of the European Union, 2012).

11. See Brett Neilson and Mohammed Bamyeh, "Drugs in Motion: Towards a Materialist Tracking of Global Mobilities," *Cultural Critique* 71 (Winter 2009): 6; and in the same issue, Paul Gootenberg's "Talking about the Flow: Drugs, Borders, and the Discourse of Drug Control."

12. On opium consumed by Southeast Asian coolies, see Carl A. Trocki, *Opium, Empire, and the Global Political Economy* (London: Routledge, 1999), 148; on alcohol in Britain, see Brian Harrison, *Drink and the Victorians: The Temperance*

Question in England, 1815–1872 (Pittsburgh: University of Pittsburgh Press, 1971); on the opioid crisis, see Anne Case and Angus Deaton, *Deaths of Despair and the Future of Capitalism* (Princeton, NJ: Princeton University Press, 2020); and Sam Quinones, *Dreamland: The True Tale of America's Opioid Epidemic* (New York: Bloomsbury, 2015).

13. Lauren Berlant, "The Commons: Infrastructures for Troubling Times," *Environment and Planning D: Society and Space* 34, no. 3 (2016): 393.

14. AbdouMaliq Simone, "People as Infrastructure: Intersecting Fragments in Johannesburg," *Public Culture* 16, no. 3 (2004): 407, 408. See also *City Life from Jakarta to Dakar: Movements at the Crossroads* (London: Routledge, 2010).

15. See Stefanie Graeter, "Infrastructural Incorporations: Toxic Storage, Corporate Indemnity, and Ethical Deferral in Peru's Neoextractive Era," *American Anthropologist* (2020): 21–36; Michelle Murphy, "Distributed Reproduction, Chemical Violence, and Latency," *S&F Online: Life (Un)ltd: Feminism, Bioscience, Race* 11, no. 3 (Summer 2013); and Rahul Mukherjee, *Radiant Infrastructures: Media, Environment, and Cultures of Uncertainty* (Durham, NC: Duke University Press, 2020).

16. Macarena Gomez-Barris, *The Extractive Zone: Social Ecologies and Decolonial Perspectives* (Durham, NC: Duke University Press, 2017).

17. Anna Lowenhaupt Tsing, *The Mushroom at the End of the World: On the Possibility of Life in Capitalist Ruins* (Princeton, NJ: Princeton University Press, 2015), 270–74.

18. Sandro Mezzadra and Brett Neilson, *The Politics of Operations: Excavating Contemporary Capitalism* (Durham, NC: Duke University Press, 2019).

19. Kalindi Vora, *Life Support: Biocapital and the New History of Outsourced Labor* (Minneapolis: University of Minnesota Press, 2015).

20. Oswaldo Zavala, "Dispossession by Militarization: Forced Displacements and the Neoliberal 'Drug War' for Energy in Mexico," in *Liquid Borders: Migration as Resistance*, ed. Mabel Moraña (New York: Routledge, 2021), 339.

21. For an analysis of McLean's innovation, see Alexander Klose, *The Container Principle: How a Box Changes the Way We Think*, trans. Charles Macrum II (Cambridge, MA: MIT Press, 2015), 85–91.

22. Jeff Kinkle and Alberto Toscano, *Cartographies of the Absolute* (Arlesford: Zero Books, 2015), 200.

23. Alan Sekula, *Fish Story* (Rotterdam: Witte de With, 1995), unpaginated Kindle edition.

24. For a more detailed account of the fluidity between the informal and formal economies, see Abril Trigo, "Transmigrants as Embodiment of Biocapitalism," in *Liquid Borders,* 95.

25. Rajeev Syal, "Drug Money Saved Banks in Global Crisis, Claims UN Advisor," *Guardian*, December 13, 2009.

26. As a contrast, consider Shaylih Muehlman's nuanced and locally specific *When I Wear My Alligator Boots: Narco-Culture in the US-Mexico Borderlands* (Berkeley: University of California Press, 2013), which describes the lives of several villagers in the drug corridor north of the gulf of California to illustrate the larger political economy of drug trades.

27. Shaylih Muehlmann, "Clandestine Infrastructures: Illicit Connectivities in the US-Mexico Borderlands," in *Infrastructure, Environment, and Life in the*

Anthropocene, ed. Kregg Hetherington (Durham, NC: Duke University Press, 2019).

28. "Nonfiction novel" is more a colloquial or marketing term than a technical name of a literary genre. Passing descriptions refer to its focus on crime and relation to journalism, citing Truman Capote's *In Cold Blood* (1965) as its origin.

29. Joseph Conrad, *Heart of Darkness* (London: Penguin, 2017), 59.

30. Roberto Saviano, *Gomorrah: A Personal Journey into the Violent International Empire of Naples' Organized Crime System*, trans. Virginia Jewiss (New York: Farrar, Straus and Giroux, 2006), 210–11. Further citations to this novel appear in parentheses in the text.

31. Walter Benjamin, "The Storyteller," in *Illuminations*, trans. Harry Zohn (New York: Schocken, 1968), 83–85.

32. Benjamin, "The Storyteller," 87.

33. Robert Saviano, *Piranhas: The Boy Bosses of Naples: A Novel*, trans. Anthony Shugaar (New York: Picador, 2019).

34. Oswaldo Zavala, "Imagining the U.S.-Mexico Drug War: The Critical Limits of Narconarratives," *Comparative Literature* 66, no. 3 (2014): 340–60.

35. Scholarship at the intersection of critical Indigenous studies and infrastructure studies also makes stories the social technique for obtaining an equitable future: "Stories insist on the ethical, embodied, and affective dimensions of knowing, refusing imperial systems of knowledge that divide fact from fiction, mind from body, and the sacred from survival." Cowen and LaDuke, "Wiindigo Infrastructures," 245.

Afterword

✦

Rediscoveries of the Ordinary; or, All That Is Solid . . .

Jennifer Wenzel

In thinking between literary studies and infrastructure studies, to what extent, and with how much friction, do the concerns and assumptions of one field translate to the other? In this afterword, I consider this question by tracing notions of "the ordinary" and what it signifies in examples from each disciplinary domain. What are the possibilities and the perils of undertaking such interdisciplinary bridgework?

Let me begin with a beautiful passage from "The Lesanes of Nadia Street," a short story published in 1956 by the South African writer Ezekiel (Es'kia) Mphahlele: "Outside there in the street the young folk were dancing. Dancing as if yesterday they didn't have a riotous beer-spilling raid; as if tomorrow they might not have a pass and tax raid. For them today was just a chunk of sweetened and flavoured Time. And in all this there was a spirit of permanence which they felt, without thinking about it."[1] For me, that poignant phrase "just a chunk of sweetened and flavoured Time" captures a sense of the ordinary as a sustaining daily rhythm of community life, amid the horrors and indignities of apartheid in its first decade. This period saw the creation of a massive state apparatus and infrastructure of racial classification, in the service of the legislated racialization of every aspect of life and what was called the *canalization* of migrant labor, which aimed precisely against any "spirit of permanence" for settled Black urban communities. Between 1956 and his exile from South Africa in 1957, Mphahlele published several short stories set on Nadia Street in *Drum* magazine, which became an important vehicle for narrating and visualizing Black urban life in the South African 1950s. Fiction, photography, and journalism in *Drum* made discursive claims upon a right to the city at a moment when such rights were being legislated away. By the end of the decade, the "spirit of permanence" was shattered by the brutal enforcement of this legislation in the form of forced removals from

Johannesburg neighborhoods like Sophiatown and Newclare to new, poorly serviced sites on the urban perimeter.

Mphahlele's gritty yet lyrical account of dancing today—not only despite, but indeed *because of*, the raids that happened yesterday and those sure to happen tomorrow—anticipates an important debate that emerged in the 1980s about the role of literature in the antiapartheid struggle. The point of contention in this debate was not *whether* culture was a weapon in the struggle but instead *what kinds* of literary representation were most appropriate to it. In a series of essays in the 1980s, the writer and critic Njabulo S. Ndebele argued against the dominant mode of contemporary Black South African writing, which he described as a literature of protest and spectacle: this literature of spectacle, catalyzed by the Black Consciousness movement and the 1976 Soweto Uprising, aimed to document the moral wrong of apartheid, a gesture that could be revelatory only for a white audience. Ndebele deemed this literary mode counterproductive because, he argued, it created an image of Black South Africans solely as victims and sufferers—in effect, running from one raid to the next—rather than recognizing them as "makers of culture in their own right," attentive to the full range of human experience, both under apartheid and in the world that the antiapartheid struggle sought to bring into being.[2] (Notice the affinity with the editors' aim that *The Aesthetic Life of Infrastructure* will disrupt what they see as a tendency in infrastructure studies "to render racialized subjects abject rather than agential.") Against the literature of spectacle, Ndebele urged what he called "a rediscovery of the ordinary," for which, I argue, Mphahlele's writing of the 1950s is an important model and precursor. For Ndebele, and for Mphahlele before him, the short story genre was a technology of literary representation with profound implications for how Black South Africans understood and imagined themselves, against the modes of racialization (with their attendant bureaucratic and infrastructural machinery) undertaken by the apartheid state.

Mphahlele's commitment to the ordinary is evident even in his decision to set his stories about the Lesane family in the Johannesburg neighborhood of Newclare, which was never glamorized in same way as nearby Sophiatown, the epicenter of the fabulous jazz culture of the 1950s until it was bulldozed by the apartheid state in the forced removals that began in 1955. Newclare, in other words, was "perhaps more representative" of the realities of Black urban life than Sophiatown, which was "seen by many as encapsulating everything romantically dangerous in the life of the 'new African' " and celebrated in the pages of *Drum*.[3] In the first fictional sketch that he set on Nadia Street, Mphahlele describes its chronotope in terms of spatial mobility and temporal stasis, as if awaiting new infrastructural arrangements one might take for granted elsewhere: "The hawker's trolley *still* slogs along in Nadia Street, and the cloppity-clop from the hoofs of the over-fed mare is *still* part of the street" (emphasis added).[4] Another passage from "The Lesanes of

Nadia Street" relates how the news of a couple's decision to marry travels through the community:

> The news had shot up and down Nadia Street like electric current. Along the rows of dilapidated houses that stood cheek-by-jowl as if to support one another in the event of disaster. It had no fences to jump because there are no fences in Newclare. The flies hovering over the dirty water in the street seemed to buzz it around without being involved in the joy of it. The news had percolated through wooden and cardboard paper windows, lashed about from tongue to tongue in the greasy, sticky darkness of Newclare rooms. It took a turn up and then down the next cross-street.[5]

Mphahlele vividly portrays both the buzz of neighborhood gossip and the grim, flyblown details of overcrowded slum life. And yet, I had read and taught this story many times before I recognized the full import of that opening simile, "news . . . [shooting] like electric current." Like most Black neighborhoods in mid-1950s Johannesburg, Newclare probably did not have electricity; at most, it might have had streetlights for policing and surveillance, but not household connections for domestic convenience.[6]

The social and historical life of the electrical grid in South Africa challenges fundamental ideas about infrastructure as "ordinary" or "boring," as articulated in the 1990s by seminal scholars of infrastructure like anthropologists Geoffrey Bowker and Susan Leigh Star. Both Bowker and Star observed the tendency of well-functioning infrastructure to recede from social attention: to become, in other words, ordinary, boring, taken for granted, invisible. More recently, however, anthropologist Brian Larkin and other scholars in infrastructure studies (as well as many of the authors in this collection) have complicated these ideas about infrastructure's putative invisibility by attending to myriad ways in which infrastructure *isn't* invisible and often isn't *meant* to be, as, say, in the spectacle of monumental dams that index postcolonial national arrival. As I have written elsewhere, "Infrastructure cannot be invisible to those charged with its maintenance and repair . . . and certainly not for marginalized communities consigned to inhabit a state of intimate disconnect—a form of life that entails living in close proximity to infrastructure while at the same time disconnected (or excluded) from its circulatory systems."[7]

The sweet and unthought thrum of the ordinary on Mphahlele's Nadia Street ("a spirit of permanence which they felt, without thinking about it"[8]) is precisely this state of disconnect, which is the inverse of the anthropologists' erstwhile "boring" infrastructure. The buzz of electricity on Nadia Street exists solely in the realm of metaphor, the "as-if" counterfactual rhythm of life without the inevitable daily raid. This contradiction epitomizes the complex politics of the ordinary in apartheid South Africa. While the state strove to depict and establish its racial hierarchy as ordinary (i.e., normal, natural, God-given), writers like Mphahlele in the 1950s and Ndebele in the 1980s understood that meaningful survival required holding on to a sustaining sense of ordinary life as a "spirit of permanence" amid what turned out to be decades of spectacular oppression and heroic resistance. For literary studies, however, this contradiction points to another important and underrecognized aspect of infrastructure's lenticular flickering within multiple regimes of visibility: not merely *now* you see it (or don't) but also *how*. This is what the editors of *The Aesthetic Life of Infrastructure* have in mind by reorienting infrastructure studies' seminal visibility thesis toward inquiring into the *legibility* of infrastructure, a pivot from (not) seeing to reading that has been important in my own work in environmental and energy humanities.[9] A reader's own capacity to plug in, as part of the unthought horizon of the ordinary, can shape what they notice on the page: even the likely *absence* of access to the grid in Mphahlele's short story long escaped my attention, until I started reading for infrastructure.

Any notion of the electric grid in South Africa as ordinary or invisible was exploded in December 1961, when a pylon near Durban was targeted and toppled in the launch of a campaign of sabotage and armed struggle by Umkhonto we Sizwe, the armed wing of the African National Congress. Apartheid-era priorities for electrification included industry (particularly the massively subsidized, coal-generated electricity provided to the mines), the convenience of white South Africans, and surveillance and policing of the areas to which Black South Africans were forcibly removed. In the transformations of the postapartheid era, the electrification of rural and previously underserved urban areas collided with post–Cold War neoliberal cost-recovery schemes, with the incapacity of the electric grid to meet democratic demands, and with the susceptibility of the national electric utility, Eskom, to "state capture"—South African parlance for diverting the levers of the state away from (good) governance and toward systemic corruption and looting of public goods. Since 2008, all of this has meant periodic "load shedding," a phrase that denotes the more or less planned interruption of electricity when demand far exceeds supply ("rolling blackouts" is the US equivalent) but that also evokes metaphorical notions of state withdrawal from carrying the burdens of citizens' infrastructural needs.

If, as scholars of infrastructure tell us, access to the electric grid entails and enables forms of social inclusion and empowerment associated with citizenship, then the interruptions entailed in "load shedding" might offer a way of understanding the contradictions of energy infrastructure in contemporary South Africa. In an inverse parallel to the apartheid-era struggle tactic of "bringing the struggle to white areas" as part of an effort to make apartheid South Africa "ungovernable," load shedding makes clear to all (and not just the chronically underserved racialized majority) the democratic incapacities of the grid as well as the precarity of grid citizenship. Examining the "suggestive symbolic and psychic dimensions" of the phrase *load shedding*, Sarah Nuttall and Liz McGregor consider how the electricity crisis that began in 2008 reflects and evokes broader shifts in the "burden of being South African," "the feeling that we are living at the end of the dream years, at the tail end of our big Idea, and that we would need to find a different form of politics and new forms of personal resilience in order to move forward, both with the life of the country and with our own lives."[10] Among the personal essays collected in *Load Shedding: Writing on and over the Edge of South Africa* (2009), Achille Mbembe and Sarah Nuttall each reflect achingly on the relationships between infrastructural failure and the politics of "everyday" life in South Africa.

The electrical grid, in other words, offers a material/metaphorical through line for tracing historical trajectories of racialization, democratization, and stalled (or interrupted) liberation in terms of the complex politics of the ordinary. In *Democracy's Infrastructure: Technopolitics and Protest after Apartheid*, anthropologist Antina van Schnitzler aptly describes the *intransigence* of apartheid infrastructure in contemporary South Africa, arguing that the putative transformation of South Africa into an "ordinary" country involves conflicts and misrecognitions over the meaning of *politics* itself. As a ruling party, the African National Congress has treated as *criminal* forms of mass action that are not dissimilar from those it had once encouraged in the antiapartheid struggle. In other words, citizens in the "new" (if now fraying) South Africa have used tactics of boycott, nonpayment, pirating, and sabotage that originated in the apartheid era, precisely in order to protest post-1994 failures of "service delivery": that is, inadequate or unaffordable provisioning of water, sewerage, and electricity. For many South Africans, both under apartheid and after, infrastructure is hardly ordinary, in the sense of taken for granted, invisible. What van Schnitzler's analysis shares with the notions of the ordinary as imagined by writers like Mphahlele and Ndebele is an impatience with too-narrow notions of politics or "the struggle." To valorize and recognize only spectacular oppression or heroic action is to miss the quotidian terrain of domestic life, in which daily contact with the electricity or water meter, rather than the longer rhythms of the ballot box, is a site of politics where citizens interact with (or are intimately disconnected from) the state.

This affinity does not mean, however, that we can translate easily between infrastructure and literature. The short story is not a technology of racial representation enabling the infrastructure of labor canalization in the same way that the passbook was, although Peter McDonald's excavation of the workings of apartheid censorship in *The Literature Police* (2009) would warn us not to draw too strong a line between the representational technologies of prose fiction and those of the apartheid state, given the vast, if unpredictable and quixotic, powers of that privileged reader who was the apartheid censor. Still, the antinomies of the "ordinary" under apartheid and its intransigent afterlives might point to some of the difficulties of thinking infrastructure across disciplines, particularly as literary studies now turns in earnest to the questions of temporality, materiality, circulation, desire, and power, which anthropologists in critical infrastructure studies have opened up in such exciting directions over the past decade.[11] This turn to infrastructure represents an opening to bring aesthetic modes of intelligence more fully to bear on matters of form, figuration, and narrative.

Infrastructure is good to think with, as anthropologist Ashley Carse has remarked, because of its simultaneous "conceptual plasticity . . . and undeniable materiality."[12] That dual imbrication with matter and metaphor has made infrastructure a topic of increasing interest to literary critics. Yet on this veritable playground for the literary-critical imagination, the suggestive and plastic possibilities of metaphor have revealed that it is in fact quite possible (even if not desirable) to deny the materiality of infrastructure. In other words—to shift by way of conclusion into a more prescriptive and provocative mode—I want to argue that what Ramesh Mallipedi and Susan Zieger have called the "material matrix" of infrastructure demands that we humanities scholars be somewhat more mindful of our metaphors.[13] What follows is a plea for circumspection and rigor in the interdisciplinary bridge work required to think between literature and infrastructure.

"Poetry," wrote Audre Lorde, "is not only dream and vision; it is the skeleton architecture for our lives. It lays the foundations for a future of change, a bridge across our fears of what has never been before."[14] Poetry is architecture for living: it bridges the present and the future; like infrastructure at its literal and historical root, it is foundational, a subterranean act of ground laying, ordering, and enabling. But the power of Lorde's claim for poetry as infrastructure hangs on what the meaning of *is* is. To be sure, skeletons, buildings, foundations, and bridges (are images that) tend toward the concrete, as compared with the airy ideations of "dream and vision." Nonetheless, to say that a poem is infrastructure is to lay claim to the power of metaphor, in its life-sustaining, world-building capacity to assert, startlingly, that *x* is *y*. The revelatory power of metaphor inheres in the until-that-very-moment tacit certainty that *x* is in fact not *y*, nor even very much *like y*. A poem is a bridge; a poem is like a bridge; its poemness means that ultimately it is (or was) not (just) (like) a bridge. The news shoots up and down Nadia Street like electric current. There is no electric current on Nadia Street. The simile does not make it so.

To hold fast to the "undeniable materiality" of infrastructure is to worry over literary-critical theorizations in which tenor is untethered from vehicle, floating free. An important precursor to *The Aesthetic Lives of Infrastructure* was a 2015 *Modern Fiction Studies* special issue on "Infrastructuralism," edited by Michael Rubenstein, Bruce Robbins, and Sophie Beal, which considered what the recent ferment in critical infrastructure studies meant for studies of literature. In her essay in that issue, Carolyn Levine argues that the dispersed and iterative aspects of racism make it "infrastructural" rather than "structural"; this formal observation about racism's spatial and temporal patterns leads her to posit that "racism and other structural factors emerge as more infrastructural than what we typically define as infrastructures. . . . Racism seems at least as fundamental as the networks it encounters, having the power to shape the infrastructures of roads, mass transit, and clean water. . . . Racism is in this sense as much or more infrastructural than the electric grid or water supply."[15] Consider the boldness of these claims, a kind of antitautology: *racism is more infrastructural than infrastructure*. Reading etymologically, Levine takes the prefix *infra-* to mean simply *fundamental*; in her analysis, "infrastructural" means a primary force of form-shaping that functions something like an unarticulated synonym for what others might call "ideological." Although consistent with the definition of *form* that Levine offers in *Forms*—"an arrangement of elements—an ordering, patterning, or shaping"[16]—this line of argument about infrastructure ignores the historical and ideological entailments (and material affordances) in the early twentieth-century emergence of the term, as Carse explains: "The infrastructural portion of a project (below/before) was built by the state and the superstructure (above/after) constructed by private contractors."[17] Infrastructure in this historical mode of ground laying entails relations between state and parastatal, public good and private enterprise, engineer and bureaucrat. These constitutive relations, along with the ground of materiality, are missing in the assertion that racism is ur-infrastructure.

I do not mean to single out Levine here, nor to deny the powerful connections between race and infrastructure (as detailed above and throughout *The Aesthetic Lives of Infrastructure*), but instead to consider these argumentative moves as emblematic of a broader tendency in humanities (and particularly literary studies) discourse as it casts its interpreting eye beyond the literary text and across disciplinary boundaries. I read the claim "racism is more infrastructural than infrastructure" as a moment of rhetorical excess, by which I mean not only an argument taken too far (certainly an occupational hazard for all of us!), but also, and more precisely to the point, a rhetorical figure (like metaphor) shorn of its illuminating figuralness, with tenor and vehicle collapsed like a dead star, denying the "undeniable materiality" of infrastructure.

Like Audre Lorde, I reach for the image of a bridge when I figure the act of thinking between disciplines or modes of discourse as "interdisciplinary bridgework." Metaphor, like infrastructure, is good to think with. Yet I worry that an unconsidered relationship to metaphor is one reason why traffic on the bridge between disciplines seems to be largely one-way at the moment, as literary critics (myself included) turn toward disciplines like anthropology, political ecology, science and technology studies, and media studies for new concepts and modes of thinking to undergird our analyses. Within this promiscuous reading over the bridge lies the risk of literary critics reducing the hard-won insights and material objects of other disciplines (not to mention life beyond academic discipline) to *mere* metaphor, in a mode at once underthought and overimagined, shedding the load of referentiality. (This is another way of saying that *structure* itself tends to function as an underthought metaphor in the humanities.) This tendency is by no means limited to the environmental and energy humanities, and it's particularly vexed with regard to proliferating conversation on the Anthropocene, another matter of concern that demands what the editors aptly call "creative interdisciplinarity." But to return to the concerns of this collection, infrastructure is not (just) a metaphor. In the spirit of AbdouMaliq Simone's indispensable concept of "people as infrastructure," the gestures toward a "broadened conceptualization of infrastructure" in this collection tend to name relations that coalesce within states of disconnect from (or interruption or inadequacy of) infrastructures as conventionally defined and materially instantiated.

"Underthought" is a word that I borrow from Alan Liu's late-1980s assessment of the conceptual, and therefore political, limitations of New Historicism. Liu observes that metaphor (or Foucauldian "resemblance") had been enlisted as the default hinge between text and context, or literature and history. Metaphor was thus deployed, according to Liu, in such an unhistoricized, untheorized way that this methodological bridge amounted to a "connection of pure nothing . . . a relation of pure suggestiveness. Physical concepts originating in positivist explanations of reality—'power,' for example, drift over the gap to figure the work of texts. . . . While driven to refer literature to history, . . . [New Historicism] is self-barred from any method able to ground, or even to *think*, reference more secure than trope."[18] Anticipating much recent debate about the limits of critique and the politics of form, Liu urged his fellow New Historicists in their late 1980s heyday to fill the gap of nothing that the underthought bridge of metaphor had papered over. Today, we may be far beyond a Derridean *il n'y a pas de hors-texte*, and one could rightly say that the ascendancy of an object-attuned new materialism leaves the textualized carnival of New Historicism in its dust, dirt, or rubble. Still, something happens on that bridge that tends to turn objects to figures: metaphors cut free from their material ground. How, then, can we scholars of literature and culture attend imaginatively and responsibly to what infrastructure is and does—or, as it happens, does not do, as we see in Mphahlele's vivid depiction of Nadia Street as a site where electricity *is* just a metaphor? My readings of Mphahlele, Ndebele, and van Schnitzler aim to offer some sense of the stakes of grappling with infrastructure and its politics *as infrastructure*; to their warnings against too-narrow notions of politics that miss the life-sustaining power of the ordinary, I would add a warning against too-broad notions of infrastructure that miss the concept-grounding power of the material.

Notes

This afterword originated as a paper presented at the special session "Infrastructure, Race, and Literature," organized by Ramesh Mallipeddi and Susan Zieger at the Modern Language Association Annual Convention in Seattle, January 9–12, 2020.

1. Ezekiel Mphahlele, "Lesane [The Lesanes of Nadia Street]," in *The Drum Decade: Stories of the 1950s*, ed. Michael Chapman (Pietermaritzburg: University of Natal Press, 1989), 134.

2. Njabulo S. Ndebele, *The Rediscovery of the Ordinary: Essays on South African Literature and Culture* (Johannesburg: Congress of South African Writers, 1991), 33.

3. Rob Gaylard, "'A Man Is a Man Because of Other Men': The 'Lesane' Stories of Es'kia Mphahlele," *English in Africa* 22, no. 1 (May 1995), 76; Kelwyn Sole, "Class, Continuity and Change in Black South African Literature, 1948–60," in *Labour, Townships and Protest: Studies in the Social History of the Witwatersrand*, ed. Belinda Bozzoli (Johannesburg: Ravan Press, 1979), 155.

4. Bruno Esekie [Es'kia Mphahlele], "Down the Quiet Street," in *The Drum Decade: Stories of the 1950s*, ed. Michael Chapman (Pietermaritzburg: University of Natal Press, 1989), 95.

5. Mphahlele, "Lesane [The Lesanes of Nadia Street]," 133.

6. See J. Edward Matthewson's *The Establishment of a Bantu Township* (Pretoria: J. L. Van Schaik, 1957) for a glimpse of the practical and ideological considerations regarding electrification and other infrastructural and service provisioning in Black neighborhoods and townships.

7. Jennifer Wenzel, "Forms of Life: Thinking Fossil Infrastructure and Its Narrative Grammar," *Social Text*, forthcoming.

8. Mphahlele, "Lesane [The Lesanes of Nadia Street]," 134.

9. See especially Jennifer Wenzel, *The Disposition of Nature: Environmental Crisis and World Literature* (New York: Fordham University Press, 2020), 14–15.

10. Sarah Nuttall and Liz McGregor, foreword to *Load Shedding: Writing on and over the Edge of South Africa* (Johannesburg and Cape Town: Jonathan Ball, 2009), 10.

11. For an invaluable account of the intersections of literature and infrastructure that precedes the recent efflorescence of anthropologists' critical infrastructure studies, see Michael Rubenstein, *Public Works: Infrastructure, Irish Modernism, and the Postcolonial* (Notre Dame, IN: University of Notre Dame Press, 2010). At the 2020 Modern Language Association Roundtable where I presented an early version of this afterword, Rubenstein offered a productively ambivalent account of infrastructure. Given that things like clean water are (or should be) inarguably necessary for public life, which aspects of infrastructure are worth fighting for, he asked, and which are violent and oppressive?

12. Ashley Carse, "Keyword: Infrastructure: How a Humble French Engineering Term Shaped the Modern World," in *Infrastructures and Social Complexity: A Companion*, ed. Penelope Harvey, Casper Brun Jensen, and Atsuro Morita (New York: Routledge, 2017), 35.

13. Ramesh Mallipeddi and Susan Zieger, panel abstract, "Infrastructure, Race, and Literature," Modern Language Association Annual Convention, Seattle, January 9–12, 2020.

14. Audre Lorde, "Poetry Is Not a Luxury," in *Sister Outsider* (Berkeley, CA: Ten Speed Press, 1984), 37.

15. Caroline Levine, "The Strange Familiar: Structure, Infrastructure, and Adichie's *Americanah*," *Modern Fiction Studies* 61, no. 4 (Winter 2015): 599–60.

16. Caroline Levine, *Forms: Whole, Rhythm, Hierarchy, Network* (Princeton, NJ: Princeton University Press, 2015), 3.

17. Carse, "Keyword," 30.

18. Alan Liu, "The Power of Formalism: The New Historicism," *English Literary History* 56, no. 5 (Winter 1989): 743–44.

CONTRIBUTORS

GEORGIANA BANITA is an associate professor of North American literature and culture at the University of Bamberg, Germany. She is the author of *Plotting Justice: Narrative Ethics and Literary Culture after 9/11* (2012) and the coeditor of *Electoral Cultures: American Democracy and Choice* (2015).

YANIE FECU is an assistant professor of English at the University of Wisconsin–Madison and the author of *Sonorities: Decolonizing Vocal Labor in Post-1945 Caribbean Culture* (2018).

JANICE HO is an associate professor of English at the University of British Columbia, Vancouver, and the author of *Nation and Citizenship in the Twentieth-Century British Novel* (2015).

JEANNIE IM is a clinical associate professor in the Expository Writing Program at New York University.

RAMESH MALLIPEDDI is an associate professor of English at the University of British Columbia, Vancouver, the author of *Spectacular Suffering: Witnessing Slavery in the Eighteenth-Century British Atlantic* (2016), and the editor of *Eighteenth-Century Studies*.

LOUIS MORENO is a lecturer in visual cultures at Goldsmith's College, University of London, and teaches in the Centre for Research Architecture.

RAHUL MUKHERJEE is the Dick Wolf Associate Professor of Television and New Media Studies, associate professor of English, University of Pennsylvania, and author of *Radiant Infrastructures: Media, Environment, and Cultures of Uncertainty* (2020).

SANGINA PATNAIK is an assistant professor of English at Swarthmore College.

SAMANTHA PINTO is a professor of English at the University of Texas at Austin. She is the author of *Difficult Diasporas: The Transnational Feminist Aesthetic of the Black Atlantic* (New York University Press, 2013), which won the 2013 William Sanders Scarborough Prize for African American Literature and Culture, and *Infamous Bodies* (2020).

KELLY M. RICH is an associate professor of English at Harvard University.

NICOLE RIZZUTO is an associate professor of English at Georgetown University and the author of *Insurgent Testimonies: Witnessing Colonial Trauma in Modern and Anglophone Literature* (2015), which was shortlisted for the Modernist Studies Association Prize for a First Book.

JENNIFER WENZEL is jointly appointed in the Departments of English and Comparative Literature and of Middle Eastern, South Asian, and African Studies at Columbia University. Her recent book, *The Disposition of Nature: Environmental Crisis and World Literature*, was shortlisted for the 2020 Book Prize awarded by the Association for the Study of the Arts of the Present. With Imre Szeman and Patricia Yaeger, she coedited *Fueling Culture: 101 Words for Energy and Environment*. Her first book, *Bulletproof: Afterlives of Anticolonial Prophecy in South Africa and Beyond*, was awarded Honorable Mention for the Perkins Prize by the International Society for the Study of Narrative.

SUSAN ZIEGER is a professor of English literature and cultural studies at the University of California, Riverside. She is the author of *The Mediated Mind: Affect, Ephemera, and Consumerism in the Nineteenth Century* (2018) and *Inventing the Addict: Drugs, Race, and Sexuality in Nineteenth-Century British and American Fiction* (2008) and the coeditor of *Assembly Codes: The Logistics of Media* (2021).